Beyond
you and me

Social Key

Editors
Kosha Anja Joubert
and
Robin Alfred

Beyond
you and me

Inspirations and Wisdom
for Building Community

Permanent Publications

Published by:
Permanent Publications
Hyden House Limited
The Sustainability Centre
East Meon
Hampshire
GU32 1HR
United Kingdom
Tel: 01730 823 311
Fax: 01730 823 322
Overseas: (international code +44 - 1730)
info@permanentpublications.co.uk
www.permanentpublications.co.uk

Distributed in the USA by
Chelsea Green Publishing Company
PO Box 428, White River Junction, VT 05001
www.chelseagreen.com

First published 2007, reprinted 2013
© 2007 Gaia Education

Edited by
Kosha Anja Joubert and Robin Alfred

Designed by
Two Plus George Limited
www.TwoPlusGeorge.co.uk

Cover design by
Alexandre Pereira
semearcriatividade@gmail.com

Printed and bound in the UK by
CPI Antony Rowe, Chippenham, Wiltshire

Printed on paper from mixed sources certified by the
Forest Stewardship Council

The Forest Stewardship Council (FSC) is a non-profit international
organisation established to promote the responsible management of
the world's forests. Products carrying the FSC label are independently
certified to assure consumers that they come from forests that are
managed to meet the social, economic and ecological needs of
present and future generations.

British Library Cataloguing-in-Publication Data
A catalogue record for this book is available from the British Library

ISBN 978 1 85623 038 4

The Four Keys to the Design of Sustainable Communities

Gaia Education, a project of the Global Ecovillage Network (GEN), is an international team of educators developing curricula and courses on the Sustainable Development of Urban and Rural Settlements.

Our team of leading edge sustainability educators has developed the Ecovillage Design Curriculum (EDE). The EDE provides the basis for a four week comprehensive course on the fundamentals of ecovillage design. The Ecovillage Design Curriculum has the endorsement of the United Nations Institute for Training and Research (UNITAR) and is an official contribution to the UN Decade of Education for Sustainable Development (UNDESD).

Beyond You & Me is the first in a series of four books that introduces the curriculum. It is for anyone seeking sustainable solutions to the complex problems of climate change, peak oil and the global inequalities of North and South. These volumes are also intended to supplement to the Ecovillage Design Education (EDE) teaching programme for both students and teachers and are edited by ecovillagers from all over the world who designed the EDE.

Other titles in the series:

The Song of the Earth: A Synthesis of the Scientific and Spiritual Worldviews
The Worldview Key of the EDE
Editors: Maddy Harland, Will Keepin

Gaian Economics: Living Well within Planetary Limits
The Economic Key of the EDE
Editors: Jonathan Dawson, Ross Jackson, Helena Norberg-Hodge

Designing Ecological Habitats: Creating a Sense of Place
The Ecological Key of the EDE
Editors: Maddy Harland, Max Lindegger, Lloyd Williams

The editor and publisher of the Four Keys is Maddy Harland of Permanent Publications, UK, while the inspirer and overall coordinator of the series is Hildur Jackson of Gaia Trust, Denmark.

The Social Key, *Beyond You and Me*, has been sponsored by Gaia Trust www.gaia.org and Permanent Publications www.permaculture.co.uk

Enjoy!

Ross and Hildur Jackson, Gaia Trust
May East, Program Director, Gaia Education
Maddy Harland, Editor and Publisher, Permanent Publications

Contents

2 Communication Skills: Conflict, Facilitation & Decision Making

Facilitation of Meetings & Decision Making

Communicating for Peace

3 Personal Empowerment & Leadership Skills

Personal Empowerment

Integral Leadership

4 Health & Healing

5 Local, Bioregional & Global Outreach

Bioregional Outreach

Educational Outreach

Global Outreach

The Editors

KOSHA ANJA JOUBERT was born 1968 in South Africa and grew up under Apartheid. This experience brought her to study intercultural communication and become an expert at building trust and a sense of deep connection in groups. After a period of extensive travelling, she has settled in the Ecovillage of Sieben Linden in Germany. A member of the original GEESE-Group, she has written a large part of the Social Dimension of the EDE-Curriculum. She organizes international EDE-courses in Germany and works as a consultant and facilitator of community and organizational learning and development processes. She is mother of two children.

kosha@siebenlinden.de · +49-39000-90860 · www.gemeinschaftsberatung.de

ROBIN ALFRED worked as a trainer, educator and social work manager for 15 years in London, prior to coming to the Findhorn Foundation Community, Scotland in 1995. At the Foundation, Robin was initially responsible for a 'reinvention' process – building consensus around the fundamental direction, practices and values of the community. He went on to chair the Foundation's Management Committee, is founding director of the organization's Consultancy Service and is also a Trustee.

Robin has been a faculty member of the Findhorn Foundation's Ecovillage Training for the past six years, leading modules focused on group dynamics, working with diversity, conflict facilitation, leadership, and all aspects of the social dimension of creating a thriving ecovillage.

ralfred@findhorn.org · +44 (0)799-097-2827

Introduction

This book was conceived and birthed as part of Gaia Education and as a deepening of the Social Dimension of the Ecovillage Design Education (EDE) curriculum. Many people, including all the writers have given their energy freely, in order to support this project, because it was worth it to them. They have wanted to reach out to you with their experience and their knowledge, hoping to inspire you and ease your way into building sustainable community wherever you are.

> The next Buddha will not take the form of an individual. The next Buddha may take the form of a community; a community practising understanding and loving kindness, a community practising mindful living. This may be the most important thing we can do for the survival of the earth.
>
> THICH NHAT HANH

> We need a more peaceful world, growing out of more peaceful families and neighbourhoods and communities. To secure and cultivate such peace, we need to love others, even our enemies as well as our friends.
>
> HOWARD W HUNTER

Archaeological evidence shows that the primordial pattern for human beings is to gather together in relatively tightly knit, clan-sized groups closely aligned with nature. Today, we need consciously to reinvent cooperative and harmonious ways of living together. For people raised within the hyper-individualized paradigm, or in settings where people come from diverse or even warring factions, learning the subtleties of constructive and mutually beneficial interaction within a community setting may take a major effort. Rebuilding human community is an endeavour whose immense challenges should not be underestimated.

Sustaining community necessarily involves a healing process in which we step out of the cycles of pain, mistrust and violence that run through human history, and take responsibility for initiating new patterns. Most of us have been educated in a way that has made us believe that we are fundamentally greedy and selfish, and that the good life consists of a constant battle against evil forces within and without. We have come to mistrust the inherent goodness of human beings. This is a paradigm that breeds violence, instead of peace.

Watch yourself next time you spend time in a public place in a city somewhere. Watch your heart's reactions to passing people. Watch your judgments. How much trust and compassion do you bring to the situation? Watch for the part in you that feels that human beings are somehow worse than nature, destroying nature, that the world might be better off without us. How are we going to build loving communities and effective movements for a peaceful world from such a standpoint?

Rediscovering the beauty, compassionate nature and innate power of human beings is part of our journey through this book.

In addition to offering inspiration, the book also has a very practical orientation. Often we hear people say, 'I want to create an eco-development, a real ecological alternative to the mainstream. You know, eco-houses, windmills, solar panels, organic veggies, recycling – all that kind of thing. A way of living that will work for the 21st century.'

One aspect is often missing – the people, the social aspect. How will we come together as humans and live happily and sustainably into our future? What will be the rallying call – the vision that will help our projects be coherent and inspiring? What will be the glue that will help to bond community members to one another? How will decisions be made and conflicts resolved? How will we walk that delicate line between being an individual and growing in a sense of personal empowerment, and surrendering our wishes and desires to the collective, or even to something beyond that?

Will we be able to celebrate our diversity or will we find our differences too challenging and uncomfortable? How will we care for our elders, and celebrate life's transitions – births, deaths, weddings, separations – and what will happen to us when we are sick or unhappy? Finally, will our community, settlement or bioregion, be a world unto itself, a self-sustaining bubble on the face of the earth, or will it reach out to the local community, building bridges, learning and teaching, giving and receiving?

The EDE wishes to inspire holistic design processes, that pay good attention to the people side of things, alongside the work on economics, ecology and our worldviews. On the threshold between vision and reality, an integrative design can set the course for a healthy and sustainable reality. We need to broaden our minds to encompass these different dimensions as well as inner, structural and outer, material aspects of each.

In the Ecological Key, the material aspects of Social Design (settlement patterns, communal living spaces, etc.) will be deepened. In this book we have focused on the structural, systemic and process aspects.

We have arranged the book in five sections:

1. Building Community and Embracing Diversity
2. Communication Skills: Conflict, Facilitation and Decision Making
3. Personal Empowerment and Leadership Skills
4. Health and Healing
5. Local, Bioregional and Global Outreach

Within each section you will find short articles written by leaders in their fields. We hope this will provide you both with practical knowledge to help you in your work, and inspiration through the examples of the writers' own work. We have attempted to bring you case studies from around the world, from diverse cultures and embracing diverse value systems. Still, there is an imbalance in this book, a leaning towards voices of 'the North'. This imbalance mirrors where the Global Ecovillage Network stands in its movement towards a deeply balanced diversity that encompasses all cultures equally.

There is no 'one right way' to do this work. One size does not fit all. Everybody is different. Every settlement will be different. The response to each situation will be different.

We hope there is something in here for everyone and that this book will serve you and your work for well-being on our planet.

Kosha Anja Joubert and Robin Alfred

1 Building Community & Embracing Diversity

Dieter Duhm reminds us of how natural and even necessary for survival it is for humans to live in community. He states that true community today involves the flowering of individuality, and that trust is a basic necessity.

Community as a Universal Way of Living

Dieter Duhm

> Only tribes will survive
> VINE DELORIA JR. (Native American spiritual teacher)

The original community of humans is not the family, but the tribe. The original community is the human vessel, into which human life, including the family, is embedded. It is part of what I call the sacred matrix, inherent to life. In it, the cosmic order connects with the social order. It is not bound to certain times or cultures, rather it is an integral part of our human social existence that lies beyond history. It could only be destroyed through violence, and it is only when we have found a full equivalent to it that is aligned with our times, that we again can enter into full and wholesome relationships with each other.

Community is the natural social entity that has experienced the greatest damage. It is a necessary part of the whole, which was destroyed worldwide. Wherever people were abducted, enslaved or sold, communities were annihilated, thus destroying the life nerves of entire peoples. This process started with the Kurgan people's invasion of Neolithic river settlements 7,000 years ago. It continued with the annihilation of the Native American peoples by the European invaders during the 17th century, and continues to the present day, when the last indigenous peoples on all continents are being driven out of their natural habitat in the name of commercial interests.

The disappearance of human community left behind a festering wound in human civilization. It was through the destruction of community that humans lost their authentic morality and sense of responsibility. People were torn away from organic communities. Piece by piece, this also separated them from their own higher selves, from their higher knowledge, and from the higher orders of life. Community was and is the natural breeding ground for trust and solidarity. If this humus is missing, the uprooted human being becomes violent.

Community is an intermediate stage in the scale of life, and it cannot be skipped. It connects the individual with a higher order and sharpens her/his sense of the whole. A healthy community reflects a universal order, with which we can then connect easier. It is through this connection that a functioning community gets its high field-creating power.

A natural community is similar to an organism, and the individual people and groups are its organs. The organs of a healthy organism have different tasks and functions; the liver acts different from the kidney and the brain acts different from the heart, and yet they all belong to the same organism. When living in such an organism, people gradually stop living according to principles of comparison and competition, and start living according to principles of supplementing and supporting each other. The system could not function otherwise.

As this organism emerges, a new mental-spiritual subject develops: the communitarian 'I'. This 'I' is at a higher level order in the spiritual hierarchy of life than the individual 'I'. The communitarian 'I' contains the knowledge and the power of all individual 'I's'. All co-workers that are solidly a part of the community are connected to the communitarian 'I' and its mental-spiritual powers, and they can therefore access survival abilities that they would not have as individuals.

When the first humans enter into this state of community again and start thinking and acting based on this connection, this will have a high healing impact on the morphogenetic field of humanity. In a living community, peace knowledge is developed. We learn the laws of universal peace by learning the universal rules of community.

The Morning Attunement – a daily gathering in the Aula of Tamera

Individual and Collective

Today, communities have a bad reputation. It is believed that they are not compatible with a developed individuality. It is one of the core beliefs of the whole Western world, that individuality and collective are two irreconcilable opposites. In reality the situation is much more complex. Nature does create collectivist communities, in which the individual hardly plays any role at all (herds of animals, etc.) But nature also creates communities, in which the development of a highly specific individual is a prerequisite for the functioning of the whole (biotope, etc.). I call them 'communitarian' communities. If people today resist communities, then they are thinking of collectivistic, not communitarian, forms of community. In reality, in human history to date, only collectivistic communities have existed. In the past, the development of the individual and the historical process of individuation had not progressed far enough to make communitarian communities possible.

The natural form of community is a communitarian community. The community, seen as an organism, is a unified system, and the organs are characterized by their individuality and their differences. The unity of the organism is achieved by the individuality and diversity of the organs. In other words, it is only when the full individuality of the members is developed that a healthy community can emerge. Community and individual are not opposites; they are prerequisites for each other. The prerequisite for a natural community is an autonomous individual, and the prerequisite for an autonomous individual is a natural community. This is the natural order in the building plan of Creation.

… a deep process of individuation leads human beings naturally to see themselves as organic parts of a human community instead of private persons.

The ability of communities to survive and be future-oriented is closely connected to the self-growth processes of the individuals involved. The more the individuals embrace their individuality and the less they let themselves be ruled by preconceived dogmas and false authorities, the easier it is for them to recognize how their personal growth can be enhanced by the community. At some point a deep process of individuation leads human beings naturally to see themselves as organic parts of a human community instead of private persons. For it is through individuation that human beings experience not only what separates them from others, but also what connects them at a much deeper level. They dare to rediscover and accept this. It is as individuals that they find their universal dimension, and it is as individual human beings that they experience their connection to the universe.

Without individuation a healthy community organism cannot develop. Conforming collectivism comes into being when individual differences are not promoted but instead suppressed. Collectivistic systems do not tolerate individual autonomy. Instead, both inwardly and outwardly, they fight everything that does not fit into their ideology. Inner cohesion is achieved by war against common enemies. This is how collectivistic systems in history up to today have operated, be it within the framework of the Christian church, Islamic fundamentalism, orthodox communism, National Socialism, or racism and sexism. Today, as a collective, humanity is being trained by the media to react to other symbols – the symbols of fashion, lifestyle, consumerism, and commerce – but the principle remains the same.

Today, we are facing a historical turning point when it comes to the creation of communities. Old structures no longer function and new ones need to be created. The extents to which such structures can be developed determine whether human beings can regain the basic values of living together: truth, trust, solidarity, and mutual support. Functioning communities of autonomous individuals are the basis for a humane world. Within them, love, both emotional-spiritual love and sensual love, will be able to develop in a new way, for love begins to blossom wherever we begin to recognize each other in our specificity and individuality. A mature community will always protect this love.

Art as healing power: Dieter Duhm gives regular art courses for Tamera community members

Trust as a Life Quality

Communities flourish if there is trust between their members; they do not function, or only seemingly function, if this trust does not exist. They break down quickly if the social glue was brought about through conformism or hypocrisy. Trust is the core power of a community. Without trust it can maybe take forceful action in the short term, but in the long run it will perish.

The amount of mutual trust that is present is determinative for everything that is important in the community. Trust determines whether true healing can occur, whether the community grows and flowers in the personal, mental-spiritual, and political realms, I am speaking of trust between men and women, in love relationships, between adults and children, trust in leaders, trust between the centre of the community and the periphery, and between different project groups.

Creating trust is not easy. Falling into each other's arms as often as possible is not a suitable method. Many groups fall apart because of too much sweetness, with which they cover their wounds without healing them. Creating trust is an unprecedented adventure and the qualities that we bring to it from existing society are not very helpful. We have learned to disguise ourselves in order to survive. Finding the courage to stand up against these old habits of concealment and hypocrisy is not always easy and we need to be very persevering. We need a clear set of values in order to be able to create true trust. If instead, we hope to follow the spontaneous development of positive emotions, the old powers will ultimately win. Almost all groups in the 20th century fell apart because of their inability to deal with conflicts in the areas of sex, love, power, money, and recognition.

The methods that a community uses to further its inner cohesiveness must be judged by their capacity to increase the substance of trust. What forms of relationships are helpful for a community depends on what forms

Music and celebration in the 'Umbigo' – the navel of Tamera

produce the deepest trust. Whether a common economy is helpful or not depends on the same. If an organization is good or bad depends on the trust of its members.

Trust can grow through many activities. It depends less on what you do than on how it is done. In Tamera, we have prepared theatre productions, travelled, gone ice-bathing in winter, played volleyball for long stretches of time, fasted, been ill, and celebrated together. Especially within the framework of our art courses and spiritual courses a special feeling of belonging was created. Our most outstanding method to create transparency and trust within the group was through the method of Forum (described later in this book). There are no simple answers on how to create trust. We have tried walking unknown paths to create a life without fear and, through time, trust has emerged.

Trust is deeply related to human truth, transparency, and the ability and willingness to allow myself to be seen. If I can truly be seen, this means that I can be loved and accepted. It is a requirement for trust to arise in community for all essential processes in the group to be made transparent. Hidden fights and complicities regarding money, power, or sex will break up any community.

We need functioning communities in order to learn to trust again so that peace can ripple out, allowing us to survive on this planet. In Tamera, we consciously seek to access our connection with the universal powers and the higher orders of life. We thereby seek to enter into the highest level of trust: the trusting cooperation with the divine powers.

Dieter Duhm was born in 1942 in Berlin. Doctorate in Sociology. Art Historian and Psychoanalyst. Author, Initiator of the 'Plan of Healing Biotopes' and co-founder of Tamera/ Portugal. He has dedicated his life to the creation of an effective forum for a global peace initiative, which is powerful enough to counteract the destructive forces of the capitalistic globalization.

His books include: *Fear in Capitalism* (1972), *Towards a New Culture* (1982), *Eros Unredeemed* (1991), *The Sacred Matrix* (2001), *Future Without War* (2006)
www.dieter-duhm.de

Malidoma Somè lets us share in the African way of understanding community. He shows how in community every person can be supported to bring their gift out into the world.

The Global Village
Living in Community with the Ancestors

Malidoma Somé

This text is based on an interview by Sarida Brown for *Caduceus*
Reproduced with kind permission from *Caduceus*, issue 61 (November 2003)

For many years now, you have been working in the West. Could you explain what your purpose is?

My purpose is the reclaiming our intrinsic human nature – our humanness. We have to start by recovering or reinventing family and community, and redefining what a purposeful life is. For this I rely on ancient, indigenous wisdom.

In the West I work to heal wounds, and to restore the values that are intrinsically human through connection with ancestors and spirits, and emphasis on family and community.

This might appear to be simple, however, the chaos of the current system creates a lot of obstacles. The power of our humanness needs to confront these obstacles so that the true self of the human being can be honored, respected and uplifted once again.

What can your particular traditional wisdom contribute to conditions here?

I am drawing from the tradition of the Dagara people now situated in Burkina Faso, central West Africa and Ghana. Their culture is profoundly rooted in a connection to the earth, to nature, and to ancestors.

In the interest of continuity, the Dagara have designed a sophisticated way of involving the ancestors in their daily lives. They believe that it takes the other world to shed light on this world so that we can transform our fascination with harmful actions into one with healing actions. Then, the community is able to affirm life, joy and abundance.

The body of man is very small compared with the spirit that inhabits it.
African Oral Tradition

The Dagara people have an elaborate cosmology to support this. It begins with the idea that every child has returned from the world of the ancestors with a specific purpose to fulfil, which is regarded as a gift. So, there is the assumption that people are born with a gift that they are bringing to the family, people and culture that they are born into.

Members of the community do everything they can to support the child and bring their gift out into the open. Initiatory rites of passage allow the young ones to grow into their full purpose. A variety of other rituals have been created to support the concept of a life purpose and to allow it to continue to grow and be fulfilled.

This is the cosmology that I am bringing to the West; in the midst of the chaos that modernity is experiencing. It has proven to be a very useful tool that allows people to look at each other from a new perspective, and to reconsider the ancient possibilities of community and family.

In our culture we have little sense of the child entering the world with a purpose and gift. How do you bring this concept to western consciousness?

The Dagara assumes that the child is a traveler who has arrived with luggage. What luggage? The gifts. How do you find them? In the Dagara culture there is a ritual that precedes birth in the course of which it is possible to identify the nature of the gift. These rituals are conducted by the elders in the presence of the pregnant mother. Using the voice of the mother who is put into trance, the elders converse with the ancestor who has taken on human form inside the body of the mother.

For this ritual to journey from the Dagara to the West it had to undergo some changes. In the West, we use the date of birth to situate the newborn within a cosmological chart, which then reveals the gift that is intrinsic to that person.

The Dagara cosmology categorizes this gift into five types: vision, peace, reconciliation, nourishment, and comfort. These are essentially connected with home, story telling, and communication of idea.

The prebirth ritual will communicate encouragement and ask for the journey to this earth to be blessed, as you would for a person who is going to fulfil a mission. The actual expression of the ritual will vary widely. To approach an unborn human as a gifted person, as a carrier of something precious, sends a clear message that this world is worth coming into, that it is worth dedicating oneself to improving it, and contributing to its blossoming.

In the West the idea of communication with ancestors appears 'spooky' and primitive. Can you explain to a westerner what the presence of the ancestors means?

It is important to accept at least a remote possibility that the dead, those who have preceded us in this world and are no longer in physical forms, still have some residual energy, and are able to influence the quality of our day-to-day lives. It is that energy that we refer to as ancestral.

Indigenous people regard ancestors as spirits, in the sense of humans who have returned to the state of spirit after shedding their physical bodies and joined a community that is 'other worldly'. They have left their footprints on this earth and have descendants who are looking for ways to build on their legacies. Ancestors look forward to becoming involved in how we continue what they have started.

Those of us who are conscious of their helpful presence among us, like to precede any initiative with an invocation. In this, we invite, request and sometimes even demand that ancestors be the source of our inspiration, and that they be involved in whatever we do so that our own clumsiness can be made sacred and precious.

It is a matter of awakening to the reality that someone without a body is on standby to walk alongside us, to work with us and to be with us in times of joy and sorrow. Their presence can dissolve any isolation or aloneness we might experience.

It is a matter of awakening to the reality that someone without a body is on standby to walk alongside us, to work with us and to be with us in times of joy and sorrow.

Is it a wasted potential not to work with the ancestors?

It is a force that is left dormant. When ancestors are ignored, we may find ourselves struggling with the same old problems in our day-to-day life, wondering why nothing is really changing. It is like continually banging at the same door and using the same tools, thinking that eventually some day we will find a solution. There's an African saying that a log does not turn into a crocodile by staying long enough in water!

It is important to reconsider certain tools that we habitually use, and possibly abandon them for others that might yield better results. A stronger connection to the ancestors may offer a resolution to the impasse that modern culture finds itself in.

The impasse of social disintegration?

That's right. Being on the brink of disintegration is a sign of this separation between the living and the dead. The world has reached a point where globalism is gradually imposing itself on us – a globalism which is still defined in economic terms. This has to change, and globalism must emphasize community beyond economics. In order to arrive at the possibility of such a global village it is important to look back into the past to heal all the problems and ills that are stored there, and that are continuing to affect the current quality of life. They leave behind an energetic signature that acts as

Dagara village life

the underlying cause of wars, slavery, famine, and all the deaths caused by human carelessness and hatred.

The way to create a global village has to begin with a massive healing of all these aspects. We cannot keep looking to create a healing in the future while painting over the ills that have happened in the past. Radical honesty is required, and an acknowledgement of all those moments in which humanity has taken wrong and painful steps. These steps have caused such rifts that they continue to have impacts on the psyche today: a propensity for separateness, disparity, violence, isolation, and division – you name it!

These effects have to be dealt with through the help of the ancestors, particularly those who were the primary victims and perpetrators at the time. The prevailing consciousness on this side is divisive, violent and unsupportive of community and family. When one sheds one's body and becomes a spirit, a different consciousness comes in.

The human power to generate change is boosted manifold when assisted by the wisdom of the ancestors. We can gather all the intelligence necessary to implement something, but always fall short of implementing the solution. It is always a good and humble gesture to acknowledge that we are limited, and therefore that we are seeking the contribution of higher powers. By doing that we become the beneficiaries of ancestral participation in our own transformation.

What is your vision of the new global village?

We need to come together to grieve all the evil that has littered the roads of human evolution. We have to be able to express this emotion in a sacred way. We have to acknowledge the fact that we have not always done things in the best interests of human continuity. As a result we need to seek reconciliation and healing to stop us from carrying this weight into the future and passing it on to future generations. This acknowledgment has to lead to a commitment to repair or mend. It is a daunting task.

I dream of a world in which the global village is interested in drawing together all traditions of the world, to synthesize them into a tradition that is not compartmentalized, hierarchical or competitive; one that does not say that one tradition is better than the other; one that looks towards the kind of beauty that each culture has. It is possible that once synthesized, this global village would reflect a cultural universalism. It is a big task and won't happen overnight. But it is worth tackling.

So how do we start?

It cannot be done individually; it has to be done collectively, by people gathering together, like the groups that I gather, to address the wisdom of ancestors, which open hearts and spirits. I am suggesting that as a first step people gather together in their own neighbourhoods to begin to transcend their own individualism and isolation into something that is more community-based.

It is important this process begins with an acknowledgment of each other, with curiosity about the gift that each person brings and has to offer for the enrichment of the whole. This model has a naturally expansive quality. Once there is such an acknowledgment, the human psyche expands and immediately new ideas come in and new directions show.

Grieving all the ills, as you suggest, sounds like a very deep process. Does it need the power of ritual to accomplish it?

In modern culture it is not usual for people to allow emotional outpouring, for people to express themselves from the heart. And yet it is the repression of human emotion that needs to be revisited, for repressed emotions take on violent and dangerous forms. When locked in, emotion becomes amplified and finds its way out in anti-social types of behavior that endanger society.

The current brink of self-destruction we have reached is symptomatic for this kind of self-repression in the face of situations that called for the humble relief of whatever feeling was evoked. Grieving is a very daunting task because it is inviting people to act in a non-traditional fashion, in a way that might show their human frailty and weakness.

So is this the way beyond current violence, for example, in the Middle East?

The way beyond that is ritual and the revision and expansion of sacredness. It can be summed up in a few simple words: prayers and involvement of the ancestors in the resolution of the crisis. When over a million people walking in the streets in London failed to stop the war against Iraq, you have to ask why? My answer is that we are being told that the message we would like to send to the government and military hierarchy is best understood when delivered by our ancestors.

It is no longer possible for us human beings to be the carriers of the kind of message that can avoid violence, prevent death and save lives. That is why

… the message we would like to send to the government and military hierarchy is best understood when delivered by our ancestors.

I envision a day of ritual, involving the same number of people who came out on the streets in February 2003, in the course of which we offer our grief to the sacred shrine of our ancestors, with the request that our prayers be taken to the right place in order to affect the right kind of change.

So you envision a million or more people coming together in a union of humans and ancestors together to forward the desire for peace, the desire to go beyond divisiveness and violence?

Yes. Peace is an inalienable right bestowed upon us. When it starts to dwindle in our lives it is important that we consider whether it is the result of something that we did that was wrong, or whether it is a message sent to us by forces beyond our human world showing us what we need to pay attention to.

I believe that in such a situation, a movement that begins with the creation of sacred shrines, where each individual is able to surrender his or her feelings, visions and wishes, carries a better chance of reaching the powers that be, in a manner that is not conventional and promises more lasting results than anything else. That's why I am saying that the next cycle of human consciousness is going to be held by what I call spiritual activism.

Our streets have to be cleared of vehicles and decorated with sacred shrines. People could then go into prayers, requesting that these prayers be received and transcended into gems of peace that will last a thousand years. It is important that we see our activism not as being directed by humans against other humans, but being transferred from this world to another world where it is processed and then returned here charged with the capacity to change the climate and spirit of our world.

How do you understand evil?

I understand evil as the energy that counter-acts the simplest, positive, life-giving thoughts that rule our lives – the thoughts of loving and of being loved, the thoughts of contributing something to this world. The greatest harm that can be done to a human being is the elimination of a person's potential. Evil is that which has little consideration for the sacredness of human life, which maintains a status quo of tension, sleeplessness and stress in a culture and society that deserves better than that.

Evil comes about because life was disregarded and respect was thrown out of the window. I know evil when I see it: that which is insidiously trying to obstruct human creativity and human desire to expand in a life giving way towards community and family.

When we become witness to violence, death, hatred, segregation, racism, etc. the question is worth asking: why are these things easier to do than the opposite?

It is very likely that such energies are directly the result of some kind of negligence that is destabilizing a situation and sending out all kinds of vibrations into human nature, systematically converting good into bad. That becomes what we call evil. Evilness is not something that can be cornered somewhere as a separate entity and combated, but an energy that eventually arises as the result of something we are not paying attention to.

We notice that more of our media is oriented towards violence simply because, most of the time, violence sells; it gets people's attention. Why? There are ways in which violence attracts and galvanizes attention. Therefore, if it is possible to view violence as a message that something needs our attention, but not our indulgence, it makes it possible to transcend evil into good, bad into positive. I am certainly not looking at it in the Christian sense of the devil scheming to make people's lives worse. I want to look at it as a signal pointing to something that has been neglected.

Is there a final message you would like to give to our readers?

We are living in a very fragile time. It is important that we humans renew our trust in ourselves and our capacities, that we don't give up hope, that we revisit our power to generate change – and affirm life over the threat of death.

This interview was originally published in the British journal *Caduceus* (www.caduceus.info), issue 61, November 2003, from which it is reprinted with permission.

Malidoma Somé, PhD, is one of today's most eloquent masters of indigenous wisdom. His life and teaching form a bridge between the traditional ways of his people, the Dagara of West Africa – among whom he is an initiated elder – and the modern world. He has been 'initiated' into the West as a scholar with a remarkable academic career, being professor of literature at the University of Michigan until the beginning of the '90s.

He is a gifted medicine man and diviner, as well as a compelling teacher and author. For more than twenty years, Malidoma has shared the ancient knowledge of his tribe with people in the West who are increasingly disconnected from their ancestors, spirit, and the richness of life in community. His voice awakens in our hearts recognition that we are all born with a life purpose to fulfil and that we can do so in a deep and abiding relationship with all beings.

In Europe he is working with the intercultural researcher Dr Helga Weule and the anthropologist Manfred Weule MA in Tingan institute in Austria since 2000. Their work on life purpose brought them together. Dr Somé shared his medicine with them, to practise and to teach his way of West African cowrie shell divination as a navigation tool for individuals and for community building in the West.

Dr Somé is the author of several bestselling books, including *Of Water and the Spirit*, *Ritual: Power, Healing and Community*, and *The Healing Wisdom of Africa*. He is currently completing two new books: one on the ancestors and our relationship to them; the other on gatekeepers between this and the spirit world.

www.malidoma.com · www.tingan.info

Hildur Jackson recalls the beginning time of the Co-housing Movement in Denmark. She acknowledges how the power of living in community serves children. And how community has made it possible for her as a mother to be active in, amongst other, the setting up of the Global Ecovillage Network.

Children Need 100 Parents

Hildur Jackson

Do Women have a Choice?

In 1969 I was sitting in my new house in Copenhagen with my two bouncing baby boys of six months and 18 months. I had just finished my law degree and was speculating over how my life might unfold. Should I seek a career as a lawyer or civil servant, and leave the children in daycare with strangers for many hours every day? Or should I give up my career and stay at home to take care of my children myself? There was no apparent third option. When I was 14, I had vowed to remain single and independent. All the women I saw around me were dissatisfied with following either of these choices. I was now with a man in whom I had confidence, and I wanted to avoid falling into the same trap as my mother and other women in her generation. Were there really no other choices than a full time career – thus penalizing my children – or staying home and cutting off a part of my energy that wants to flow into the world?

In 1968 I decided to continue my studies, now in cultural sociology, to find out more about human nature, and in particular to learn if there were societies in other parts of the world, or throughout history, which had found better solutions to this dilemma. I joined the feminist movement, which was just starting at that time. With one baby on my lap and my husband looking after the other, I attended meetings in which women shared their concerns. One day I read a newspaper article in *Politiken* (a major Danish newspaper), 'Children Need 100 Parents'. A lightning bolt struck me. Of course! Many women had the same problem. Together we could create something new.

So I took the initiative to establish a living situation in which several families combined private homes with common open space, had no fences, and shared some facilities – a concept which later came to be known in English as co-housing. I founded a group with friends and we started looking for property. Within three years we had created a small co-housing community of six families and converted an old farmhouse near Copenhagen into common space. Basically, the initiative was a social experiment, and a very successful one. It was called Hoejtofte – after the farm we bought. We learned later that two other similar initiatives had come into existence as a result of that same newspaper article. They are still both well-functioning co-housing groups along with more than 200 others. This was the beginning of the co-housing movement which has spread over the world and also inspired us to be part of birthing the broader ecovillage movement. Co-housing started as a way of creating a better childhood for children, a fact which is sometimes overlooked. Did they achieve that and what is the situation today?

Inventing Co-housing as We Went

We developed the idea of co-housing as we went along. Living with six other families and their children was fun and quite different from living an ordinary suburban life – even though our project was situated in the middle of an ordinary suburb near Copenhagen. We chose to have no borders between our gardens. We had two giant lawns for games and a common house and stables. We raised chicken, tended a large common vegetable garden, and had fruit trees and berry bushes. Quite often all the men, and occasionally a woman or two, would play football with the kids – and all the other neighbourhood kids too.

We also had three Icelandic horses, which were a lot of fun. Our neighbours' girls helped to look after the horses and often looked after our youngest son, too. Every Sunday we went horseback riding in the forest. The children had many friends, as Hoejtofte was a natural centre of activity in the larger neighbourhood. We could meet and have celebrations in our common house. Over time we became quite good at celebrating using music and theatre. It is much nicer to be celebrated than having to put on your own party! On summer afternoons we would often run or bike to a nearby lake in the forest and go swimming.

As the old farmhouse was in constant need of repair, we held monthly work weekends. These helped to strengthen the glue of community between us. These are some of the dearest childhood memories of our sons. Our life was fun and rich. When my husband Ross travelled on business, which was quite often, I never felt isolated. Twelve years after the first two, I had a third son and experienced the joy of being mother of 'our first co-housing baby' with 12 parents to look after it. I could always get help. Having a child in such a setting was a constant blessing.

The local school often commented that children from our community were good at sharing and solving problems. They learned direct democracy at Hoejtofte as they were part of the decision-making processes. Also, they benefited greatly from having many adult role models. My boys learnt from the neighbours what they could not learn from me or my husband. And they easily accepted that house rules were different in different houses. We shared responsibilities and the joys and sorrows of life. The adults supported each other in various ways. For example, when one man had a mental breakdown, three of us stayed with him for several nights and days (and stayed home from their jobs), thus avoiding his needing to be hospitalized.

I believe women are naturally good communicators, and do well in community settings. In communities like ours, women weren't suppressed in any way. For me this was an important step forward in the process of achieving equal opportunities between men and women. It allowed me to find a middle way between having a job and staying at home. I studied, did activist work, wrote. In 1981 I joined the Nordic Alternative Campaign – 100 Nordic grass roots movements working with the scientific community trying to create a vision of how to solve the global, social and ecological problems with a single vision and finding ways to realize this vision. For 10 years I co-ordinated this project on a voluntary basis. We held exhibitions, competitions of ideas, set up preliminary projects, meetings, and seminars in Denmark, Norway and Sweden. Without the co-housing community as a stable base and without a husband willing to pay the phone bills and buy the stamps this could not have happened. And it was the prerequisite of later initiatives of a Danish and then a global network of ecovillages.

And it was great for the kids. Ask the children today and they all want to live in co-housing communities. Some already do, although it is as difficult today as it was then to build one, for still in Denmark there is little local encouragement (but also no active resistance), no support from our politicians, and suitable land is scarce. In spite of this there are more than 200 family co-housing groups, many ecovillages and many co-housing groups for seniors. They sell easily.

The children of Hoejtofte have all moved away, but they have kept contact. Many have their own children. We continue to meet once a year – the last three years at the co-housing community of Bakken, where one of the Hoejtofte children now live with her husband and three children. At the last count there were 45 of us, with 28 children under eight years old.

We all learned a lot about conflict resolution, about love and solidarity. Co-housing communities offer an alternative way to solve social problems without involving public institutions – and at much lower cost!

We all learned a lot about conflict resolution, about love and solidarity. Co-housing communities offer an alternative way to solve social problems without involving public institutions – and at much lower cost!

Children in other Co-housing & Ecovillages

Although ours was small, I believe that our experience is fairly representative of what children experience in other co-housing communities and ecovillages as well. I have been visiting projects in many countries and find the same patterns. Bakken, a 25-year-old co-housing community has a small gym which is heaven for children. Several places have nurseries and schools in the community. We decided that our children would be strange enough as it was and they joined the local school, which was very good. Knowing so many other adults and being welcomed in so many homes makes children very open and confident. They can move around alone from an early age which makes for more independence. Opportunities are so abundant, and friends so accessible, that they watch less TV than average. They are free to take their own initiatives and create their own games. Relationships to the animal and plant world allow them to gain the respect and understanding of beings other than themselves. You always find some animals (chicken, rabbits, horses, sheep) in communities as they can be looked after in holidays by others.

What is the Situation for Children now in 2007?

Raising children in Western society has not become any easier than in our younger days. All our children now have their own children, so I watch many children grow up. I love to spend time with them and only wish that they could all live in a co-housing project. The women of my children's generation are under more pressure than before as they all work full time with professional, responsible jobs. Children are placed in institutions from early on and spend most of the day surrounded by many other children and a lot of noise. Their inner impulses are heavily regulated by what the institution offers and by the shortage of staff. In their free time children watch a lot of television and play electronic games. They often have TVs in their rooms, gameboys and mobile phones. On TV they see the news of war and conflicts, violent cartoons in a constant flow and commercials that aim at turning them into big consumers. The food they get is often junk and fast even while parents struggle to get them to eat properly. Traffic limits their capacity to roam.

I am deeply worried about these conditions under which children grow up today in our country. Employees in Denmark have six weeks' holiday a year and this is often the only time during which children experience nature in a more direct way. This way of life is not enough to teach children about nature and life and to develop the kind of democratic, self-confident, loving people we need to change the world.

The co-housing movement, and subsequently the ecovillage movement, which I believe are really just two variants of the same basic impulse, represent an idea that offers a solution for children. I still think that if for nothing else we should build them for our children. I would say it takes a village and at least 20 parents to raise a child. Co-housing communities and ecovillages have laid a firm foundation for the future and are ready for broader recognition and support as disillusionment with the negative consequences of so-called 'free markets' and consumer society spreads. People are beginning to realize that we must move forward to a sustainable and just global society, based not on the needs of commercial entities and their allies, power-hungry politicians, but on the needs and desires of real people everywhere.

Hildur Jackson. Born 1942. Married to Ross Jackson for 40 years, they have three sons and five grandchildren. Hildur is a lawyer, a cultural sociologist, an ecovillage designer and a writer. Together with Ross and others, she co-initiated Danish National Network of Ecovillages (LOS in 1993) and GEN, the Global Ecovillage Network.

Her books include: Hildur Jackson and Karen Svensson (ed.), *Ecovillage Living, Restoring the Earth and her People 2002*; articles in *Permaculture Magazine* and LOS'NET on single ecovillages; Hildur Jackson, *Creating Harmony, Conflict Resolution in Community*, 1998
www.gaia.org

1 Building Community & Embracing Diversity

Robin and Kosha describe how we can care for the seedlings of our dreams and visions in order to watch them grow into a strong reality. They inspire us to share our visions in a way that respects their aliveness and need to be constantly recreated.

Vision in Community

Robin Alfred & Kosha Anja Joubert

There is nothing more powerful than an idea whose time has come.
VICTOR HUGO

All our projects, all our communities have unfolded into existence from single seeds – ideas that were envisioned and nurtured until they could start growing.

An idea comes from somewhere. We are taking a shower and suddenly we have an idea – *I need to do this*! Sometimes it happens alone – *I need to write a poem about my walk in the forest yesterday afternoon*. Sometimes, we need to find others to help us manifest our idea. Perhaps it is a little dreamy – *I want to create a new way of dealing with human waste* – and we need help grounding it and making it real. Perhaps it will require money – *I want to share my knowledge about local currencies with more people* – and it needs access to networks and publicity. Perhaps it is born out of desperation – *there must be a better way for us to make decisions than this!* – and you need more ideas and an environment conducive to lateral thinking.

However it starts, an idea appears in us. We can choose to see this in many different ways. We might like to think that this is 'my idea'; it comes from my training and my experience. We might prefer to say that an idea is right for its time and it happens to land in me. We might believe it is a combination of both me and something beyond me that creates the idea. We might conclude that there is nothing more personal than vision yet, at the same time, the power that a vision carries to transform reality, springs from its connectedness to the larger whole. Real visions are uncovered, not manufactured.

However we see it, our experience has taught us several things about how to care for, and nurture, this idea, and how to grow it into a vision that will inspire ourselves, encourage others to join us, and sustain us when the going gets tough.

Develop, Refine & Hold your Genuine Intention

Clarify what it is you want to do. Create a strong image of where you want to reach. Make it so inspiring, that you can't help but keep coming back to that image with joy again and again. Ask yourself questions about it: How does this connect to my purpose in life? How does this reflect my deepest values? How might life look once this vision has fully unfolded? Dip into the shadows too: Are there parts in me, which do not believe that this is possible? Can I reconcile them? Do these voices have worthwhile contributions to make or are they nagging old habits that need to be told to shut up?

This process of refining the idea functions like a broadcast of intention. Through this process, an idea grows into a vision. It will pull reality towards you. Instead of starting straight away with working your butt off, take time for the magnetism of your idea to unfold. Clear intention is a powerful force.

Keep the vision close to your chest until your sense of it is strong enough that it (not you) can withstand its being shared with others. Often people have come to one or other of us and said something like this:

> I had this great idea – to create an eco-housing development. I put an advert in the paper and 20 people came to the first meeting. I was thrilled. But now, two years have passed, and we seem to be spending all our time arguing about the details – how people join, money and work in the community, is it even a community, is there a spiritual side to all this … on and on it goes. And we haven't even found a site yet!

The problem here is sharing the idea too early, with too many people. In our experience, a vision arrives in the hearts and minds of between one and three people, and clarity of direction, purpose, intention, needs to be developed and held in this small group, and this small group alone. Only when this core group is clear about the major aspects of the venture –

- The vision – what exactly is the purpose of this undertaking?
- The key processes – membership: joining and leaving; decision-making; finances
- The core relationships – leadership and hierarchy;

– can others be invited to join it? Then, it is clear what they are joining – your project and your vision. We cannot think of any successful venture that was started by a committee. Vision doesn't work like that. It needs a clear channel for its expression in the world, be it The Body Shop (Anita Roddick); Virgin (Richard Branson); Microsoft (Bill Gates); the Findhorn Foundation (Peter and Eileen Caddy and Dorothy McLean) … if you can find a vision that manifested through more than an initial group of three, we'd like to hear from you!

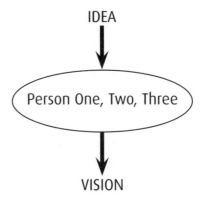

Don't Confuse the Vision with the Mission!

The vision of your project is the aspirational goal. It is the contribution your project wants to make to the world. If you write it as a Vision Statement, the statement needs to be

- Memorable
- Inspirational
- Clear
- Achievable, i.e. something you can 'live into'

And not measurable!

There may need to be all sorts of measurable targets and goals along the way and that's fine and very helpful, but if your vision is measurable too, where do you go when the measurements are not being achieved? You have nothing left. The vision needs to remain like the North Star – drawing you on, providing direction, something to remember when the targets are hard to achieve, or the finances are running low.

Vision

Vision is seeing the potential purpose hidden in the chaos of the moment, but which could bring to birth new possibilities for a person, a company or a nation.

Vision is seeing what life could be like while dealing with life as it is

Vision deals with those deeper human intangibles that alone give ultimate purpose to life

In the end, vision must always deal with life's qualities, not with its quantities.

Van Duisen Wilhard

Everyone in the Project Needs to be Connected to the Vision

Having said that you need to keep the vision close to your chest and in the hearts and minds of only a few in the early stages, once you are embarked on the process of manifesting and living your vision, everyone needs to know what it is, and be connected to it. In some projects, it is written down and stands clear for everyone to see e.g. new arrivals at Zegg, an ecovillage in Germany, cannot fail to see a huge billboard in the centre of the campus, that sets out the core principles underpinning the project. Other ways include regular meetings to discuss the vision; including the vision statement as a strap line to notices, emails, agendas.

Only when people are connected to the vision, and when their own individual sense of purpose can find expression in the larger, collective sense of purpose we call the vision, will they want to work late, do the extra unseen chores, 'go the extra mile' for the benefit of the whole.

The Vision Needs to be Re-created Continuously

In the end, a vision is not made up of the sentences that express the vision statement of a project. Vision is the power behind these sentences to focus our intention on a common higher goal. Sometimes the words of the sentences themselves might have lost their meaning from over-usage. Or we might have forgotten their deeper meaning and lost ourselves in an everyday interpretation that fails to inspire us any more. The only meaningful criteria for judging a vision are the actions that spring from it, and its power to sustain us when we face hard times.

We need to give space in our communities for continual reconnection with the source behind our vision statement in order to keep it sparkling. And we need to keep in mind that vision is always an answer to the present, an expression of what we want to create, how we want to shape our reality now and take on responsibility for an emerging future. Visioning is an ongoing process of focussing intention, which will never be completed.

> Never doubt that a small group of committed citizens can change the world.
> Indeed, it's the only thing that ever has.
>
> MARGARET MEAD

For authors' biographies, see page x.

Prescription for the Heart

Sheikh Din Muhammad Abdullah al-Dayemi

- Perform a serious, relentless and moral inventory on yourself.
- Repent and seek forgiveness of your errors and weaknesses.
- Determine an approach that allows you to live according to your core values.
- Make a commitment.
- Develop a practice to foster a continual invocation of praise and gratitude.
- Cast fear, discouragement, discontent, pessimism and reactive rebellion aside and treat these things as your enemy.
- Surround yourself with the company of truth and those who support you unconditionally in your process of self-completion.
- Rid yourself of your defensive posture.
- Practise humility by making yourself vulnerable to God and those you love.
- Do all these things even if you don't feel like doing them.
- In order to be able to function through these things we have to be able to stay present.
- Let go of this list because it's not a list – but first, do the work.

Sheikh Din Muhammad Abdullah al-Dayemi is the current western spiritual representative and religious leader of the Dayera Sharif, a 750-year-old Islamic dynasty with its headquarters in Dhaka, Bangladesh. He is also the director of the Dayemi Tariqat, a religious and service organization that operates an intentional spiritual community in Southern Illinois with branches across the United States, Europe and Bangladesh.
DayemiTariqat@aol.com

Geseko von Lüpke describes the Vision Quest, a powerful initiatory ritual that, by helping us find a deeper sense of ourselves, can help prepare us for the challenge of living in community.

Feeling Connected Through Being Alone

Solitary Fasting in the Wilderness as an Initiation to Community Life

Geseko von Lüpke

Why are people seeking life in an intentional community? Often, they hope to be able to cope better with their problems than while living in a nuclear family. Or they look to community as protection against loneliness, as a substitute for extended family, as a womb for undeveloped potential waiting to be expressed. And quite often all this neediness of the group members leads to crises in intentional communities, if not to total break-up. A community is not a substitute mama for grown up children nor a therapist. What a community really needs are grown up, responsible people aware of their potential, with a strong vision ready to face all the challenges that may be encountered on the way to its realization. How can people from the post-modern age, raised in an atmosphere of competition, alienation and separation become fit for community? How can we mature in a society promoting childlike consumerism and using the material world to compensate for meeting our inner needs? How can we learn to lovingly accept ourselves with both our inner beauty and our shadows? How can we make our potential contribute to the whole?

Traditional societies have developed methods and rituals to end child-hood, which allow a young man or woman to claim their potential and contribute to the life of the tribe as mature adults. The solution for rendering a community sustainable lies in a simple paradox: 'At times you need to leave everything behind in life. Time to walk away and be alone with God, with nature and her beings' says American psychologist Steven Foster, who worked for 30 years with his wife, Meredith Little, to rediscover old rites of passage and adapt them for the modern world. 'And in this lonely place one turns inside and as a gift receives answered, clarity, a vision to take home to one's community, so it will prosper and flourish and life will go on.'

*Creating Sacred
Space – a Medicine
Wheel*

Our own ancestors in the forests of Europe sent their young men and women into the wilderness too. The adventures they encountered have been transmitted by stories some of us are still reading our children today: fairy tales! Almost all fairy tales follow an archetypical pattern: A young person leaves the security of home and walks alone into the dark forests where he faces dark forces, inner and outer demons, giants and witches. When he overcomes them, he returns to the human world changed and born anew to take a new position in society. The anthropologist Hans Peter Duerr writes in his book *Traumzeit*: "The archaic peoples knew that, in order to gain insights into our world, we need lo leave it behind; in order to be 'tame' we need to be 'wild'; to live fully we must have been prepared to die; to know the meaning of 'inside' we need to have been 'outside'."

What is a Vision Quest?

The modern vision quest is a 12-day ritual involving four days of preparation; four days of being alone in nature while fasting; and four days of integration. It is a ritual of symbolic death of old roles, a retreat to the knowledge of the soul beyond socially adjusted patterns of behaviour, to silence and insight, that allows us the see the path of our lives more clearly, and an exercise for all the crises that lie ahead of us.

The vision quest is an archetypical ritual known to all cultures in the world that enables us to step out of the tightness of an ending phase of life and give birth to a different person into the future. These phases have been honoured with different ceremonies in the past – as passages, crossroads, changes, thresholds – to give way to a new form of life with a new role, new responsibilities and new privileges. All these initiations had to do with the holistic human being and with how to express our full self in order to enable the community to survive. In a group, social responsibilities have always been given to those who passed the initiations. French ethnologist Arnold van Genepp discovered that all over the world these rituals consist of the same three parts: letting go of the old, a period of testing, and finally a return to society.

Traditional cultures that live in close connection with nature experience the phases of life as part of the cycles of nature. Since humanity started to observe nature people have been trying to harmonize their social life with the universal laws – in the Savannas of Africa, the deserts of Australia and the Siberian Tundra. Just as nature proceeds through the cycle of the seasons, men and women pass through the cycles of life. Spring, summer, autumn, winter – childhood, adolescence, adulthood, and old age. The changing of the seasons was linked also to the four directions:

- Innocent sensuality and pure emotions of childhood were associated with summer and the South.
- Doubts, insecurities and dark depressions of adolescence are likened to Autumn and the West, where life retreats.
- Sober clarity and the analytical planning of the responsible adult arise in the North, similar to a snowy winter landscape.
- Old age, death and rebirth are assigned to Spring and the East, which gives new life to barren land.

This archaic psychology, known today as the Medicine Wheel, lays the foundation for understanding the processes of human transformation: every human being is living these seasons of life, ending each one of them with initiations and rituals. But not only in the big cycles of life did the healers of past ages find this matrix of human maturation. In every relationship, every day, even every hour a human being seems to move across the Wheel: a steady process of pure emotion, doubtful inner searching, responsible clarity and detached wisdom – South, West, North, East. One is following the other, just like the seasons and the four directions, even if some phases seem to last forever.

All those familiar with community living know from experience that almost all intentional communities dance around the Medicine Wheel as well: the euphoric and effervescent love for all at the very beginning (South) is followed by a phase of disillusionment, blame, doubt, criticism (West). At best this leads to structural clarity, common rules, deepened communication and more responsibility (North). This, for the first time, gives rise to real community in a mature state, including tolerance for diversity (East). Then the dance goes on, new crises arise and are not to be feared, as they serve for further growth and maturation.

The Medicine Wheel lays the foundation for understanding the processes of human transformation: every human being is living these seasons of life, ending each one of them with initiations and rituals.

Does this mean that we, like our forebears, need to be alone in order to be able to live in community? Over the past 20 years, more and more people have decided to cut their umbilical chord to civilization – for this limited time of four days – to be alone, fasting, without shelter, in the wilderness, to encounter their self. They sense the value of the old knowledge. They are looking for the purpose of life, want to move through crisis, begin a new phase of life, grow roots or simply decide which community they want to join. The vision quest is a rite of passage that does not primarily serve personal growth but serves the community, to which the person returns after his experience. The community needs people who know who they are, who are not afraid to be alone, who effortlessly switch from 'I' to 'We' and who accompany others on their own path with tolerance. It seems we need to learn to be alone to be able to construct a new world together.

How Does a Vision Quest Work?

In a contemporary vision quest a group of people who usually don't know each other gathers in a lonely place – desert, forest, mountains. There, they prepare together for the days spent alone, fasting, equipped only with a sleeping bag, mattress, warm clothes and a diary to go into the wilderness. Ten people meet in a moment of transition with a common purpose – to grow. They openly share their hearts, their beauty and hopes, as well as their shadows and crises – independent of status or social roles. They listen to one another and to themselves, learning from the others and beginning to acknowledge who they are and where they are at in their lives. Community develops almost inevitably when up to ten people show themselves openly and eager to change. Exercises in nature deepen this process, the natural diversity mirroring the daily rising of new facets of inner wisdom. The purpose is to look at current reality and acknowledge it. Only then, after ceasing the usual fight against our own inadequacy, will it be possible to step into a new phase of life.

The purpose is to look at current reality and acknowledge it. Only then, after ceasing the usual fight against our own inadequacy, will it be possible to step into a new phase of life.

After four days of intense, led preparation every member of the group takes off to find a place in the wilderness that represents in the outside world whatever has been recognized in the inner landscape of the soul. Every participant is accompanied into the wilderness with a ritual – to the place of inner sight, reconnection and challenge. What follows are four days and four nights in a different world – a world with no socially defined rules, distractions, agendas, useless encounters. Now the moment has come: this moment we have been preparing for over months and especially the last four days. Everything is coming together now: the fear of loneliness and the joy that the inner calling is finally being answered; a childlike curiosity and insecurity facing a world with its own rules; the longing for deep experiences and respect for the three taboos that characterize this time: no contact with people, no food, and no shelter except the clothes to keep us warm.

> The first day I was simply happy to be there, to be there alone sitting in the sun, naked. There was no hunger and no loneliness. I felt at home.

As the participants learn more about their environment, they simultaneously discover more about themselves. They might find unknown caves and recesses, soft rolling hills, hard grounds and soft moss beds, the broad sky and narrow passages. In the wholeness of the natural world they discover their own wholeness. Insecurity about how to handle all the winged, crawling and creeping neighbours, into whose territory we venture forth, mirrors our life in human company. And here may lie the first lesson:

> In my usual way albeit unconscious until now, I had not taken care for the future. During the first night I realized that marvelling at the stunning sight I had not taken care of my needs. The hilltop was sloping on all sides and I was sliding downwards on my mattress. No rest, no peace. Therefore I moved on, despite all rules, and this is my life's issue: a nomad searching for her place.

The deeper we plunge into ourselves, the more rises from below the surface. All sorts of things move into our consciousness: old images, longings, moods, fears, needs, loneliness, pain, love, creativity, plans and boredom, intense and rapidly changing. We are alone with our perceptions looking at the mirror of our inner life. This can feel threatening but is utterly normal. Difficult as fasting alone in the wilderness may sound, it actually only recognizes the fact that we are alone in our everyday lives as well, although this is usually hidden by relationships, work and entertainments.

We are alone and we are not: ants crawl on our legs; flies buzz around our head, a squirrel is moving in circles around our place. In this loneliness we feel watched by a thousand eyes, perceived without any sound.

> I knew I wasn't alone. As I sat there I heard a rustling sound right next to me and got a fright. A little while later I heard an animal squeak not far away from me, as if it was in danger. I didn't know how lively it was in the forest at night. I only knew that I felt threatened.

The vision quest is a real bodily experience, not an esoteric adventure. Being in the wilderness means entering the living room of slugs and snails, being exposed to the heat of the sun and frosty nights. No house, no roof over our head, no tent, only a sheet of plastic often difficult to set up. Being exposed to the elements in this way can bring deep insights: When a thunderstorm is bearing down on shivering people in the dark of night, the everyday dramas at home seem irrelevant, a luxury some of us don't want to afford any longer. The value of having shelter is appreciated as well as the community around us. Whoever is exposed to wind, rain, heat and cold feels the grandeur of nature and the fragility of our self-images and roles. Without shelter the opportunity to experience something knew opens up. Nature becomes the projection of our inner worlds. She can be both a place of horrors or a paradise full of unexpected gifts. The perceptions are stimulated, the senses are sharpened, the mind clearer. Fasting is a secure way to widen consciousness. Our senses open up to the interactions of the elements and the natural rhythms, the separation between the self and the world is dissolving. We chew on naked life and digest the past.

We go back and forth between inside and outside, experiencing reality as unity and ourselves part of it. The living world is looking at us. Everything is mutual and exchanging. Whatever we touch – water, wind, earth, trees, stones – is caressing us. Being is central, with all our senses. Because the usual roles are absent, we see what is: the majesty of the starry sky at night, the splendour of a desert flower, the playfulness of a rodent under the rocks, the delicious drinking water, the miracle of our own body. Being alone is not a problem anymore when we feel the unity with all things.

> The clear simple beauty of nature is beginning to transform me. I become simple. For hours I just sit and gaze, seeing nothing, drinking water and feeling how I get weaker because of the fasting, observing how thoughts appear, words and sounds, that spontaneously come together in a small song. Suddenly I talk out loud about some anger. As there are no witnesses, I forget to pretend. At some point I fall into the obvious meaningfulness and uselessness of the natural processes and laugh, amazed. For a moment I feel the certainty that beyond every purpose I just am like a tree, a rock, a flower, a human being, a lizard. And a little later this moment becomes a treasured memory.

During this time outside we symbolically pass through the crises and transformations of our lives, discover the foundations of our strength as well as fragile illusions. Nature serves as the screen on which we watch this drama. Nature never judges. The doubts and blaming, judgement and sadness that

The power of Introspection in Nature

come up, arise from within us. There is no one to hold responsible. We see that the negative aspects of our lives are linked to our perceptions. There is more than enough time to battle our own demons and shadows. There is no escape from our naked self, our will and wanting. No guru is there to save us, no priest to pray for us. It is up to us to do this. That's how the searchers come to the source of their power.

> What is happening? I am here, but it neither feels sacred nor otherwise very special. I am alone, I rattle, I hear the crickets, and little flies are tickling my forehead. I am part of it all, no doubt. I am at home here in the wilderness, and I am feeling at home here.

The whole process during these four days leads to closing a chapter of our lives and symbolically opens a new space in order to consciously pass on to the next phase of life. The structure of this ritual, its archetypical purpose, mirrors what we know about the process of death and rebirth from myths around the globe: We die in our old role, digest and 'compost' the experiences of the past and come back to the world anew. The more consciously participants close their old life, the more likely they will be to step effectively into a new life at the end of this process.

When the vision seekers meet again for the first time after those four days and nights of loneliness there is an atmosphere of awe and inner turmoil. We see tanned, thin, beautiful faces, shining eyes that transmit the passed wild experiences. Some long embraces express the longing for the human world that accompanied all during the time of loneliness. The participants are quiet, validating themselves and the others. A new quality of community is experienced when people meet after such a time, connected to their authentic power, without the need to be seen, compete for appreciation, to pretend what we are not, in order to be loved. In the following days everyone will tell their story, share their experience, and receive the mirrors of the listening community. Together we work on recognizing and understanding new identities that have formed during the days in the wilderness and develop ways to integrate our transformed understanding of our self into our everyday life. For many people who undergo this process a whole new model of community forms: they experience it as a meeting of different grown up and mature people who support, complement, and appreciate each others growth.

The capacity to be alone has opened a new level of connection for them. Instead of falling into the traps of codependency, they come back to their people knowing about their own personal myth. The transformation is much more than losing the fear of being alone. Who dares to enter the 'other world' of the wilderness also leaves behind a purely rational worldview. While experiencing the magical world out there, where inside and outside seem to mix, the vision seekers are reintegrating a separated aspect of their souls. The limited, rational worldview opens to a trans-rational space where mind and heart cooperate. Nature itself becomes the measure for our inner values,

Together we work on recognizing and understanding new identities that have formed during the days in the wilderness and develop ways to integrate our transformed understanding of our self into our everyday life.

for a functioning community. Out there we have experienced ourselves as part of a much bigger community, the community of all living beings. This deep reconnection can carry us through moments of loneliness and chaos in our community. Our focus is not the Darwinian struggle to survive but the subtle net of ubiquitous cooperation, where everyone finds their niche and contributes to the grand network of life. The dance through the Wheel of Life that we experience so consciously during these days teaches us that challenges and crises are not disasters, but steps on the path of growth.

Vision quest helps us realize what our potential really is, to acknowledge it and to dedicate our life to integrating our gifts into our life. South African president Nelson Mandela, who went through his own lonely journey during his time in prison, warned in his inaugural speech that there is no bigger sin than not letting our light shine and not developing our abilities. The late Steven Foster said: 'I am sure if we all had the chance to send every human being in the wilderness for three or four days without food, alone, just being there, this would bring about an enormous change on our planet.'

Dr Geseko von Lüpke was born in 1958. He studied Political Science, Cultural Anthropology and Journalism and travelled the world. For many years now he has been researching and describing processes of spiritual growth and human development. He specializes in holistic worldviews and designing of political structures for a sustainable future. The seeming paradox between political involvement and spiritual growth brought him to Deep Ecology. As a father of three children, he works as a journalist and writer. As international networker he connects pioneers and activists from many cultures and organizes conferences. He leads Vision Quests in Europe.

Dmitry Morozov, founder of Kitezh Children's Community, Russia, describes what inspired him to set up a spiritual community dedicated to raising orphaned children. He writes both of the passion and transformative energy that underpins it, and highlights some of the pitfalls. Set in the unpromising cultural context of Russia in the 1990s, Kitezh stands as testimony to the power of vision.

From Vision to Reality
A Home for Children in Russia

Dmitry Morozov

An extract from the book *Kitezh Community*

Origins

I am often asked how I first conceived of Kitezh, and indeed, what is Kitezh? Is it a cooperative community of foster families, an attempt to revive the Russian tradition of community, an effort to change our way of life or some kind of spiritual venture? The very name of our settlement is taken from folklore. Kitezh is a mythical invisible town that was transformed by the will of God into a vessel of spiritual energy.

It took some years for the idea of Kitezh to grow within me, as gradually and naturally as a shoot sprouting from the Earth. Time passed by and the tiny seedling germinated, the sprout burst through to the light, broke away from the seed and began to grow according to a law unto itself, revelling in the sun and getting battered by the rain and the wind.

At first I dreamt, or rather I sensed, that I would not be able to give my life to the fight for material wealth; that possessing things, a career and even happy idleness would in essence be a waste of effort in the brief snippet of the Earth's journey that is my life. I felt then, and know now, that there is nothing higher for a human being than to see himself as a part of the cosmos, to love and to be loved, to do good by learning and making an effort. I felt that I would not be alone on that path, because after all these are simple truths and, however cloudy they may seem, they are to be found everywhere and by everyone who looks for them. You only need to create the conditions for your life to become a path that can embody the will of the Creator.

It is not competition but love that should become the main source of creative energy. Once we have arrived in this *mir*, our community, we should establish within it service to God, in the company of others, not as a form of escape, but by deepening our involvement with His laws. To serve God means to create, to work, to carry out a plan that is invisible to us. The goal that I set before the community was therefore the most fundamental that there is on Earth: to raise orphaned children.

In the Beginning

In Kitezh there was an empty field and the idea was a blank slate. Just what you need to create a new world. The idea was to create ideal conditions for the development and education of abandoned children. To do this we needed people to come and live with us who were ready to serve the idea. And for those people the first things we needed were houses, roads, and electricity.

Why was a community the best form to create a developing environment? Because it is precisely this type of social structure that demands from a person a consciousness of doing good.

Whenever I talk about the first years of building Kitezh, I am always struck and surprised by the common consciousness we have developed. My narrative comes from the most fresh, recent layers of my memory. In fact I find myself recounting not what actually happened, but I repeat the most successful parts of previous accounts. And so I do not even remember very well what actually happened. This is how myths start. Our adults and children hear these stories and pass them on, referring to the 'wonderful first years of construction', turning mythology into a heroic epic.

Creating the Community against the Background of Contemporary Russia

You must realize that in Russia for many years there were no alternatives to State provision. Also, because of our history, the problems in our country with regard to orphaned children were possibly the biggest anywhere in the world. The term 'orphan' in our country describes children whose parents have died as well as what we call 'social orphans' who have been removed from their parents for their own safety. Ninety-five per cent of all children in institutions are social orphans, with at least one living parent. Kitezh is a distinct move away from a system that has been creaking and crumbling for decades and which takes little or no account of the spiritual or individual needs of the child. Kitezh is small, believes strongly that education is an essential therapeutic tool and believes too that the very fabric and rhythm of our daily lives is our therapy. Kitezh adults share fully with each other the raising of all children and the therapeutic leadership in which our young adults now share is very real and very powerful.

Everything seemed so simple in the beginning. We used psychological tests to select community members from those who expressed an interest in living with us. After a trial period, a group of people was formed who were to become the teaching staff. Every community member became a foster parent, a teacher and a mentor. The most difficult task was to raise enough money to build houses, dress and feed the children.

Of course, in any period in Russia, raising money for charity has never been a simple matter, but I really didn't imagine that I would be investing my life's savings into setting Kitezh up, nor that what I wanted to do would be going against the mindset of society, the economic reality or flawed human nature.

For the first year, things went pretty smoothly. We acquired 40 hectares of land in the Baryatino region of Kaluga district. We had a number of volunteers who heard my inspired call to arms on national radio and came from all corners of Russia to start a new life in the name of higher aims. We were even donated enough money and building materials to construct our first houses. We got up early and worked till late, hurrying to get the roofs on before the snow started, and we sang songs around a campfire surrounded by our tents, making plans about how we were going to live as one big family, raising children, reading books, making beautiful artefacts, in harmony with nature and the environment.

That was more or less how 15 people, adults and children, spent the winter up to January 1994, in one finished and two almost built houses. And at our New Year celebration, there were 37 people, including those who had helped out in the summer and abandoned their cosy Moscow and Kaluga flats to be with us. How happy we were! Surrounded by uninhabited snow-clad forests and fields, we truly felt like creators of a new world. We were delighted to be together and that our efforts were starting to bear fruit. Golden candlelight flickered in windows frosted over with ice.

How happy we were! Surrounded by uninhabited snow-clad forests and fields, we truly felt like creators of a new world.

Setbacks

And then there were the humdrum working days, when John, a great optimist and a master with his hands, took to drink, not from despair or disappointment, but simply from an inability to deal with deep emotions. This was something new for us. The farmers in the local villages drank in a truly Russian way: many drank regularly and from despair. Their lives really were without the slightest cause for joy, without higher aims. We couldn't imagine that this epidemic could infect our community. Another Kitezhan, Nikolai, who had worked as a businessman in St Petersburg, could not keep his enterprising nature to himself. Suddenly we discovered that he had been selling trainers from the back of a lorry at the local market. He was not a bad person. He simply could not understand the importance in the community of consulting the others before acting. For the locals, Kitezh was a strange creature. They saw us as foreign and incomprehensible, and they used to spy on us. And then suddenly: 'Kitezhans involved in black market trainers!' The conditions for our existence demanded extreme awareness and support of one another. You cannot build a new world with the tools of the old one.

Then other things happened. We genuinely did not have money, often not even enough for food. Sometimes we had to trade a bottle of vodka to borrow a tractor, haggle with local peasants to help us put the roof on a house or build a chimney. We were also borne of this world, and to break away from its laws was no easier than it is for a blade of grass to break through asphalt. Fortunately, I understood then the importance of learning to wait. The time comes for everything: for every person and union of people, for every community.

Helping Children Grow

In the 14 years of Kitezh's existence we have discovered that it is essential to create a special developmental environment for children who have psychological problems. This is an environment that helps them to develop in accordance with their instincts and compensates for their problems and shortcomings. By 'environment' we mean not only the natural world, but also material, spiritual and cultural phenomena that are influential in society and that can both reinforce and negate parental influences. For example, good poetry aids development, whereas little poems made up by criminals have the opposite effect.

The Kitezh developmental environment consists of three elements:

- The foster family, which gives the homeless child that which is most important, namely a sense that he is needed and loved. This perception is essential if the child is to develop properly.

- The community of competent adults, which provides the child with a safe environment in which s/he can develop the ability to live and work as part of a collective, and which at the same time recognizes the right of each and every person to their own individuality.

- The natural environment and the architecture, which benefit the child spiritually, guide him to look for beauty and harmony, reduce psychological distress and provide surroundings that are conducive to therapeutic work.

Communication between an adult and a child is a creative process, based on love and inspiration. We consider that raising a child is an art that is impossible without love, compassion, inspiration and other artistic attributes. Only then can professionalism play a positive role. No foster parent can manage without both.

The first condition that we seek to fulfil in Kitezh is that there is an inner harmony among the adults and that they have a common conviction in the truth and integrity of the values they teach. In our therapeutic community we ask all the adults to adhere to one, uniform value system. The 'world view' should be one that is shared by everyone and as such it should represent the democratic will of the community as a whole.

Building a social organism is in no way similar to building a car or a house. The main problem is that people have free will and the ability to develop. They don't want to fulfil one and the same function year in year out, but rather they aim to fulfil their own ambitions. The stumbling block for many people in the community is the need for a 'common vision'. Because Kitezh is a therapeutic community, a place where children receive treatment for emotional problems, Kitezh residents must recognize a certain limit to their democratic freedoms. To bring up children whose entire value system has already imploded once and who need a holistic reliable, consistent and safe world, it is essential that adults observe certain principles in their interaction with others.

Raising children is an art requiring intuition and empathy. Only by intensively feeling sympathy and by sharing their children's fortunes and troubles can adoptive parents or teachers really identify with them and picture their inner world. Intuition is as important for a teacher as for an artist. It is a special talent that opens up in a person. It can be reached by different paths: by immersing oneself deeply in ones inner world, by meditation or psychoanalysis. The main thing is to learn to reach an inner peace that opens the door to empathy, or identification, with other people.

The Physical Environment as a Reflection of the Purpose of Community

If you were to find yourself in Kitezh right now, you would see log cabins with turrets, pine, carved porches and ornamental carved window decoration. You would also see delicate little wooden bridges. It is just as if a picture by the Russian artist Vasnetsov had come to life. We are proud of our 'fairy tale' architecture, as we believe that it plays a vital role in enabling children to be receptive to fairy tales. Why this interest in fairy tales? Simply, it is only in the world of fable that metamorphoses, miracles and transformations are possible. Strictly speaking, the settlement that we have built functions as a mere physical instrument, which allows us to work with the sub-conscious.

Traditional Russian architecture makes the child conscious of the good and equitable world of fairy tales. It allows him (or her) to feel a sense of affinity with his native land and people and it reconnects him with his 'roots', thus helping to prevent him from feeling lonely and lost. The style of the architecture, the pictures on the walls of the houses, our tradition of dressing in embroidered Russian shirts and singing folk songs on festive occasions all have their part to play in alleviating emotional problems. We turn to the most deeply embedded images from folk culture, and to fairy tales and myth to build up a picture of the world. We are no more inclined to talk about Jung's theory of the collective unconscious than a fish is to analyze the water in which it swims. Nevertheless, there are grounds to believe that this collective unconscious is an extremely powerful force that is worth harnessing for the benefit of the developmental environment.

What lies at the heart of most of our beloved fairy tales? It is the idea that magical transformations are possible! And the most important thing that happens at Kitezh is the magical transformation of our children …

To create a permanent natural background that testifies to the existence of beauty and order in the world, we draw upon the charm of the limetree-lined avenues of the ancient park, the calm of the shady ponds, the carefully laid out and well-kept paved paths and the flower-beds around the houses. The children participate actively in the creation of this beautiful environment, and in doing so they discover a simple truth: that it is within their power to change their world and that they themselves can fill their lives with beauty and order. Thus the foundations are laid for feelings of love towards one's native land. At the same time the children learn to draw energy from their everyday physical surroundings.

Every normal person can expect at least once in their life to experience the curative force of nature, the way that it sharpens the senses and quite literally satiates one's being with energy. Sometimes the ability to contemplate beauty and to feel at one with the mighty forces of the sky and the earth becomes a means of survival, a way to maintain a healthy state of mind.

Our fields, park and forests are more than just our habitat and the basis of our material survival. They are also a source of our inner strength. They remind us of the great and endlessly changing flow of life and provide welcome signs of the everlasting nature of the world of which every Kitezh resident feels they are part.

Kitezh Children's Community – Key Facts

In 2006, Kitezh Children's Community in Russia celebrated its 14th anniversary. Kitezh is a home and a source of inspiration for 50 adults and children. A second children's village, Orion, was started in 2004 and will be home for a further 50 adults and children. The vision to build a network of therapeutic villages for Russian orphans is becoming a reality.

Kitezh's second achievement, which is unique in the international experience of child-raising, is that it combines the advantages of the family construct with a collective form of social organization and child-raising.

The foster parents of the Kitezh Community have together conducted a unique educational experiment. We called our organization a 'community' because it is simultaneously an educational complex, a social experiment, a form of local administration and an absolutely real way of living.

The basic unit of Kitezh is the adoptive family. In Kitezh there are currently ten families. All the families share a common financial source, legal protection, common household management, and a united approach to education. Every adult fulfils a variety of functions, managing the community or in education, at the same time as being an adoptive parent or guardian. The combination of adults of various professions and the involvement of the children in the day-to-day work (e.g. teaching in the school, working in the kitchen, chopping wood) allows us maximum efficiency in the use of human and financial resources.

The highest legislative body is the Council of Members of the Non-Commercial Partnership. The highest executive body is the Head of the

Community, elected annually. All questions relating to the children's education and upbringing are decided by the Teachers' Council, of which all adoptive parents and schoolteachers are automatically members.

The first wave of young adults who spent a number of their formative years in Kitezh are playing an active role in the life of the community and in the therapeutic task. They participate in a highly intensive, well-supervised and consistently applied programme of mentoring and group discussion. Members of the 'Small Council', consisting of five 15 to 18 year olds, are gradually being inducted into practising the skills with younger children that have so far eluded some of the adults.

People who are right for Kitezh

Working in a therapeutic community means accepting the importance of inner work, being able to accept help and criticism from colleagues, the teachers' council, and the elected director. A colleague who has not resolved his inner problems and complexes cannot be a good teacher and psychologist. Being ready for lifelong development, a good-hearted nature, inner peace, clarity and purity of mind: all are essential qualities that earn someone the right to work with the inner worlds of children.

Therefore, we can only accept into our community people who are genuinely ready to open themselves up to those around them and who can share their real inner world and not some abstract ideal. It is difficult and painful. You have to have a strong will, determination and discipline.

Every adult in Kitezh agrees to try to meet the following demands on them as members of the therapeutic community:

- They should discuss all problems of relationships with children and other adults openly with other adults. They should put the unity of the community and the interests of the children before themselves.
- They should avoid remarks and actions that could prompt the children to form a negative view of the world.
- They should involve their feelings in their work and continually exchange ideas and information amongst the group.

It is creative people that we seek. We need creative adoptive parents, creative bakers, and creative farmers. The common wealth depends on everyone involved, and so does, more importantly, the general atmosphere in the community. Everyone chips in with building houses, taking decisions, moulding the contours of our common future. We all have to be able to perceive problems as they arise, to find creative solutions and harmonize our vision with that of everyone else in order that the turns and twists don't topple over our common ship.

Dmitry Morozov was born in Moscow in 1959 under Khrushchev and studied history at the Institute of the Countries of Asia and Africa of Moscow University while Brezhnev was in power. He became a journalist during the height of stagnation. For this reason, it is not surprising that the ideals of collectivism and reconstruction of the world formed the basis of his World View, which is embodied by the Kitezh Children's Community. As a journalist he travelled in many countries but finally decided that raising children and building his own world in Russia was the most interesting challenge.

1 Building Community & Embracing Diversity

Dieter Halbach tells us a story that might sound familiar to many. How can we survive the phases of disillusionment and disappointment that accompany the growth processes of most ecovillages and intentional communities? The seven steps to building community give us some helpful guidelines.

The Community-Seeker – A Story

Dieter Halbach

The Bookstore

Stopping by a small bookshop recently I came upon different books with interesting titles like *Eurotopia: An Index of European Communities*, *Diggers and Dreamers* or *Communities Directory*. Each of them held thousands of addresses of community projects. My heart skipped a beat: with all these addresses is must be possible for me to find a place to start the life of my dreams? The salesman behind the counter looked at me through his nickel-rimmed glasses, his eyes half sympathetic, half amused, and said: "Good books for people looking for community! Yes, I searched for community once myself … and when I found one at last, I lost it again. But I recently rediscovered something I'd lost."

After this somewhat nebulous introduction, he began to relate his odyssey across the globe from one community to the next. He was nothing if not critical: no one could satisfy him on his quest for the perfect community. The politically correct communities had stressful lives and lugged around heavy ideological baggage; the economically successful ones were sandbagged with work and management and had become far too conventional; the freaks were too stoned and chaotic for his taste; the spiritual communities were so obsessed with love that they had thrown sexuality out the window, and the sexually liberated communities had done the same with love.

My bookseller was just getting into high gear when suddenly a wistful, almost mystical smile appeared on his lips: "But after so many years of searching I finally found it: my community! They were just a handful of people, but somehow they had managed to integrate all aspects of life in perfect proportion."

"Right, so why didn't you stay there?" I asked him.

"They didn't want me," he replied. "I wanted the perfect community, and they wanted the perfect human being!"

A short time later, after many more questions, I stepped onto the street, the book under my arm. I felt strange. A blend of pain and joy, spiced with a pinch of fear, had settled onto my heart – which in turn was beating like a drum. Is this what the poets call 'yearning'?

"Only sunny eyes can see the sun," my bookseller called after me, laughing.

And what about the butterflies in my stomach? I wondered.

So, I stepped into the adventure called life … looking for myself and looking for community.

Euphoria and Chaos

When I got back home I had to sit down. What to do with so much energy?

Then it struck me: I would found a group! My own community! I would shape it according to my own ideas. This would save me the frustration of searching and of having to compromises. I got into designing an advertisement for our local alternative newspaper immediately and invited all those interested to a first meeting.

This was the starting point: one month later we sat together in the backroom of a café. More than 30 people had come, the avant-garde of community seekers of this region. We seemed to be a fine selection of human beings: half-enlightened, old hippies, single mothers, students in search of a suitable subject for their thesis, retired people trying to find a fulfilling way to live the rest of their lives, singles in search of a partner, jobless needing work, activists in need of a revolution …

However, these finer nuances and differences became apparent later. That very first evening all I could see was shining faces, beautiful people inspired by a common dream: the dream of an ecologically sustainable life, of living together in solidarity and peace. In other words: it seemed like a fulfilment of my longing to dream together instead of alone!

But we had so many dreams … their number seemed to grow from meeting to meeting. And at the same time, their importance seemed to shrink while our list of points to be discussed became longer and longer. Dialectically opposed dreams started to show up including the necessity of arguing about right and wrong.

Then the nagging question came up: where was the money going to come from? And who was ready to truly commit him/herself? Our discussions became endless while our dreams withdrew. We desperately tried to find a consensus for our common vision, and the process ended in more or less superficial commonplaces. By that time 'we' mostly meant 'I', and 'you' was used in interjections such as 'you've interrupted me!' and 'you are late!'.

We all wanted the same, but it was always different from what the others wanted. Maybe we were simply too diverse! Were we wasting our time? Some of us started thinking of leaving the group. Should we keep on meeting?

How could we have come this far, when the beginning seemed so promising? Not so long ago we all shared our vision of a better world and it made us feel so light! We started interpreting: unfortunately, 'the others' had betrayed our common dream! When I stood up to remind us all of our original unity and vision (after all I was the founder) the rest of the group started criticizing me for thinking I knew better! I was accused of having invited the group solely in pursuit of my own self-realization. That night I left the meeting in anger and in tears.

I was not going to spend my precious time with such an ungrateful group! Anyway, they would never succeed in finding a suitable place. And they had no money. An inner nightmare of angry accusations raged in my mind: it became clear to me, that they (there followed a list of names …) were simply not on the right track. They were trying to push their own interests and favourite ideas. And nobody understood why I could not possibly share a kitchen with a meat-eater …

At that very moment I had an intuition. I saw the man in that bookshop twinkling at me calling: "Only sunny eyes are able to see the sun."

Community: from I to We

Could he, by any chance, have meant my eyes? Had I become blind to the light in others? I was about to lose my own dream of community. Was there something I could do? Or should I simply let go of a dreamy dream that stood no chance in reality?

First of all I tried to remember: What was my deepest longing? Slowly a thought crystallized into a sentence: I yearn to be seen by others. I long to feel at home in a group. I wish for a group in which I don't have to hide or put on a mask in order to belong.

However, had I managed to see the others? Had I made them feel at home? I decided to share these questions with the rest of the group. Suddenly, new hope arose in me. Maybe they were feeling the same turmoil? How would it be to start every meeting with a sharing of how we were feeling?

I didn't want to rush into new concepts. First of all I would have to meet my worst adversaries, meet them over a cup of tea and listen to them. Maybe this would enable me to see things I hadn't seen before? And maybe we could then prepare the next meeting together (instead of me doing it by myself?).

Maybe we could create some sort of deeper exchange that leads to different experiences? That would help us understand each other in a deeper way? Could we create a space for compassionate perception? For listening to dreams and visions?

Stages in community building

The above story has taken place in many different variations and in all sorts of groups. Many initiatives fail in the beginning stage or get stuck in permanent conflicts. The sequence is typical not only for communities but for love relationships in general. Scott Peck researched and described the above phases in a systematic way in his book *The Different Drum* (see also

Ed Groody, Dieter Halbach). According to Scott's observations building a community usually follows a rhythm of four stages:

- **The pseudo-community**: the euphoric phase of the first meeting, feeling as one.
- **Chaos**: discovering the differences and accusing others.
- **Emptiness**: assuming self-responsibility and beginning to see each other.
- **Community**: accepting the differences and holding one's space within a field of 'unity in diversity'.

Ed Groody, a longtime trainer of the 'Foundation for Community Encourage-ment', summed up his experiences of this 'model of phases' as follows:

> Experiencing 'community' can take hours or minutes or days. Some say that on a deeper feeling-level, the feeling of renewal and connectedness with other members lasts forever. In our normal state of understanding and experiencing however, this phase of 'community' gradually retreats to that of the status quo, that is to say to 'pseudo-community' or 'chaos'.

The good news is that, thanks to extensive work within the community movement techniques have been rediscovered and developed that sustain groups in the process of building or reestablishing communities.

Ninth Continental BioRegional Congress in North America, held at Earthaven Ecovillage in North Carolina in 2005.

Alejandra Cardoza

The bad news is: the process never ends: we have to build and rebuild again.

Personally I work with community projects whenever I can. I believe that their work contributes to social change and thus has an important function in a culture of separation. Experiencing community often has a healing, supportive and renewing effect on individuals. This experience brings with it a temptation of becoming spellbound by its inner intricacies. However, after a genuine experience of life in community the question of our contribution to the rest of the world comes back strongly. What can healthy communities give to the planetary community? Jelalleddin Rumi, a 13th-century poet has put this thought into verse:

> An evening of hurting verbal exchanges,
> my best kept dark secrets.
> All have to do with love and non-love.
> The night will end,
> then we have work to do!

Important First Steps in Building a Community

> The matter is understood and has been judged to be good, the idea takes shape and is about to be put into practice – and suddenly people are standing in each other's way. Humanness founders on humanity.
>
> ERICH MÜHSAM

Unfortunately, this diagnosis from 1919 on contemporary attempts to achieve a better life is still frequently accurate. Many well-intended community initiatives fail soon after they are started.

Luckily, a considerable body of knowledge has grown around the issues of building community. The following seven steps condense some experiences and suggestions on the first founding of communities and projects. They are based on my experience in the ecovillage of Sieben Linden in Germany and on my work as a consultant for organizations and intentional communities. Here are a few suggestions on how to approach the matter intelligently:

Clarify your own inner vision and personal motivation

The basis of your group communication must always be clarity on your own goals and competencies. You particularly need an honest analysis of your deficiencies, your hidden motives and the compensatory expectations you place on others. Sadly enough, the group's beautiful official goals often do not match your personal expectations and self-doubts. Both need to be laid bare from the beginning.

Look for a small group of like-minded persons whose motivation and group chemistry are in harmony (no more than 5-12 persons)

If the group is too large it's very difficult to arrive at a clear consensus. On the other hand, a small family or other symbiotic structures are too small to serve as a sole nucleus. What is important is the inner agreement and mutual recognition within this 'core group'. The determination to act together in full awareness of thematic and personal differences is the inner task of this group.

Determine the essential principles in common, i.e. formulate the vision clearly but leave the individual paths open

Using a powerful vision as a foundation. This group should proceed to develop a basic concept which formulates all essential common goals but which also allows for sufficient individual freedom. If the project's fundamental goals and focal points are defined clearly enough, it becomes much easier for interested people to decide whether or not to join. This also means that there will be fewer rules, and less debate on how to implement them, as the community progresses. Rules on communication, decision-making structures and the necessary steps toward realising the project should be laid out at the beginning.

Look for capable core members with good people skills who want to share and realize the goals

This core or start-up group has the right to select further participants and determine the criteria for joining. It is important to develop a sense of one's own centre – a 'healthy' sense of self – in order to take on a certain executive function which doesn't exclude others or appear arrogant (no more debates on principles).

Create a culture of trust through internal group work, appropriate communication methods and rituals

No concept, no structure and no vision can replace our ability to achieve authentic perception and communication. Internal peace work and personal growth are the essence of community formation. If conflict arises, it is worth seeking help from experienced people, e.g. coaching, consulting or facilitation.

Get to know each other through shared work in practical projects

Life itself is our greatest teacher. No group should move in together without having experienced one another over an extended period of shared working and living (e.g. in other communities).

Define the starting group and create the path as you go

The expanded core group becomes the project's sponsor when it assumes the risks of direct action and establishes legal and financial commitments (particularly in regard to joining and leaving and between the first residents and sponsors/financiers). Competencies and leadership qualities must be recognized and areas of responsibility defined. A social sculpture emerges in which all the components demand to be seen and acknowledged.

But for all our enthusiasm and earnestness we should never forget our sense of humour and the fact that we are all seekers on an unknown path. All the errors we make are a gift to the group as long as we are prepared to look at them without bias and with courage.

Dieter Halbach (born 1953 in Berlin) is a sociologist, community builder and author. He is the editor of *Kurskontakte/Eurotopia*, a broadly published German journal about communities and sustainable living (www.kirskontakte.de). In 1995 he founded the German community-network 'Come together'. He cofounded the Ecovillage of Sieben Linden and coordinated the development of this project as manager of the cooperative over a period of 10 years. Presently, he is living in Sieben Linden. He gives seminars on community-building and is part of the consultancy team 'Hand in Hand' that supports projects and networks.
www.gemeinschaftsberatung.de

After years of visiting and researching ecovillages and intentional communities in North America, Diana Leafe Christian identifies nine issues that, if they were addressed at the outset, would help avert many future conflicts, and thus improve the chances of a great idea growing into a thriving community.

Starting a New Ecovillage
'Structural Conflict' & Nine Ways to Resolve It

Diana Leafe Christian

Since the early 1990s, I've been researching what helps founders of new eco-villages and intentional communities to thrive, socially and interpersonally. (Since many ecovillages are a form of intentional community, I use the terms interchangeably in this article.) It's one thing to get an ecovillage established physically; it's more challenging to do that *and* create a 'spirit of community' – a sense of deep trust and connection with a new group of people who feel like family. Fortunately, as editor of *Communities* magazine in the US throughout the 1990s, I was in a position to visit, telephone, and email the founders of dozens of intentional communities in North America. I wanted to know what worked, what didn't work, and how not to reinvent the wheel.

I was surprised and dismayed by what I found. No matter how inspired and visionary the founders, only about one out of ten new communities actually seemed to get built (and only one out of four co-housing communities). The other 90 percent seemed to go nowhere, sometimes because of lack of funds or not finding the right property, but mostly because of conflict. (And sometimes accompanied by lawsuits!)

This was heartbreaking. Here were people inspired to create a new way of life based on ideals of ecological sustainability, shared resources, and cooperative decision-making. And yet 90 percent of them not only did not establish their new communities, but also often ended up punching it out with their hired gladiator lawyers in a court of law.

So what was the missing social 'glue'? What factors helped the successful 10 percent not only get up and running, but get along well with each other?

'Structural Conflict' – & how to Reduce it

I learned that the purely structural steps of starting a new ecovillage – establishing a core group with a specific vision and purpose, choosing a decision-making method, choosing a legal structure, finding and financing property, creating a membership policy – have *everything* to do with the interpersonal aspects of ecovillage life later on. The degree to which ecovillagers get along well with each other is affected by two things:

- The quality of their interpersonal interactions, their communication skills, their willingness to be open, honest, and kind with one another, and
- How the above-named structural steps do or don't set up the ecovillage for major conflicts down the road.

... structural problems are like time bombs. Several weeks, months, or even years later, the group explodes in major conflict that could have been prevented if they had considered these issues at the outset.

After years of interviewing founders and hearing their stories of intentional community break-up, I began to see a pattern. Most failures seemed to result from what I call 'structural' conflict – problems that arise when people don't put certain processes in place or make certain important decisions at the beginning, creating one or more omissions in their organizational structure. These built-in structural problems are like time bombs. Several weeks, months, or even years later, the group explodes in major conflict that could have been prevented if they had considered these issues at the outset. Of course these 'structural conflicts' trigger a great deal of interpersonal conflict at the same time, making everything much worse.

While interpersonal conflict is normal and expected, I believe that much of the structural conflict in failed intentional communities could have been prevented, or at least greatly reduced, if the founders had paid attention to the following crucial elements in the beginning. If *not* addressed in the early stages, each of these can generate structural conflict 'time bombs' later on.

1. Identify your ecovillage vision, and mission/purpose, and create vision documents

One of the most devastating sources of structural conflict in ecovillages can occur when various members of your group have different reasons for why you're there in the first place. This can erupt into arguments about what seem like ordinary topics – how much or how often you all work on a particular community project, or how much money you allocate for it. It's really a matter of underlying differences (perhaps not always conscious) about what the ecovillage is *for.* (I use the term 'vision' to mean how the group wants to see the world be a better place, and the term 'mission/purpose' to mean what *your* particular group will do to help achieve that vision.) All your community members need to have the same vision and mission/purpose from the beginning, and know that you all support it. It should be thoroughly discussed, agreed upon, and written down from the beginning. When a group doesn't have a common vision and mission/purpose, severe conflicts can erupt later in meetings, as different people passionately advocate for what they want, not realising they're arguing from different underlying images of what their ecovillage is really about. And, when people who are already living in community discover that they have two or more different versions of a common mission/purpose, who is 'right' and who is 'wrong'? Who gets to continue living in the ecovillage and who has to pick up and move? (See 8, below.)

2. Use a fair, participatory decision-making process.

If it's consensus, get trained in it first. If one leader or small group makes all the decisions in your ecovillage, people will resent the power imbalance and this will cause conflict (unless you're forming a spiritual, religious or therapeutic ecovillage with an acknowledged leader – and you all agree to this in advance). Resentment over power issues can create huge conflicts in community. Decision-making is the most obvious point of power, and the more your decision-making method is fair, shared, and participatory, the less this particular kind of power-imbalance conflict will come up. This means everyone in the group has a say in decisions that will affect their lives in the ecovillage.

Another source of conflict is using the consensus decision-making process *without* thoroughly understanding it first. What often passes for consensus in many groups is what I call 'pseudo-consensus' – a misunderstood attempt at consensus but with no real understanding of its principles or methods. This can include trying to use consensus without the group's first having the basic criteria for using consensus: a common vision and mission/purpose, or equal access to power (meaning one person is not the landlord and the rest tenants, or one person is not the boss and the rest employees), and the deep understanding that one blocks a proposal rarely, and only if there is a principled objection to the proposal. Pseudo-consensus wears people out, drains the group's energy and good will, and generates a great deal of resentment all by itself. So if your group plans to use consensus, you can prevent a great deal of structural conflict by getting trained in it first! (See 8, below.)

3. Build trust and connection, 'community glue,' right at the beginning.

Starting an ecovillage is not only about ecological sustainability, but is also about generating a sense of community – a spirit of group well-being in which you've connected with each other emotionally and know each other deeply. Feeling connected to others, feeling trust in your relationship with them, itself reduces conflict – not because conflict won't come up, but because when it does it doesn't hit you as hard. Conflict between people who don't know each other well or trust each other can feel frightening and hurtful; the very same conflict between people who know each other well and trust one another can seem mild and easily resolved.

What builds trust and connection? Working together, eating meals together, telling each other your stories, speaking from the heart about personal or interpersonal issues, singing, dancing, doing rituals, and celebrating together. Many forming ecovillage groups host weekly or monthly potluck meals, often associated with business meetings, which certainly contributes to community glue, as do making decisions together and emotionally rich conversations and sharing from the heart. In North America, one of the best ways for people to experience a sense of community glue is to spend the weekend in a rustic lodge with kitchen facilities: preparing food and eating meals together, hiking and swimming, playing sports, making music and singing, and telling stories around the campfire.

Storytelling is a wonderful way to create intimacy on deeper levels, especially if the topics are self-revealing and personal. You each can tell your life stories, focusing especially on life-changing events or those that affected you deeply. Or each person can share for 20 minutes or so about mildly 'taboo' subjects such as attitudes and practices about religion, money, or social class in your family of origin. Such sessions can not only lead to a much closer sense of connection, but can also help you understand how each group member might approach such ecovillage issues as sharing common property or handling community finances.

One of the best emotionally rich, community bonding processes I've experienced is the Gifting Circle. (For details, see below.)

4. Make clear agreements – in writing

(This includes the legal entity for owning land together.)
People remember things differently. This is not a moral failing; it's just a characteristic of human memory. One person may remember the middle of a discussion; another may remember the actual decision; a third may remember a subsequent conversation about the issue over dinner. Your community's agreements – from those about chores to the most legally and financially significant documents about property – should absolutely be written down. Then if later you all remember things differently you can always look it up. Problem solved; conflict averted. The alternative – 'We remember this right but you're mistaken (and maybe you're even trying to cheat us!)' – can lead to dreadful conflicts and even community break-up.

5. Learn good communication and group process skills; make clear communication and resolving conflicts a priority

My definition of 'good communication skills' is being able to talk with one other about sensitive, emotionally charged subjects and still feel connected, including methods for holding each other accountable for agreements (see 6, below). I believe it sets up structural conflict later on in community life if you *don't* address communication and group process skills and conflict resolution methods in the early days of your group. Then, you'll have workable procedures already in place when conflicts may erupt later on.

6. Help each other stay accountable to community agreements

Ecovillagers can help each other stay accountable to their agreements in a few simple, guilt-free ways. These methods rely on the principle that it's more difficult to forget or ignore responsibilities if they're publicly visible – when the 'community eye' is on us. People tend to want the appreciation of other people, and to experience ourselves as contributing to the group, not letting it down. Therefore, because other people are watching, the task tends to get done. Social pressure can often accomplish what good intentions cannot!

Here are four 'community-eye' methods.

- In ecovillage business meetings, make agreements about which people will do which tasks, and the date by when they will do them, and keep track of these tasks from meeting to meeting. At the beginning of each meeting, have a task review – the people or committees who agreed to take on these tasks report whether they have been done, and if they haven't been finished yet, when they will be done. This is *not* a time to make people wrong if they didn't do their tasks: it's a chance to inquire publicly, and offer support and encouragement. (This method doesn't work if people use the language of guilt or blame!)

- Create a wall chart of tasks and people assigned to each task, with the expected dates of completion each. Someone has the job of keeping the chart current and making sure it's visible to everyone at meetings.

- Institute a buddy system, where everyone with a task is assigned another person with a task who will call and courteously inquire, 'Did you move that pile of lumber yet?' or 'Have you found out how we can join that CSA farm?' This is not about blaming or assigning guilt; it's about helpful inquiry and mutual encouragement.

- When someone finishes a task, thank and acknowledge the person publicly at the next ecovillage meeting. When someone doesn't accomplish a task, the group as a whole asks the person to try again. After a while, the simple desire not to let others down tends to become a strong motivation for more responsible behavior.

7. In choosing co-founders and new members, select for resonance to your mission and purpose, and for emotional maturity

A wrenching source of conflict is when a new member enters your ecovillage who is not aligned to your group's vision, mission/purpose, and values (see 1, above). Or when someone joins whose emotional pain – surfacing weeks or months later as disruptive attitudes or behaviors – can end up costing your group many hours of meeting time and draining you all of energy and well-being. A well-designed process for screening and orienting new people into your group, and saying 'No Thank You' to those who don't resonate with your values, mission/purpose, or behavioral norms, can save a great deal of conflict in the months and years ahead. (See 8, below.)

8. Establish a balanced relationship between vision and purpose, decision-making method, and membership criteria

Here's what I mean by 'balanced relationship':

- First, as you know, one of the criteria for using consensus decision-making is that the group has a common mission/purpose, and they all know what it is.
- Second, one of the best ways to help new members join a new ecovillage is to orient them to the place first, while they're still checking it out and haven't 'made the leap' yet and joined. This includes making sure the new people understand and support the community's values, vision, and mission/purpose.
- Third, one of the best ways to help spread power widely in a group and prevent certain kinds of conflict later on is to use consensus decision-making (with everyone well trained in it first).

However, if a group does not have a common mission/purpose, or if it thinks it does but it is stated so vaguely that it's open to wide interpretation, *please* don't use consensus decision-making! This will only mire the group in conflict as different people passionately advocate completely different strategies, and are baffled and upset why those other people aren't seeing that we should obviously do it *this* way. Because the group is using consensus, and all must agree before a proposal can be adopted, often someone will block a proposal that doesn't resonate with *their* interpretation of the group's mission/purpose. This frustrates and hamstrings the group and makes people feel crazy. The problem is that two separate kinds of structural conflict are intersecting and exacerbating each other. You either need an agreement-seeking method that isn't pure consensus, such as 90 percent voting (*not* majority-rule voting), or, to all agree on the common mission/purpose in the first place.

Further, if your ecovillage has no stated criteria for membership in the group, and no clear membership process that orients new people to your group's values, vision, mission/purpose, financial and self-governance agreements (and thereby screens out those who don't understand or support these), please don't use consensus, for the same reasons. It doesn't matter if your group has fine agreements and a clearly stated mission/purpose if new people coming in don't know what these are. Or if new people know what these are but don't agree with them.

Final tip: Require all new members to take a consensus-training workshop before they have full decision-making rights (the ability to block a proposal) in your meetings.

9. Learn the head skills and heart skills you need to know.

Starting an ecovillage is like simultaneously trying to begin a marriage and start a new business – and it is just as serious as doing either. It requires many of the same planning and financial skills as beginning a successful business, and it also requires the same capacities for trust and honest, kind communication as a love relationship. Founders of successful new communities have learned this. Founders of failed communities have usually leapt in without a clue. The latter didn't *know* what they didn't know. So the ninth major way to reduce structural conflict is to take the time in the beginning to learn what you'll need to know.

Founders of new ecovillages must cultivate both heart skills and head skills. This means learning how to speak from the heart, make fair group decisions, how to how to face and deal creatively with conflict; and how to make cooperative decisions and create fair agreements. It means learning how to create budgets and strategic plans, and how to evaluate the choices for legal structures to own property together or operate business or educational activities. It means learning the property market in your desired area, local zoning regulations, and, if when necessary, how to get loans with reasonable terms. It means learning about site planning and land development. And it means doing all this with a sense of connection and shared adventure. Plunging into the property-search process or trying to get a loan without first understanding these interrelated areas can lead to structural conflict later.

Community founders with spiritual vision and wonderful ideas flounder and sink because they had no idea how to buy property or negotiate a bank loan.

Ecovillage founders tend to be specialists, but they must in fact also be generalists. I've known community founders with spiritual vision and wonderful ideas flounder and sink because they had no idea how to buy property or negotiate a bank loan. I've seen founders with plenty of business or technical knowledge who hadn't yet learned to speak honestly and from the heart.

Not everyone in your community group needs to be equally skilled. Nor must you possess all this skill and knowledge when you begin – you can always hire training for your group or expertise in whatever you need- whether it be a communication skills trainer, consensus trainer, meeting facilitator, accountant, lawyer, project manager/developer, land-use planner, permaculture designer, and so on.

The Gifting Circle: A Feedback Process that Feels Good

For creating more trust, and connection, I highly recommend the Gifting Circle process. It's based on the idea that kindly delivered feedback is a gift, and it's all good. It is an opportunity for people to not only give thanks and appreciation, but also to share concerns they've been withholding, or address situations that they want to clear up. Doing so ritually, with everyone doing it at the same time, seems to make giving and receiving feedback easier. And obviously, the more skilled the actual language used – telling real feelings, using 'I' messages, choosing neutral language to describe other people's behavior – the better the process generates connection. Here's how it works:

Everyone sits in a large circle in a big room, but with some space between the chairs for sound privacy. Soft music plays in the background to help set the mood of respect and sacredness, and to give more sound privacy. Candles and any of the group's ritual objects are placed in the center, with the intention of creating an honored, safe, and friendly atmosphere. The following four statements are written large and posted where everyone can see them.

- Something I appreciate about you is …
- *[Optional]* Something that is (or has been) challenging for me with you is …
- Something I know about myself is …
- Thank you for listening.

The facilitator explains the guidelines and how much time there'll be for the process. (For a group of 20 or so I recommend no less than 90 minutes.) At the end the facilitator asks if people would like more time. It takes some people time to give enough minor feedback messages to get up the courage to give more significant or emotionally charged messages.

Each person chooses a small object to place in front of them on the floor. It can be a special stone, or just their wallet or keys. It serves as the signal, 'I'm available to listen'. The Gifting Circle involves Givers (speakers), Receivers (listeners), and Gifts (the feedback). When it begins, each person willing to hear feedback at that point places his or her object in front of him or her on the floor. Anyone who wants to give feedback crosses to someone who has their object on the floor, and sits, kneels, or crouches before them. This is a simultaneous process; so many people will be going to and from other people in the circle.

The Giver picks up the seated Receiver's object and hands it to them as a symbol of the Gift they're about to give. Some facilitators suggest that the object be handed to the Receiver with both hands, and the Receiver take the object with both cupped hands, as a physical reminder that the feedback is a gift. The Giver whispers or in a low voice makes the four statements to the Receiver. The statement about what may be challenging for the Giver about the Receiver is optional. The Giver may not want to talk about such challenges at that moment, or there may be no challenging situations – the Giver may simply want to give the Receiver appreciation and acknowledgement. (Note: this process is as much for sharing appreciation as it is giving critical feedback.) The 'something I know about myself' statement invites the kind of intimacy that arises when people freely reveal something about themselves to another. The four statements are meant to be heard only by the Receiver, and not audible to anyone else.

The Receiver just listens. When the Giver is finished, the Receiver doesn't respond but simply says, 'thank you.' The Giver returns to his or her seat. The Giver can put their object on the floor and become a potential Receiver, or go to a different person with another feedback Gift.

The Receiver may put their object on the floor again, meaning 'I'm open to receiving more feedback.' Or they may continue holding the object and just sit there for a while, feeling what they feel and considering the feedback. This gives the Receiver control over how much, and how often they receive feedback, which seems to increase willingness and tolerance for hearing it. Or the Receiver can put the object away and become Giver, giving feedback to someone else in the circle. Anyone who wants to respond to what the Giver said can do so later, if they wish.

It's suggested that people pause a bit for silence and contemplation between the actions of giving or receiving. People will be constantly changing roles, crossing back and forth across the circle as they decide to give feedback, or to remain where they are and receive it (or not). The facilitator is available to explain the process again, or clarify any misunderstandings. The facilitator rings a chime five minutes before the end of the session, and again at the end. (Once the group knows the process well, the facilitator's role can be eliminated and someone can serve as timekeeper.)

The group can, if it wishes, evaluate the process at the end, but only the process, not anyone's content. The Gifting Circle seems to generate as many loving expressions of appreciation as it does expression of concern and requests for change. There is usually a hushed atmosphere during the process, and often, smiles, tears, and long hugs.

Diana Leafe Christian is author of *Creating a Life Together: Practical Tools to Grow Ecovillages and Intentional Communities* (New Society Publishers, 2003), about forming successful communities and ecovillages, and *Finding Community: How to Join an Ecovillage or Intentional Community* (New Society Publishers, 2007) about researching, visiting, evaluating and joining a community. From 1994 to 2007 she was editor of *Communities* magazine, a quarterly publication about intentional communities in North America, and she now publishes an e-newsletter about ecovillages and sustainable communities. Diana speaks and leads workshops on ecovillages internationally; her articles have appeared in publications ranging from *Mother Earth News* to *The Encyclopedia of Community*. She lives in an off-grid homesite at Earthaven, an aspiring ecovillage in the mountains of North Carolina.
  www. DianaLeafeChristian.org

Weaving the Community Fabric

Liz Walker

Walking Iris

As Allegra and Sarah (aged 9 and 4) pass my house, I call them over to see something special: my walking iris has a beautiful, orchid-like bloom. "It only lasts for one day," I explain. "You can watch it unfold its petals in the early morning, and by nighttime the flower has shriveled up and died. When I lived downtown, it only flowered once a year. That day was so special, I would stay home from work to see it. But now that we live at EcoVillage at Ithaca, it flowers a lot. It likes the extra light it gets in my passive solar home."

Allegra is part Hispanic and has wide brown eyes and black hair. Sarah is Jewish, and her hair is a tousled golden mane. The girls lean toward the delicate white blossom with its bright purple center. "Mmmm," they murmur. "That smells so good!" The iris has a sweet, almost spicy fragrance, as lingering as a gardenia. It is intoxicating. I offer each of them a cutting from the mother plant.

"Why is it called a walking iris?" Allegra asks.

"Because it is really a tropical plant that grows fast and sends out shoots like a spider plant. Each new shoot puts down roots, and then that sends out more shoots – almost as if it is walking forward."

The girls leave, and I reflect on the symbolism of the walking iris. When a walking iris sends out a new shoot, it also sends out a two- to three-foot-long stem, exploring new territory. If the shoot doesn't find soil or water, then the stem develops sticky scales and gradually dies back. If the shoot finds what it needs, then the whole plant develops fully.

When I first got my plant, it flowered so rarely that I hoarded the joy of its blossoms. Later, as the plant sent out more shoots, I gave well-rooted cuttings to my best friends. Now it is thriving, and I have several large plants around the house.

I have discovered that when I plant or give away a shoot from my walking iris, I am contributing to its overall health and growth. Likewise, when I give freely of my love, my attention, my time, and even my money, I am contributing to the overall health and growth of my community. It makes me feel happy and healthy, too. Such sharing is not a sacrifice but a celebration, an act of love that has an immediate ripple effect, sending happiness back to the giver, multiplied many times. Like the walking iris, our momentary, everyday acts of kindness permeate the community with a sweet and spicy scent.

At Ecovillage at Ithaca we have set up our lives to foster connection. We share meals together several times a week, participate in work parties, and create our own on-site entertainment. We get to know and enjoy our neighbours – without ever having to drive anywhere. Over time we're building trust and closeness. However, we've learned that it takes at least as much work and dedication to weave the social fabric as it does to create the physical form of our community.

Using the Cohousing model gives us a head start on creating strong social bonds. In cohousing the buildings and site design encourage lots of inter-action, while still maintaining the privacy of individual homes. The densely clustered housing, pedestrian streets, and shared gardens are augmented by a Common House where people share meals, and children play. Decisions are made by consensus, leadership is shared, and there are always plenty of ways to contribute to work projects, committees, and weekly chores. How-ever, despite the supportive social and physical structures of cohousing,

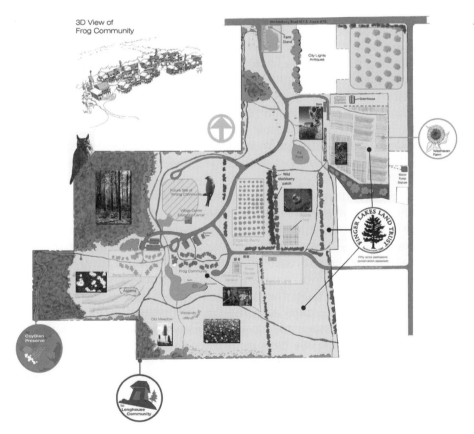

EVI envisioning plan

we've learned that it takes a special commitment to get to know each other on a deeper level – a skill that is not taught in our fast-paced culture.

In 1997, after five years of dedicated work and hundreds of meetings, our Common House was completed and all 30 households in our first neighbourhood had moved in. We had long anticipated this moment. We assumed that we would automatically feel a strong sense of community as we ate together in the Common House, landscaped the neighbourhood, or passed each other on the path. But we were wrong.

We knew a lot about going to meetings together but very little about living together. Certainly we knew each other's meeting styles intimately – who talked a lot, who had to be encouraged to share their point of view, who listened well, and who argued a point well. But in terms of really knowing what was going on in each other's lives, the situation left a lot to be desired.

'Deep Groups'

Building on another community's practice, we decided to create mixed men and women's support groups, called 'deepening relationships groups' or 'deep groups' for short. The idea was wildly popular and soon half of the adults in the community had joined, speaking to a strongly felt need for more intimacy in our lives. Each group of six to eight adults met Saturday mornings, twice a month. Everybody chipped in for shared childcare. Although each deep group developed its own creative style, they all included time for in-depth check-ins. These gave us a terrific opportunity to learn more about each other. Typically each person had five to ten minutes of uninterrupted time to talk about what was going on in his or her life. So we learned things like how someone felt about having her parents visit, what it was like to be unemployed, how someone coped with their son's difficult behavior, and whose marriage was experiencing stress. Good ground rules ensured that all sessions were confidential, and people were respectful to each other.

Simple support groups can help people to move through transformative changes, and best of all they can be replicated anywhere. You don't have to live in an ecovillage to create a nurturing support group.

I can tell you that there is nothing quite like having the undivided, supportive attention of a group of peers. The attention alone was transformative – like having a favorite friend listen to you well. It challenged me to look clearly and honestly at my own life, recognize patterns, celebrate the good things, and ask for support for the difficult times. I found it a real joy to share at this level with people whom I also saw in many other contexts and many of whom I expected to be part of my extended family for the rest of my life.

The original deep groups lasted a year, then rotated membership. After several years they seemed to disappear. Now, however, with many new members in our village, we have resurrected the idea, and once again, six years later, half of the adults are involved. The results are striking. Many people feel that it satisfies a need to be seen and accepted for who they are, and likewise to acknowledge others. These simple support groups can help people to move through transformative changes, and best of all they can be replicated anywhere. You don't have to live in an ecovillage to create a nurturing support group.

The personal growth that may start in a deep group, however, is augmented by living in community. I like to think that each of us is like a stone in a stream. As the stones' rough edges tumble against each other, they gradually wear away and take on a polished, smoother finish. A similar process can happen with people in the supportive climate of our community. People bring all their unresolved issues with them when they come to EVI and inevitably come up against the group. Those

Peoplecircle

individuals who take responsibility for their learning, take risks, and grow begin to lose their sharp edges. As they confront their issues, work through them, and come to resolution, their transformation becomes obvious – they begin to glow with an inner beauty.

'Invented Celebrations'

One of the most fulfilling aspects of our community lives is celebrating together. And it doesn't take much to spark a party – just someone with an inspiration and the energy to organize. Add some shared food or drink and a little music, dance, or ritual and voila!

We celebrate Easter with an egg hunt and Channukah with potato latkes (cooked by the dozen). Other Jewish holidays, Christmas tree decorating, a big Thanksgiving feast (complete with the option of vegan turkey), and occasionally a Buddhist-inspired ceremony or Earth-based spirituality ritual all take the spotlight during the year. We have corn roasts in the fall and a strawberry festival on the summer solstice. Birthday parties happen year round. And we don't stop at ordinary parties. What makes our community extraordinary is that we often invent our own celebrations, drawing from many traditions – or creating a new one. We live for these times of creative and meaningful fun. One of our favorites is 'Guys Baking Pies'.

'Guys Baking Pies' August 8, 2002

Early August, and the blackberries drip off their branches. One section of the EcoVillage land had a huge blackberry bramble on it when we bought it. The farmer who hayed the fields that year mowed a careful path around the brambles. "That's a keeper. That'll have good berries," he told us. Sure enough, that bramble alone often produces many gallons of purple, juicy berries.

My partner Jared puts out an email to alert people that Saturday will be EVI's seventh annual 'Guys Baking Pies' day. On Saturday Jared and a motley assortment of neighbourhood men and boys troop down to the berry patch. The wise ones wear old jeans and long-sleeved shirts, despite the 95-degree heat. The less experienced wear shorts and sandals and are soon covered with long red scratches.

The crew picks berries all afternoon then assembles piecrusts and fillings. Occasionally a woman will be asked for advice on the right texture for a pie-crust or how to make a latticework crust, but mostly these men and boys know what they're doing. Finally the pies go into the Common House ovens.

After people go home for a quick supper, the whole community (plus friends and family members) gather again at the Common House. Jared presides over a ceremony that includes the singing of songs specifically written or modified for the occasion (for instance, who will ever forget the hit, 'When the moon hits your eye like a big berry pie, that's cohousing …'). People recount the major events of the past year. Jared reads a special poem he has written about berry picking.

> Mouth or Bucket?
> Mouth or bucket?
> For a few precious hours
> my life simplified to this.
> In the bramble I am the Buddha
> my mind's chatter banished
> by senses chasing away past and future.
> All else falls away as my eyes lock on
> a black jewel, protected by the maze,
> morphed by sun, wind and rain,
> facets swelling with earth flavors …
> Oh, steady now! The fingers navigate the treacherous channel
> OUCH! They won't give up their treasure easily
> I acknowledge a grudging respect.
> The fingertips caress it
> a gentle squishiness, fully and deliciously ripe,
> drops into my hand
> an oral receipt for the price I've paid.
> I study this black bulbous gift from the soil
> but only for a moment:
> Mouth
>
> JARED JONES (excerpted from 'The Jewel in the Berry')

Then it is time for the procession. About fifteen men and boys of all ages proudly parade their pies through a gauntlet of waiting admirers. Each pie maker presents his masterpiece in turn. 'This pie has a combination of blackberries and bananas, and I've carved a face of a pirate on the crust,' says one young man.

The rest of us eagerly await the moment when we can dig in. We have 15 beautiful pies to choose from, along with vanilla ice cream, whipped cream and tofutti (a vegan ice cream). We sit at long tables and compare notes on our purple teeth and tongues. (Did you know that only wild blackberries dye your mouth? Commercial berries have somehow had this characteristic bred out.) We eat and grin wild purple grins at each other, enjoying another successful 'Guys Baking Pies' day.

Times of Crisis

Our community has learned a lot about living, working, and celebrating together; about communicating effectively; and about resolving conflicts. But I think we really shine when we're celebrating an important milestone or when we're supporting someone through a crisis. We are a large group, and milestones and crises happen with surprising frequency. People graduate, get married, birth babies, lose jobs, experience breakups, or lose their parents. As we witness each other's lives, we find in ourselves a larger capacity for loving and giving than we knew existed. We grow larger as human beings.

What we do at EVI is not new. People have lived in close-knit communities for thousands of years, whether in Australian aboriginal groups or small New England towns. The basis of our success, as with theirs, rests in strong relationships between people. We are reweaving the web of our togetherness as we learn to create a culture of deep caring and sustainability. The pain or joy that one person experiences reverberates through all of us, calling forth a deep response.

Sometimes our members face a medical crisis. Julia, for instance, recently suffered a serious accident. The mother of two young boys, Julia has epilepsy. When her husband Rod came home one day, he found her at the foot of their stairs, unconscious and with a cracked skull.

Julia was airlifted to a hospital specializing in neurosurgery. The surgeon who operated on her said that he had never before removed such a big blood clot from a living human being. Internal bleeding had severely compressed Julia's brain, and it was likely she would die or at least suffer permanent mental or physical impairment.

Our community mobilized an outpouring of love and support. We held silent prayer vigils every night. Someone accompanied Rod to the hospital (over an hour away) every day. Others cooked dinners for the family, ferried the boys to and from school, or provided after-school care. One neighbour offered to clean the family's house and wash the daily dishes. We made up a photo-board – covered with pictures of Julia, her family, and friends – signed it with our get-will wishes and took it to the hospital for her. We visited regularly. People gave her massages, took her flowers and videos, or played soothing music for her. Almost everyone helped out in some special way.

To the amazement of her doctors, Julia got out of the hospital just two weeks after the accident. She seemed to have recovered her full range of motion and, although she still felt disoriented, her mind was sharp. Her

The basis of our success, as with theirs, rests in strong relationships between people. We are reweaving the web of our togetherness as we learn to create a culture of deep caring and sustainability.

recovery was truly a miracle – one that Julia ascribed, at least in part, to all the loving care from the community.

Our community's caring – whether we are giving or receiving it – is to be treasured. It creates a safety net that, unfortunately, is not available to most of our society. We know that help will be there for us during the most traumatic moments of our lives. I like to think of it as 'community life insurance'.

Weaving the fabric of community takes dedication and time. It involves clear communication and goals, shared leadership, working, resolving conflicts and making decisions together. In addition, and perhaps even more importantly, it involves creating a soulful space to allow each other to breathe and grow, to celebrate, and to move through difficult times with love and support. At its best, living in community can help us to become the more generous, expanded human beings we are meant to be, and to feel a deep sense of belonging to something infinitely larger than our selves.

This piece is excerpted in part from Liz Walker's book, *EcoVillage at Ithaca: Pioneering a Sustainable Culture* (New Society Publishers, 2005) with kind permission of New Society Publishers, www.newsociety.com

As the co-founder and executive director of EcoVillage at Ithaca (EVI) since 1991, Liz Walker has dedicated her full-time work to bring this internationally acclaimed project from vision to reality (www.ecovillage.ithaca.ny.us). Her new book, *EcoVillage at Ithaca: Pioneering a Sustainable Culture*, has helped to introduce the concept of ecovillages to a broad audience in the US and other countries. A Korean version is now available.

1 Building Community & Embracing Diversity

The Power of Community
Finding & Sharing the Vision
Starting Community: The Essentials
Embracing Diversity

*From a baseline of 30 years' experience in political activism,
Starhawk shares her insights into the obstacles that keep our
movement from being more diverse. She offers her perspective on
how we can open up to more diversity.*

Building a Diverse Movement

Starhawk

In nature, diversity means resilience. A prairie that has hundreds of different plants growing together can resist pests or respond to storms that would devastate a field of identical hybrid corn. In social movements, too, we need diversity in order to thrive.

After Seattle, one of the key articles that circulated widely on the Internet was a piece by Betita Martinez, a Chicana activist and author, entitled 'Where Was the Colour in Seattle?' She noted how the young activists were overwhelmingly white, and posed the question: 'How can we can build a racially diverse and anti-racist movement?'

In many of the movements I've been in, from the antiwar groups of the sixties and seventies to the feminist movement and the antinuclear movement, this question has been a familiar one. Similar discussions were going on twenty or twenty-five years ago. What often astounds me is how little progress we've made in building racial diversity. Other differences have not continued to divide us so deeply. I remember agonizing conversations in, say, 1979 about whether straight women and lesbians could ever actually work together in the same organization. Today that's not an issue in most of the groups I work with. Issues still arise of course, but they don't prevent us from working together.

The global justice movement is not a 'white' movement – it's a movement inspired and rooted among people of color around the world from the Zapatistas of Mexico to the insurrectionists of Bolivia who retook their water supply from privatization. From Africa to Fiji to Papua New Guinea to Thailand to India to the US, people of color have been in the forefront of the fight against global corporate capitalism, have faced torture, prison, and death, and have also joyfully pioneered new tactics and new forms of struggle. I have no doubt that stopping the WTO or challenging the IMF is absolutely in the interests of the majority of people of color on the planet, regardless of who does the challenging. But in North America, a large proportion of the direct action movement has been white, and the question of how to build diversity is one of the overriding challenges we face.

There are certain obvious answers and some suggested solutions. As white activists, we can look at our own unconscious racism, at our lack of not just outreach but of real attempts to bring people of color into the central organizing, at our history of not working on the issues that concern people of color and of not recognizing the leadership and organizations of people of color. While the most stunning successes of nonviolent direct action are found in liberation struggles of people of color, direct action poses higher risks for those who are already targets of the criminal injustice system – to face these risks, people need to be convinced that the issues involved are direct life issues. As white activists, we can educate ourselves on the history and contributions of people of color, and learn to become effective allies.

Interlocking Systems of Oppression

Racism, sexism, heterosexism, and all of the related systems of prejudice and oppression are, in reality, interlocking and intertwined. They reinforce and feed upon each other, and to end any one of them we have to address them all. All depend on isolating the individual, on convincing people that their pain is a result of personal failing rather than part of a larger structure of oppression directed at whole classes of people.

Opposing any and all of the 'isms' is a struggle that is in all of our interests if our goal is a world of true liberation for any of us.

Racism is maintained in part by the deep sexual tensions created by a patriarchal construction of manhood. Manhood is identified with power, and that power is systematically taken away from black men, who are literally and symbolically castrated. These power dramas are enacted on the bodies of women. White men have been raping black women continuously for centuries as an aspect of slavery and a general economic and social oppression. Then that sexual violence is projected onto black men, who are feared and accused of raping white women. Racism can therefore not truly be undermined without confronting sexual oppression.

But sexual oppression also is reinforced by racism. Racism leaves the women of the target group doubly vulnerable to exploitation. It separates women from one another. And as soon as one group of women is defined as in need of protection from the sexual violence of some 'other' group of men, repression of all women is justified.

That patriarchal construction of manhood – the identification of male sexuality with violence, power-over, and the thrusting piercing weaponry of war – supports militarism.

Any one of these syndromes constricts us all; just as tying a tight band around one leg until it becomes gangrenous will affect one's entire body. So opposing any and all of the 'isms' is a struggle that is in all of our interests if our goal is a world of true liberation for any of us.

The global corporate capitalist system, the latest manifestation of this interlocking system of oppression, is a race thing – it's a continuation of the policies by which the mostly-white North has exploited the mostly-dark South for centuries. And the 'lesser developed countries' are that way precisely because of the history of exploitation and resource extraction that have subsidized the wealth of the industrialized world. 'Global apartheid' is another descriptive term for this system.

The global corporate capitalist system is also a sex thing – the average worker in the *maquiladoras* and the factories of the Free Trade Zones is a sixteen-year-old woman. Women and children are the majority of the world's poor. Women's bodies are commodified in an international sex trade. Policies that impact health services, education, and the availability of life necessities such as food and water disproportionately affect women, who are the first to go hungry, the ones who walk the dusty roadsides for miles searching for water, the last to receive education.

Obstacles to Diversity

Pamela, a young African American woman in my affinity group, comes back from the Convergence Center at the A16 action in Washington, D.C., in distress. 'It was weird,' she says. 'People wouldn't look at me.'

Katrina, another African American woman, a longtime activist and organizer and a powerful healer, anchors our healing space in the Temporary Autonomous Zone in the midst of one of D.C.'s African American communities. 'I had some great conversations with community people,' she says. 'But every time I got into a conversation, some young white activist would come up and try to get into the middle of it. Sometimes they made remarks that were so inappropriate that I was embarrassed.'

Even in groups that define themselves as anti-racist, that want to be welcoming to all people and to broaden their diversity, oppressive behavior still exists.

Even in groups that define themselves as anti-racist, that want to be welcoming to all people and to broaden their diversity, oppressive behavior still exists. The sexism, racism, homophobia, classism, etc. of the society we grow up in become embedded in our personalities. They lead us to respond to people who are different from us in ways that are often unconscious. They create blank spots where we literally cannot see our own behavior. Trying to examine and uproot those behaviors takes us out onto highly unstable emotional terrain, where shame, guilt, hatred, rage, and grief lie only shallowly buried.

In trying to confront that unawareness, people behave badly in fairly predictable ways. Some members of the privileged group – men, white people, heterosexuals, upper-class people – will not see the problem, deny it when confronted, invalidate the perceptions and feelings of the target group, grow defensive, get angry, make predictable excuses and bad jokes, blame the victim, make token efforts at reform, and find new ways to continue the old, offensive behavior. Some will also feel ashamed and guilty – so guilty you can barely stand to be around them – and go overboard trying to please, become wannabee target group members, adopt the hairstyles, slang, foods, and holidays of the target group, and snub other members of their own group while attempting to curry favor with the target group.

Some members of the target group in turn will become defensive, attack people who don't deserve it, blame everything on the ism in question, refuse to see their own problematic behavior, take offense where none was intended, sulk, get quietly hurt and simply leave without confronting the issue, play the race/sex/class or whatever card, make self-righteous judgments, and feel entitled to insult members of the privileged group.

These behaviors often give rise to the following unhelpful syndromes:

The anguished ally syndrome

The person who is most devoted to being a good ally of oppressed people, who goes to the most antiracism workshops or most fanatically works on his or her own sexism, who reads, thinks, meditates, and lives and breathes support for the oppressed, is often the first person to say something offensive under the guise of being helpful. Excruciating self-consciousness mixed with guilt makes it impossible to simply act like a human being meeting another human being whose color, gender, and ancestry are important but not delimiting factors in the complexity of who that person is.

The language police

Part of changing the syndromes of domination is changing our language, learning new ways to think and speak about the issues. Some words need to be simply banished from the vocabulary of people of conscience, and many concepts and images need to be rethought. But often in groups, someone seems to be hovering like a praying mantis; rubbing their hands in anticipation of a mistake they can pounce on.

I was once criticized, for example, for speaking of the 'victims' of the Nazis – 'victim' being a word that disempowers people. However, since I was talking at the time about the dead victims of the concentration camps, the favored term 'survivors' didn't actually apply.

The Language Police may be consciously or unconsciously trying to establish themselves as antiracist, but their efforts undermine the work of truly challenging oppression. A group in which people become reluctant to speak for fear of making some error in sensitivity becomes dreary and oppressive. Language can be challenged in ways that draw forth more creativity instead of shutting people down: 'I wonder how our thinking would change if we used different metaphors, metaphors other than darkness for evil and light for good?' That way the focus can be kept on the larger goal of creating change.

Activist paralysis

Many white people concerned with diversity have realized that our responsibility is not necessarily to recruit people of color into mostly white groups, but to raise the consciousness of the white community.

Over the years, thousands of activists have gone through workshops on diversity, on unlearning racism, on challenging white supremacy. Many, including me, have gained incredibly valuable insights and new perspectives.

But for a long time now, a disquieting observation has been whispered among trainers and organizers concerned with antiracism and diversity issues. The workshops, the consciousness raising, and the soul searching have not noticeably increased the racial diversity among many of the groups in question. What is worse, a certain percentage of the activists involved seem to come out paralyzed, unable to move forward in the work that they were doing.

In order to make space for the voices of women, people of color, working-class people, indigenous people, and people who have street wisdom rather than formal education, members of more privileged groups need to sometimes step back and shut up. It means not always assuming leadership, setting the group's agenda, or determining its priorities. And if groups want to include people of colour and women, they need to include people at the level of leadership, not just as envelope stuffers or street troops.

But for some activists of conscience, these insights become a paralyzing inner dialogue: 'If the issues that move us aren't attracting people of colour, they must be the wrong issues. If our style of organizing isn't attracting people of colour, we must be doing it wrong. We need to take leadership from people of colour. If they aren't present to lead us, all we can do is figure out how to recruit them. If we go ahead and act, we're cutting out the possibility that we could bring more people of colour into leadership.'

We can frame local struggles in a global context and link global issues to the local campaigns that touch on immediate community needs.

But a group that cannot set its own agenda, where people can't work on the issues that call to them or organize in the style that they find most empowering because they are trying to fulfill some other group's priorities, is not an empowering place to be.

The issues a group is moved to work on may not be the immediate priority for local communities of colour, but they may still be vitally important issues. Local communities may be overwhelmed by sheer survival and local struggles and may not have energy to put into struggles around global trade agreements or financial institutions. Organizers of colour may already be overwhelmed and not have time to attend new meetings or take on new issues.

But the global struggles are vitally important to people of all colours around the world, and to lay them aside would not be ultimately in the interests of any of the oppressed. We can frame local struggles in a global context and link global issues to the local campaigns that touch on immediate community needs. In fact, the local struggles reflect the impact of the global issues – they are neoliberal policy made manifest. Thus 'privatization' becomes the closing of a local hospital, a WTO ruling on gasoline additives becomes increased cancer and asthma rates in a low-income community.

Nurturing Diversity

The global justice movement has to be a diverse thing, if only because the one great advantage we have in the fight against the greatest conglomeration of political, economic, and military power ever amassed on the planet is our human creativity, and we certainly can't afford to waste the talents and vision of any one of us, let alone of women, people of color, poor, and working people, who make up the vast majority of humans on the planet.

Understanding our recent history and the interconnections of the 'isms' can help us see how to move forward. We can nurture the diversity that already exists within our movements, and expand it by consciously deciding how we frame the issues, by expanding our learning, by doing our own deep work, by making our groups and actions welcoming, and by building alliances and coalitions.

Framing the issues

The global corporate capitalist system impacts us in many different ways. For the more privileged, this may happen through the diminishment of space for alternatives, for a true public culture, for a real depth of inquiry and creativity. Or it may happen through the diminishment of wilderness, ecological diversity, or environmental health, or through the lessening of possibilities for a full, vibrant life.

But for the less privileged, the system hits full in the face with guns, bombs, torture, and the prison systems that maintain the authorities' control. Or it hits through starvation and disease. Environmental destruction may mean a literal loss of land through droughts or hurricanes or rising ocean levels, loss of a traditional seed source, a livelihood, a culture, and a heritage. The commandeering of resources may mean the destruction of ancient sacred lands and ways of life – in effect, genocide.

How we frame the issues affects who is inspired to work on them. The global justice movement needs to be loudly and clearly identified as anti-racist and anti-sexist. Or, to get out of the 'anti, anti, anti' syndrome, as a movement *for* economic, racial, and gender justice.

The global justice movement needs to draw the connections between economic hegemony and military hegemony. Indigenous peoples in their fights for sovereignty are in the forefront of the global justice struggle, and the movement in North America and in Europe needs to acknowledge their importance and be guided by their perspectives.

Expanding our learning

Oppressed groups necessarily learn a lot about the culture of the oppressors, otherwise they won't survive. People of privilege do not need to learn about the cultures of the oppressed in order to function. But if we want to build bridges and broaden our connections, we do need to make a conscious effort to expand our perspectives, and doing so will give us more ground for understanding and communicating.

Doing our own deep work

Issues of race, gender, and identity involve our core selves. To really change our groups and our unconscious behavior means to examine the construction of our selves in ways that go beyond political analysis and engage deeper powers of spirit and healing. Confronting our identity means coming to terms with our family – and all the pain and discomfort that may be present in our family history. It means looking at our own wounds and at the ways in which we have wounded others.

In fact, there is no one alive whose ancestry includes only Pure Victims or Noble Heroes of Resistance. Nor is there any group of Purely Evil Oppressors. Every one of us is born of both oppressors and oppressed. Facing those contradictions within ourselves, our families, our heritages is some of the beginning work we need to do to open up to more diversity in our communities.

In a Multicultural Ritual Group, we found that the most powerful tool we had for holding our own contradictions and bridging our differences was to simply sit and tell our personal stories. As a group, telling our stories helped us bond and know each other. Encouraging people to form small groups, to discuss not just race but their own real experiences of the economic and political realities, might move us beyond the barriers.

Encouraging people to form small groups, to discuss not just race but their own real experiences of the economic and political realities, might move us beyond the barriers.

Making our political culture welcoming

I imagine a person of colour coming into a political action might feel something of the following spectrum of emotions: Who are these people? Are they descendents of slave owners, land-grabbers, exploiters? Have they dealt with it? Are they safe to be around? Is there anyone like me here? Am I consorting with the enemy, betraying my own community? And can I make a difference here? Will I be listened to; will my viewpoint and experience be respected?

In fact, these are some of the very questions that may be brewing inside any newcomer in some form. We all come into a new group wondering: Who are these people? How do I know that I can trust them? Will they accept and understand my differences? Will I be welcome here? Will I be able to make a contribution?

If we want to build bridges across barriers of difference, if we want to show respect for others, there are some fairly simple, tried and true things that work: Look people in the eye. (Of course, in some cultures, this is an insult, so sharpen your sensitivity to body language cues and notice if you are causing discomfort.) Smile. Greet people and make them feel welcome. Pay attention to everyone in a group or a conversation, not just to those you identify as most important. Give everyone a chance to speak. Give respectful attention to every person's ideas. Don't interrupt. Don't jump into other people's conversations unless you're invited. Sense other people's personal boundaries, and respect them.

Katrina taught me a simple exercise that can also be helpful in changing our group culture: Think of a group that has more social power or privilege than you do. Close your eyes and imagine walking into a meeting full of those people. It's on an issue that's important to you, and you have a viewpoint that you vitally want to be heard.

What would they have to do to make you feel welcome? Open your eyes. Write those things down and share them with the group. Now do them for everyone who comes to your group.

There are many things we can do to make our events more diversity-friendly. But the most important thing we can do is to really be a community willing to openly struggle with these issues. We don't have to have answers, or achieve perfect political correctness. But we can clearly and visibly be asking the questions.

Building alliances and coalitions

To diversify our movement, we need to be good allies of a broad range of diverse groups and peoples. Many low-income groups are necessarily focused on the immediate local issues that most directly impact their lives. When groups focused on the global picture adopt and support these issues, we not only expand our base but also learn to address the real complexities of the global issues.

- Being a good ally means developing personal, not just political relationships. It means getting to know people in the fullness of who they are, going out for coffee or a beer, hanging Out, inviting people to dinner, not just to meetings.

- Being a good ally means raising the issue of diversity in groups that are not yet thinking about it, noticing who is included and who is not, challenging policies or practices that result in de facto exclusion.

- Being a good ally means sharing resources, media attention, opportunities to speak and be heard.

- Being a good ally means interrupting oppression, challenging racist or sexist remarks, not leaving it up to the target group to always be the ones to defend themselves.

- Being a good ally means offering support for the issues and concerns of others, without abandoning your own.

Conclusion

In the end, the diversity of our movement will be reflected not so much in who turns up for any given meeting, but in the web of alliances we can build.

When groups working on global justice issues are willing to bring their courage, commitment, and dedication to community struggles and can respect local leadership and issues, when white activists can do the hard work of self-education and transformation that leads to the sharing of power, when women activists and activists of color are willing to risk trust, *we* can begin to build those bridges that can cross barriers. When we identify the interlocking systems of oppression as our opponent, we can begin the work of true transformation that can liberate us all.

Starhawk is the author of ten books on Goddess religion, earth based spirituality and activism, including *The Spiral Dance*, *The Fifth Sacred Thing*, and her latest, *The Earth Path* (HarperSanFrancisco). She teaches permaculture design courses with a focus on earth-based spirituality, organizing and activism: Earth Activist Trainings. A committed activist for global justice and the environment, she travels globally teaching, lecturing and training.

To receive her periodic writings and schedule: Starhawk-subscribe@lists.riseup.net · www.starhawk.org · www.earthactivisttraining.org

It is time to move from a culture of domination to a culture of partnership, that integrates more feminine qualities like compassion and sharing. Dolores shows how men and women can support one another on the path to a more peaceful future.

Gender Reconciliation
From Domination to Partnership

Dolores Richter

A Look at History

Historians have explored the remnants of ancient tribal living and have concluded that egalitarian cultures existed for a long period of human history. These cultures respected diversity; they honoured matter and spirit, women and life itself. Also, within these cultures there seems to have been no cruelties or wars. Religious images were mainly based on the great Goddess, who protected and was a part of all that lived, be it plant, animal or human. The religion of the great Goddess was inclusive, honouring life and its origins.

The patriarchal revolution began around seven thousand years ago. The patriarchal revolution was a process of expansion, and violence extending over several millennia. Patriarchy attempted to destroy the Goddess cultures and their holistic perspective. The new patriarchal religions severed direct contact between the human and divine realms. Nature was seen as soulless, separate from ourselves, a commodity and resource to be exploited.

Our sexuality, which in matriarchal times, had been viewed as part of the celebration of life and as an ecstatic aspect of creation, was demonised and privatised. Sent to the hidden realms of society, our sexuality was divided into the permitted and the forbidden. The result of pushing vast parts of our sexual energy underground was a volcanic eruption of aggression against women, nature and life itself.

We need to be aware of this history if we wish to step out of the spiral of violence. Violence grows from suppressed life energies.

The demeaning of woman and her role in society is one of the factors that contribute to global violence. By transmuting the great Goddess who cared for all her children into the one God who punishes all disobedience, we have lost contact with our compassionate human nature. We have lost touch with the all-embracing quality of love itself. To regenerate a new non-violent culture we need to create new conditions that will re-integrate matriarchal values.

Women Today

> Of the world's 15 million refugees, 75% are women. Today 100 million women and girls in Africa and Asia are circumcised. In the United States domestic violence is the leading cause of injury to adult women, and one rape is committed every six minutes. SCILLA ELWORTHY, *Power and Sex*

Young women in training at Findhorn Community

In Middle Eastern countries women are punished for not hiding their body and many women on earth are denied access to education.

But even in those parts of the world where equality has long been proclaimed between men and women, large parts of society are still organized around masculine concepts. To succeed in political or professional careers women have to act like men. Globalization of companies and our economic systems are based on qualities like bigger, better, faster, richer and more powerful. It seems we have conquered our planet to possess, dominate, rule and take advantage of it.

Are we not aware that our resources are finite and therefore not sustainable? How many of us have lost contact to qualities like intuition, compassion, tenderness and caring? Have we lost these qualities because women adapted to a man's world?

> We still have a way of living dedicated by masculine values. For example, getting a big job in a company is important and is rewarded with money and honours; looking after children is not so important and is not rewarded with money and honours. Winning and getting there first is important, more important then having a good time on the way. SCILLA ELWORTHY, *Power and Sex*

So how can women move into positions of power without ending up doing things the way men do? How can men make the journey from exercising power of domination to exercising co-empowerment? How can women and men develop their feminine qualities? How can women and men become friends and lovers?

Reconciliation: from Domination to Partnership

First of all: reconciliation here has nothing to do with guilt or forgiving on a personal level. Reconciliation is becoming aware of what is, why it is this way and then healing it.

We all come from a culture of domination: domination of human beings over nature, men over women, adults over children, rich over poor, powerful over powerless people. Creating partnership in this world entails transforming a culture of competition into a culture of compassion, a culture that focuses on hierarchy and possessions to a culture that focuses on sharing and to listening to the needs of all.

Life needs a balance of male and female qualities. And since men have a feminine side, and women have a masculine side, it is an inner work of balancing as well as one that deals with behaviour in the outside world. Stepping into partnership, as I understand it, means finding a completely different attitude towards all life outside and inside of us. An attitude of partnership entails deep respect for all living beings, seeing them as equally important and beautiful. A culture of partnership is one that reconnects with the living, loving, longing life force within us and around us. It will challenge us to make ourselves visible with our innermost being.

We need to get to know ourselves from deep within, listening to our inner voice, our feelings, our heart, our body, and our sexuality. Only when we have learned to understand ourselves will we be able to understand those who are different from us: the opposite gender, other cultures, religions, and beings like animals and plants.

The wish to dominate comes from a fear of feelings around insecurity, unpredictability and weakness.

The wish to dominate comes from a fear of feelings around insecurity, unpredictability and weakness. This is one reason why the process of reconciliation starts with getting to know the unknown parts within ourselves. What we will get to find there is life – unpredictable, intense and wonderful! A culture of partnership is based on the life principles of contact, communication, and cooperation – whether we are dealing with technology, with economics, with child raising, with schools, with emotion or with love and sexuality.

Partnership in Gender Issues & Love Relationships

Modern life has brought many changes to family, village and community structures. Partnerships, marriages and families are living in isolated units. Feelings, love-relationships, and sexuality are considered being personal issues. Modern societies share the idea of romantic love: we look for the perfect partner to fulfill all our needs, and to be the one and only person we will rely on. The African writer Sobonfu Somé sees this romantic image we have of love as playing an important part in the gender conflict.

When couples live in isolation from a surrounding community and when they lack a spiritual source, so many needs need to be fulfilled by the partner, that no one is capable of living up to it. Much of the conflict between the sexes comes from the fact that we are looking for something in our partner that cannot be found in one person. Within patriarchy there is a big potential for conflict between male and female lovers.

Over decades of stepping back and hiding their inner truth and wisdom in fear of suppression and punishment, many women have lost contact with their own power and deep knowledge. Some may have found powerful positions in modern societies, – but when feeling attracted or falling in love, many layers of feelings open up: fears of dependency, of being turned away, fear of betrayal, and the urge to be protected and understood …

Sobonfu Some writes:

> The separation from spirituality and our spiritual source, as we perceive it in the industrialized world, leads to a concentration towards the idea of romantic love. It creates a strong pull or vortex of longing for one other person, for a different kind of being connected. The pattern of relationship of our tribe is based on a different principle, one where relationships are not private. When in the village we speak about 'our relationship', this concept is not limited to two people. It is strange to look at two people as community. Where are all the others?

This gives us an insight into a different way of looking at love relationship issues. The growth of deep trust amongst lovers is much more than a personal achievement of the two of them. To heal this underlying conflict of love-relationships we need intentional communities that debate issues around love and sexuality openly. They need to support partners and lovers in situations of conflict. This will help to heal the wounds that came from former times and support women in regaining their self-esteem, sovereignty and power.

For trust between men and women, for deep bonding, fulfilling love-relationships and sexual fulfillment to develop, we need a culture of support within the surrounding community.

We Support Gender Reconciliation through

- The honouring and respecting of female qualities as much as male.
- The valuing of long hidden qualities such as intuition, tenderness, feeling, sensuality and compassion.
- The integration of issues around gender, love-relationships and sexuality into our communication and exploration processes within communities.
- The creation of an environment where questions, highlights, experiences and conflicts arising in relationships between women and men can be shared with others.
- The creation of belief-systems and a culture of communication based on partnership and cooperation.
- Getting to know us as whole and holy beings.
- Training to balance male and female qualities inside of us by visualization, meditation and ceremonies.
- Developing the ability in each of us to step into real contact with

deep understanding and compassion for ourselves as well as for those who are different from us – especially from the opposite sex.

• Gathering in women's and men's circles to share, explore and understand our own sex.

Dolores Richter, born 1959 in Germany, has been involved in building community for 25 years. She lives at Zegg-community close to Berlin, which aims to create cultural conditions for a vivid and humane society. For many years she was the head of education and guest programs at Zegg. Now she runs seminars on communication, Zegg-Forum, love, sexuality and community-building all over Germany. Her interest is gaining knowledge and tools which help to ground communication in trust and clarity, love and sexuality in truth, living and working together in the awareness of 'being part of the whole'. She is mother of a 10 year-old son.

*Helena Norberg-Hodge gives us insight into
a culture that integrates all age-groups and
inspires us to see the benefit and beauty
that may grow from reintroducing these
ancient social structures.*

Integrating Age Groups
Learning from Ladakh

Helena Norberg-Hodge

With the process of industrialization or modernization, societies around the world conform to an economic model that imposes a segregation of age groups. From childhood, people are separated into groups according to age and these divisions remain throughout their lives. This is a crucial element of our global economy, which encourages competition at all levels. In many traditional societies, economic success relied on cooperation, not competition. People of different ages interacted productively and peacefully on a daily basis.

Thirty years ago, I traveled to Ladakh, or Little Tibet, an isolated region in the Himalayas, to learn the language and put together the first Ladakhi-English dictionary. Though culturally Tibetan, Ladakh is officially part of India. The region was only accessible during the summer months via unpaved rough mountain roads. Ladakh had been exposed to outside cultural influences, but they had come slowly and been adopted on the region's own terms. Until the '70s there was almost no contact with the Western world.

A Culture Attuned to the Needs of People and Environment

In this remote region I found a culture so attuned to the needs of people and the environment that it was unlike anything I had ever known. I had never before met people who seemed so emotionally healthy, so secure as the Ladakhis. They seemed to belong their place on earth – bonded through intimate daily contact, through knowledge about the immediate environment with its changing seasons, needs and limitations. There was a strong sense of interdependent community where everyone was valued and could depend on one another. Money was of little use in the local economy, which was based primarily on sharing and exchange of produce and other goods. Most families in traditional Ladakh practised subsistence agriculture and family members of all ages – from toddlers through to grandparents – took part in producing food. Everyone helped with irrigation, building houses, herding animals and all the other tasks essential to life in Ladakh.

Spending time with my friend Dolma's family, I saw something of how children were brought up. Dolma spent more time with little Angchuk, who was six months old, than anyone else did. But caring for the baby was not her job alone. Everyone looked after him. Someone was always there to kiss and cuddle him. Men and women alike adored little children, and even the teenaged boys from next door were not embarrassed to be seen cooing over little Angchuk or rocking him to sleep with a lullaby. Taking responsibility for other children as you yourself grow up must have a profound effect on your development. For boys in particular, it is important since it brings out their ability for caring and nurturing. In traditional Ladakh, masculine identity was not threatened by such qualities; on the contrary, it actually embraced them.

Children were never segregated into peer groups; they grew up surrounded by people of all ages, from young babies to great-grandparents. They grew up as part of a whole chain of relationships, a chain of giving and taking. When villagers gathered to discuss important issues, or at festivals and parties, children of all ages were always present. Even at social gatherings that ran late into the night with drinking, singing, dancing, and loud music, young children could be seen running around, joining in the festivities until they simply dropped off to sleep.

Old people participated in all spheres of life. For the elderly in Ladakh, there were no years of staring into space, unwanted and alone; they were important members of the community until the day they died. Old age implied years of valuable experience and wisdom. Grandparents were not so strong, but they had other qualities to contribute; there was no hurry to life, so if they worked more slowly it did not matter. One of the main reasons old people remained so alive and involved was their constant contact with the young. They remained a part of the family and community, so active that even in their 80s they were usually fit and healthy, their minds clear.

One of the main reasons old people remained so alive and involved was their constant contact with the young.

With the exception of religious training in the monasteries, the traditional culture had no separate process called 'education.' Education was the product of an intimate relationship with the community and its environment. Children learned from grandparents, family, and friends. They learned about connections, process, and change, about the intricate web of fluctuating relationships in the natural world around them.

Development?

Unfortunately, since I first came to Ladakh much has changed. As part of a program of 'development', a road was built into Leh. With the road came a deluge of Western influences, including media and advertising, tourism and a competitive money economy. Education became something quite different. It isolated children from their culture and from nature, trained them instead to become narrow specialists in a Westernized urban environment.

Frodo Kempf

Old and Young.

Children were split into different age groups at school. This sort of leveling has had a very destructive effect. By artificially creating social units in which everyone is the same age, the ability of children to help and to learn from each other is greatly reduced. Instead, conditions for competition are automatically created, because each child is put under pressure to be just as good as the next one. In a group of ten children of quite different ages, there will naturally be much more cooperation than in a group of ten 12 year-olds.

The division into different age groups is not limited to school. Now there is a tendency to spend time exclusively with one's peers. As a result, a mutual intolerance between young and old emerges. Young children nowadays have less and less contact with their grandparents, who often remain behind in the village.

Conclusion

Today's global economic model succeeds in creating competition by dividing people from one another. In Ladakh, the effects have been profoundly detrimental to communities and individuals, in fact, destabilizing the entire society.

To build cooperative, harmonious societies we need an approach that creates more opportunities for people of different ages to interact – to study together, work together and play together. Many schools in the West have already begun to reintegrate age groups in the same classroom. 'Buddy' programs, where an adult is paired with a child or teenager to provide friendship and support through difficult times in their lives, have been popular in the US. A healthy society is one that encourages close social ties and mutual interdependence, granting each individual a net of unconditional emotional support.

Helena Norberg-Hodge initially visited Ladakh as a member of a German anthropological film team in 1975, when the area was first opened to tourism and 'development'. The only outsider to master Ladakh's difficult language, she worked with local scholars to write down the language for the first time, and to compile a Ladakhi dictionary. In 1978 she founded the Ladakh Project, and later the International Society for Ecology and Culture (ISEC). Based in the US and UK ISEC's mission is to reveal the root causes of our social and environmental crises, while promoting more sustainable and equitable patterns of living in both North and South. Helena's work in Ladakh has been acclaimed internationally. In 1986 Helena received the Right Livelihood Award, also known as the Alternative Nobel Prize. Her book *Ancient Futures: Learning from Ladakh* has been described as an 'inspirational classic' by *The Times*, London.

In this article, Marti shares with us the unique system of education for children in Auroville, a community co-created by people from nearly 50 nations and dedicated to principles of human unity.

Growing up in Community
The Auroville Experience

Marti de Pezeral

Background

Auroville was inspired by Sri Aurobindo's experience of the evolution of consciousness. Like Gurdiev and others before him, the great Indian yogi Sri Aurobindo believed that a giant step in human evolution would occur when a few highly evolved people on Earth would reach a higher level of consciousness and a critical shift in human evolution would occur. Auroville was envisaged as a morphogenetic field, a centre of human unity were conscious work would be done collectively to make this evolutionary leap towards a truly divine consciousness. The work would focus on transforming the body at a cellular level by transmuting matter into pure consciousness. This was seen an important task to prepare for the dawn of a new world. The charter of Auroville states that Auroville is a living laboratory of evolution. It is to be a place of unending education for a youth that never ages. Nearly 50 different nations and about 80 linguistic groups co-create in Auroville. This may make Auroville one of the most diverse spiritually-intentional communities on Earth. This in itself is an immense challenge.

Learning for Children in Auroville

In today's world many children grow up without a true sense of belonging. They are a bit like strangers on an ill-adapted planet. They are sometimes herded into conventional merit-oriented school systems that do not correspond to their deep needs to explore who they really are. They don't have the space to grow into fully realized beings where mind, body, and spirit flow as one. They have lost that deep sense of community that was once so important in traditional societies. And as a result more and more children are alienated from the learning process. Some of them develop severe learning deficiency disorders and end up on the streets or in prisons.

The Mother, the visionary and founder of the multi-cultural community of Auroville in South India had a dream. She wrote:

> There should be somewhere upon Earth, a place that no nation, could claim as its sole property, a place where all human beings of good will, sincere in their aspirations could live freely as citizens of the world … In this place children would be able to grow and develop integrally without losing contact with their soul. Education would be given, not with a view to passing exams and getting certificates and posts, but for enriching the existing faculties and bringing forth new ones.

The central focus of learning in Auroville is to allow our children to develop their true potential, or what the Mother called, 'the psychic being'. And what we see today is that some of our children are highly aware beings. Many of them have a deep love for nature, share a responsibility for each other, and have a sincere concern for the Earth. They know that they have a mission in life, even if they don't know how that mission will reveal itself. They respond best to experiential learning, that is, by doing rather than listening to explanations about how things are done. They are questioning, often impatient to acquire the skills that they will need not only to survive in today's difficult world, but to make a difference. Most of them despise sham and pretense, but are usually quick to forgive an honest mistake. They will refuse to be molded into mindsets that don't honor their deepest sense of who they are. They think with their hearts and feel with their minds. And curiously each new generation in Auroville seems to resonate on a higher octave and have a more subtle awareness. The task is to respond to each child's needs by giving them an environment that nurtures their life force.

A child needs many parents

We have come a long way from the early pioneering days of Auroville with a one-room school, a few volunteer teachers and parents. From the beginning there was a racial mix. Local Tamil village children joined children coming from throughout the world to build the new city of the future. Education was rather rudimentary, but in some ways the eroded barren desert that served as Auroville's home was a school unto itself, as children learned how to thrive in the hot sun of this barren plain. In time Auroville went from an arid plateau to a lush forest. And so did Auroville's schools grow deep and sprout branches. Today there are about a dozen schools experimenting with the Mother's philosophy of education, the ideas of Maria Montessori and the Rishi School, as well as more conventional methods. We have advanced vocational training schools and a high school that prepares for the international baccalaureate and has excellent libraries and a fully-equipped science laboratory. Children from all races, ethnic groups, and classes study together in three mediums: English, French, Tamil. They do some Sanskrit, as well. Because there is a large cultural diversity from the outset, children are much more tolerant of each other from an early age. The emphasis is on learning to be in community together. Service to others is an important part of the code of life.

Indian children at Auroville

In Auroville today, as in other spiritually-intentional communities, the children who emerge seem to have a distinct awareness of having a role in life. They may not know the details of their mission on Earth, or their personal destiny, but they know they have one. Some of them manifest a strong sense of service and desire to evolve spiritually. 'As a child,' says one of the early Aurovilian youth,

> I remember wandering in the forests barefoot. We had very little, but everything seemed possible. Later on, some of us struggled to fit in outside of Auroville. It wasn't always easy, but what Auroville gave us was a basic sense of confidence in ourselves and a deep sense of community and *raison d'être* for something bigger than each of us as individuals. This has really helped me to confront and overcome obstacles on the way.

The Mother's philosophy of education focuses on the integral development of the child. Singing and sports are as important as math and physics. Martial art techniques and prana breath work develop psychic and physical equilibrium. Awareness of one's surroundings and the flow of conscious energy is emphasized. The body learns and in so doing, the mental is quietened. Conventional educational systems tend to put the emphasis on developing mental capacities. But the result is often that children begin to live in their minds rather than their bodies. Ancient Vedic philosophy is

When the body is properly trained, intuition becomes highly developed and with it, awareness of the universe. When the mental is too dominant, the person will simply not be well-balanced.

about quieting the mind to become one with the universe. *The Upanishads* describe the body as a chariot and the mind as the subtle reins that guide the chariot. When the body is properly trained, intuition becomes highly developed and with it, awareness of the universe. When the mental is too dominant, the person will simply not be well-balanced.

In Auroville, there is an emphasis on providing space and an environment for children to discover their essential being. Classes are often organized in thematic contexts where children are invited to create their own books and materials after learning about a topic. Group work is often emphasized. This means that at an early age, children learn to conceive and carry out projects together. This prepares them to be good team members, a skill that is often important later in life. Several schools experiment with the sandbox, a technique where young children choose objects from shelves and create a story in a sandbox. Teachers observe the children play. They can then see in which direction a child's imagination and intuition takes them. They can even diagnose problems and see in which ways a child may be troubled or have unfulfilled needs.

Auroville is ideal for personal development. Children wander barefoot in the forest, ride horses on back roads, build tree houses, learn to swim in the hefty swells of the ocean. They spend a lot of time in nature. A child that loves nature becomes a natural conservationist. Auroville children get practical training in environmental restoration. Many of them have instincts to defend nature when the Earth is threatened by new roads and housing projects. Children in Auroville see each other not only in school but also in community life. This means that their relations with each other have both breadth and depth. They might go to the mountains together, care for horses at the pony farm, or work on a tree planting project. They develop natural social skills that serve them in many situations. Some of the Auroville schools stress yoga and meditation as a natural part of a child's development.

Auroville has many different kinds of schools. Each child is seen as equal but all children have different learning needs. Children can be channeled into a school that meets their specific needs. One child may be more artistic. Another may be attracted towards math, engineering and the sciences. Children have an opportunity to manifest their real talents. At the same time there is recognition that each child has a capacity to develop all the aspects of its being. The emphasis is not on education to take up a career but rather on learning to engage with life. Sharing is stressed. Competition is discouraged. Beauty and perfection and integral being are seen as important values. Concepts of success and failure are relative. What is important is that a child develops according to their true potential. Leadership is seen more in terms of helping others than in terms of personal gain. Because children have a place in the community, they don't have to feel pressure to compete in life, but simply to do their best. They know they will always have a place in the community. Having said this, some of our Auroville children have gone on to universities such as Harvard and Oxford. We have had a Rhodes scholar, as well.

When parents separate or divorce, which happens in communities just as it does in the world at large, children are usually not traumatized in the same way that they may be in other contexts. This is because when the community life around the child remains stable, children know that they have a home that is larger than the fractured family nucleus. When one or both parents stay in the community the child usually adapts well because their sense of security is not threatened. They know they will see and relate to their parents and the community.

Interestingly, our young adults sometimes leave the community to work outside, but many of them come back to have their own children in Auroville. Our Auroville educational system is not perfect, but the return of the Auroville youth is a confirmation that Auroville provides youth with an important part of what they need. Today Auroville has nearly three thousand residents. As the community transits from a cluster of ecovillages to an eco-town and an important international cultural crossroads, our forms of education become more varied. But the idea is always to nourish the inner being and to provide life long education. A constant stream of visitors and residents offer workshops, seminars and in-depth training programmes in a multitude of learning areas.

I would say that the most important community values in education centre upon giving children and adults alike space to grow and develop according to their own aspirations and needs. These values are strongly based on providing a contact with the Earth that honors nature as our greatest teacher and friend. They focus on providing space to discover, invent and transform, where all life becomes yoga.

Marti de Pezeral is a former professor in applied linguistics at the Sorbonne University (Université de Paris 1.) She has also worked at the Centre Nationale de la Recherche Scientifique (CNRS) in Paris. She has written many books, including *Indigo Spirit for a Child-Friendly Planet*, a book on core values in education, and *This Earth of Ours*, which has a prologue by His Holiness the Dalai Lama. She is a United Nations ECOSOC representative to Geneva and is Chair of the International Advisory Council (IAC) of the Global Ecovillage Network (GEN). She divides her time between Auroville and Paris.

*Jan Martin Bang describes the background,
philosophy and way of life in the Camphill
Movement, possibly the world's most
radically integrated from of community
living for people with special needs.*

Integration of People with Special Needs in Camphill Communities

Jan Martin Bang

Health and wholesomeness only come
when in the mirror of the soul of man
the whole community takes shape;
and in the community lives
the strength of every single soul.

RUDOLF STEINER (1861–1925)

Background

During the 1930s a group of intellectuals brought together by Karl König began meeting regularly in Vienna. They were inspired by Anthroposophy, the teachings of Rudolf Steiner, and how these could be put into practice in the fields of health and education.

As the political situation became more threatening, they decided they had to move. After the Anschluss in 1938, when Nazi Germany invaded Austria, they dispersed throughout Europe, but came together again at Kirkton House in the Dee Valley near Aberdeen in Scotland in the beginning of 1939 and began taking in handicapped children. When the Second World War started some months later, the group was registered as enemy aliens and all the men were interned on the Isle of Man. The women carried on and a larger house was found. They moved there, to Camphill House, on 1 June 1940. A few months later the men returned. The community then comprised some 30 people of which just less than half were handicapped children. They saw themselves as political refugees working with social refugees.

During the 1940s, the community grew and by 1949 there were 180 children living in five houses. The 1950s saw the Movement grow and develop, reaching out to England, Ireland, Germany, Holland, South Africa and the United States. In the early 1950s, König began to think about more extended communities, where mentally handicapped adults would live together with co-workers in extended family situations. This was first put into practice at the Botton Estate in North Yorkshire in 1954, and the first Camphill Village, as we know it today was established. This created a model, which has been the basis for Camphill for over half a century. Today, Botton contains well over 300 residents in four clusters spread throughout a valley leading up to the North York Moors.

Throughout the world there are now over 100 Camphill Communities in over 20 countries. They are organized into seven regions, and a number of magazines and newsletters keep information flowing between them. There is a strong element of internationalism, and even in the small community of about 45 people where I live we counted 13 different nations represented at a recent cultural gathering.

Midsummer Festival

Philosophy

We often describe ourselves as living a community life, which tries to realize the ideas of anthroposophy in day to day living. The ideas of Rudolf Steiner, who founded the Anthroposophical movement, owe much to the scientific approach of Johann Wolfgang von Goethe (1749–1832). Goethe liked to put things in context, he liked to look at processes, and he looked for patterns, which replicate themselves in different places.

In Camphill we work with two parallel impulses. One consists of working with villagers (the mentally handicapped) based upon meeting people and recognising that they have physical, psychological and spiritual aspects, each contributing to the unique individual that we come face to face with. This can be considered an 'inner' work, and co-workers are encouraged to spend time studying, both on their own and in various groups.

The other impulse consists of creating an alternative society, as when co-workers talk about 'the fellowship', or 'realising a three-folded society'. Three-folding was presented by Steiner in lectures during the last part of the First World War and the years that followed. He based his thoughts on his study of the development of European society over the preceding centuries. In England, he saw the industrial revolution as the modernization of economic life, leading to demands for *fraternity*, the development of trade unionism and labour party politics. In France under the French Revolution he saw a change in the legal life leading to demands for *equality*, and in Middle Europe (later unified to become Germany) changes in the spiritual life leading to demands for *liberty*.

Steiner traced how these three great ideals, of Fraternity, Equality and Liberty had been corrupted by the rise of nationalism and the development of the centralized nation state. König further traced how this led to the insanity of Nazism, fascism and state communism after Steiner's death. The three-folded analysis was presented by Steiner as a way of rebuilding

Europe after the disaster of the First World War, but his ideas did not gain credence, and the ideas were largely dormant until taken up by König in building up the Camphill communities in the 1940s and '50s.

As far as I know, it is only in Camphill (though there are other Camphill inspired communities which are not officially part of the network) that these two impulses, the inner work of living together with people who have special needs, and the outer work of creating an alternative society, manifest together in this way. When in balance, this gives the Camphill tradition a robustness that has carried it through more than 60 years and into over 20 countries throughout the world. It combines 'doing good work' with 'building a bright future'. New communities are founded nearly every year, and young people flock to experience this amazing phenomenon.

How do these Ideals Work in Practice?

Within our communities most of us live in large extended families, co-workers (both long term people with their families, and young temporary volunteers) and villagers (mentally handicapped or otherwise in need of help), sharing our lives, our meals, our living rooms and bathrooms. There may be as many as fifteen people or more gathered round the dining table three times a day. Each house has its own budget, and is run more or less autonomously by a couple of responsible co-workers. In the morning and the afternoon everyone goes to work in a variety of workplaces. In Solborg we have a bio-dynamic farm, extensive vegetable gardens, a bakery, a weaving workshop, herb growing and drying, and a large forest for timber and firewood.

Canoe trip

In many countries, mentally handicapped people are 'looked after' in various ways, sometimes really well by caring people, in other countries kept in terrible institutions where they are hardly treated as human beings at all. In our Camphill Villages we try to find a suitable job for each person according to their ability, something useful and tangible that they can do, which contributes to the well being of others. We try to create a community where we all look after each other. Sometimes I feel that life here revolves around work, there is always too much that needs to be done, never enough people to do it. On the other hand, a sense of useful purpose is an asset. Certainly the concept of unemployment has no relevance in our community! We all have a basic need to be loved, to be appreciated, to be of use to someone, and we express it by doing things for other people, giving the gifts of our work to those we love. When someone is told that they are no longer useful, just told to sit quietly and look at the wall for the rest of their life, they will experience major trauma. Work is done both for other people, but also for ourselves.

The concept of unemployment has no relevance in our community!

Interdependence

The bonds that develop between co-workers, their children, and the mentally handicapped are many and varied. It is not always easy to share your life with people who think and behave very differently. Some co-workers find that, after a year or two, this is not a lifestyle for them, and they leave. Others experience a deeper possibility for personal self-development in their interaction with others, and remain close friends with the mentally handicapped even many years after they have left the village and created a new life for themselves. Some of those who grow up in the villages as children of co-workers can't wait to leave and find a more 'normal' life; others are eventually inspired by their village background and go back into it with great vigour. There are a number of second and third generation co-workers throughout the movement.

We eat together as an extended family three times a day, and that is a daily reminder of how various tasks are their own rewards. One of our villagers has responsibility for the chickens, collecting and counting eggs, feeding the chickens and closing them in at night. She is really proud of that job and, just as many people define themselves by their jobs, that is one of the first things she will tell a new visitor. We have a weaving workshop operating during winter months, when the gardens are deep in snow. One or two of our villagers work there, and are justly proud of the tablecloth on our table, or the waistcoat that I sometimes wear. In the summer the vegetable gardens and greenhouses produce large amounts of food, a great deal of which will last throughout the winter. These vegetables appear on our table nearly every day.

The Nature of Work

All these useful objects, and many more, are products of people's work. Made not for earnings or profits, but for the sake of making something that

It is important for each one to experience the work of others that not only is it freely given, but freely accepted. In this way every human being has worth and value, as they contribute something to the general well being of the community.

is a joy to make, and of use to other people. Work is a service to others, freely done and freely given. In our village we strive to get away from independence, instead we aim to create interdependence. It is important for each one to experience the work of others that not only is it freely given, but freely accepted. In this way every human being has worth and value, as they contribute something to the general well being of the community.

Other villages have workshops, which produce pottery, candles, dolls or wooden toys. I have eaten meals in Camphill houses where the table came from the carpentry shop, the table-cloth from the weaving workshop, the plates and cups from the pottery, the candles (which are lit at every meal) from the candle shop, and virtually all the food is produced by the village, bread, milk products, jams, vegetables, herb teas, honey, and meat. This self-sufficiency is not an end in itself, but rather a way of ensuring that each person is employed doing something that is useful to the village. In many cases in mainstream society, mentally handicapped people are peripheralized and 'looked after' and so denied an active and useful role. In the world of Camphill, every person has something to contribute, and feels self-worth even when fetching the milk or laying the table.

In addition to the work branches, there are the houses to be run, washing, cooking and cleaning. This is considered work, just as important as production, and the occupation of 'housewife', 'house mother' or 'homemaker' is as vital to the well being of the community as any other profession. Everyone has a workplace, and contributes something useful to the running of the village, according to his or her capability. Within this sphere no money changes hands, and work is seen to be something that is freely given within the fellowship, recognizing that some people have higher capabilities than others.

Finances and Money

In Norway, our villages do not earn very much of their income from sales of products. There is a highly developed welfare state here, and the government allocates relatively generous amounts of money to people 'looking after' the mentally handicapped. This is unique in the Camphill movement. Most other countries give smaller amounts to those working with the mentally handicapped, others give nothing. In each country Camphill finds its own solution. In Britain and the United States there is a well-developed funding machine, with newsletters and mailing lists. The sales of produce, and the degree of self-sufficiency both help to cut the need for external inputs. Some movements give generously to others. In this way the Norwegian Camphill movement has subsidized the founding and developing of new Camphill villages in eastern Europe over the last decade and a half, and this assistance continues in the form of cash payments and a regular building group that travels to a Camphill village in Russia every year to build and to teach ecological earth and straw bale construction.

Most of the co-workers who have made a commitment to living and working long term in Camphill have formed Economic Fellowships and share their income. This means that we put all our earnings into one account, and meet regularly once a month to discuss how to parcel it out. The basis is one of equality, we start off with the same basic amount of pocket money, but from then on things become unequal. I have two children needing schooling, my neighbour has five, and the co-workers responsible for the third large family house in the village, have no children. Clearly we three families receive quite different amounts of money in order to cover the cost of feeding, clothing, schooling and dealing with our children.

The simple way to deal with money issues is to invoke equality, to give each person the same, and tell them to be responsible for themselves. Another way, much harder, but much more educational, is to bring up our differences, look at them, and make sure that our very different needs are met. Living with equality is relatively simple, even mechanical, everyone gets the same, and everything is 'fair'. But as human beings we are all different, and have varying needs. Accepting that and living with it, is much harder, but opens up the possibility of learning more about other people, and our own response to them. Loving people who are nice and friendly is no big deal, fine in its own way, but not likely to challenge you. Learning to love your enemies is much more challenging, but more likely to make you grow as a human being. When we share our economy, the challenge of living, working and loving someone who is greedy, lazy or 'not nice' throws you back into yourself, forcing you to take stock of your own prejudices and expectations. But it's not easy; it brings you up to face all the greedy, lazy or 'not nice' features of your own personality!

Winterforest trip

Ecological Principles and Practices

The farms and gardens in Camphill Villages are bio dynamic, producing food of the highest quality while nurturing both soil and wildlife. Generally the organic waste from the kitchens is composted, usually by a village compost set-up. Horse transport is quite common, being very efficient and low cost at a village scale. Villages in England have pioneered wastewater treatment using ponds, reedbeds and 'Flow Form' water cascades. These are now standard in the Norwegian villages, and common throughout Camphill worldwide. Buildings, both communal halls and chapels, and the usually large residential houses, are largely constructed out of natural materials, and avoid the use of poisons and plastics as much as possible. However, there is still much to be done in the raising of consciousness, and in building, transport, recycling and energy use.

Conclusion

Camphill Villages are communes or intentional communities in the classic sense, attempts to create an alternative to mainstream society. We attempt to integrate a spiritual worldview into our everyday lives, to create fellowship in our economic life, and a flexible equality into our social sphere. In short, we offer an alternative way of life – both for ourselves and for those we live with and care for.

Jan Martin Bang was involved in alternative technology, health, agriculture and cooperatives in Britain throughout the 1970s. In 1984 he moved to Israel with his wife and young son. He was co-founder of The Green Kibbutz Group, active on behalf of the Global Ecovillage Network in Israel, coordinated the first Permaculture Design Course in Israel, co-founded the Israel Permaculture Group, and farmed 1,000 organic olive trees. He completed the first modern straw bale building in Israel. Jan also taught Permaculture and Ecovillage Design in Turkey and Cyprus. In 2000 he moved to Camphill Solborg in Norway with his family, where he holds domestic and administrative responsibilities. He is the editor of *Landsbyliv* (Village Life), the Norwegian Camphill magazine. He is currently secretary of the Norwegian Permaculture Association, and active within the Norwegian Ecovillage Trust. He has written a book on Permaculture Ecovillage Design published by Floris Books (Europe) and New Society Books (North America) in September, 2005, called *Ecovillages – a practical guide to sustainable communities*.

Solborg Camphill Village, 3520 Jevnaker, Norway · +47 32 13 30 51 (home) · +47 32 13 34 56 (office) · +47 48 12 96 53 (mobile) · (F) +47 32 13 20 20 · jmbang@start.no

2   Communication Skills: Conflict, Facilitation & Decision Making

Communicating for Peace

Starhawk shows us the difference between hierarchical models and models based on the image of the web – both having their foundation in nature. She cautions us to use the power of leadership wisely and always to make sure to co-empower those around us.

The Practice of Direct Democracy

Starhawk

Direct democracy, horizontal organizing, nonhierarchical structure – these are all key aspects of our movement. Putting them into practice is an art that requires a shift in our organizational modes as well as in our thinking.

The Hierarchical Model

Hierarchy is the model of leadership and organization most people are familiar with and surrounded by from the moment they are born into a modern hospital through their education in a public or private school and beyond, whether their later life includes attendance at a university, a job serving burgers at McDonald's, rising to management at a large corporation, a stint in the military or attendance at the neighbourhood church. Although to many of us, hierarchy has negative connotations of disempowerment and lack of freedom, the word actually describes a certain pattern that exists both in nature and in human affairs. A hierarchy is a branching pattern. Go look at a tree and see how the twigs connect to one branch, the branches to one larger limb, the limbs to the trunk.

This branching pattern is extremely widespread in nature. It's the same pattern found in the way that small rivulets combine into brooks, streams, and mighty rivers. It's the pattern of our capillaries, veins, and arteries. Nature repeats this pattern over and over again because it is so useful. A branching pattern functions for collecting, concentrating, and dispersing. It branches out to fill the widest possible space as completely as possible. Notice how a tree fills the maximum volume of space with leaves or needles that can collect sunlight from the largest possible number of surfaces. The energy from the sun is transformed into sugar and then collected and concentrated, and eventually dispersed to feed the cells of the tree and the roots, which in their structure mirror the branches. The roots collect water and nutrients, which in turn are concentrated and then dispersed out to the branches and leaves.

A branching pattern links the trunk to the furthest leaf in a clear line, but it doesn't allow the leaves to directly feed each other. Salmon cannot leap from the headwaters of one stream to the headwaters of another.

For a branching pattern to be sustainable, the flows both ways must be balanced. The energy collected by the leaves is balanced by the water and nutrients collected by the roots. The trunk, the place of concentration, is merely a conduit that serves this balance.

But in human societies, branching patterns are often used to collect wealth, resources, and labour from one group and to disperse them to another group. Barely enough is given back to insure survival. The value produced by labour is collected from the workers, the leaves of the corporate tree; then concentrated into the hands of various levels of management, and eventually dispersed to owners and shareholders.

In such a hierarchy, power and decision-making flow in opposite directions. Decisions are made by a few in the top echelons and communicated downwards to those who have no say in the decisions.

A Different Model: the Web

When we begin to organize around the principle of direct democracy and real equality, we need to look for a different model, a different pattern. It's no accident that the global justice movement has grown along with the Internet and that the most common metaphor for online communication is that of the web. A web implies a pattern of connections that are complex and flexible in ways that a branching pattern is not. In a classic spider web, spokes radiate out from a central point, linked by a spiral of sticky thread. A web can also concentrate information: any point on the web can communicate with the center. But it can also communicate with other points on the periphery.

The World Wide Web is a familiar model of this pattern. It allows multiple forms of communication: one to one, one to a selected few, one to a whole listserve. It allows the posting of information on a website for many to access, and responses can also flow in many directions,

Most antiauthoritarian groups work by some form of consensus, Consensus does not mean unanimity; it means that everyone's needs and concerns are listened to and taken into account. Consensus works best as a creative thinking process, when enough time is allowed for open discussion of an issue as well as for synthesis and revision of ideas to occur. At best, consensus fosters an attitude of openness, of respect for each person's position, and of flexibility. Consensus can be time-consuming and frustrating – but so can any decision-making process in which there are real differences to be resolved. Glossing over those differences or allowing one side to simply outvote the other doesn't actually resolve them, and the splits then show up when the group tries to enact its decisions. There are many resources available for learning consensus process, and a skilled facilitator can be a great help to a group.

Example: Reclaiming

I've worked with one group, organized around these principles, called Reclaiming, for over twenty years. Starting in 1980 as a small collective of five women, we've gone through many evolutionary stages as we've grown and expanded.

Reclaiming began as a tight-knit circle of friends who started teaching classes in earth-based spirituality and Witchcraft together. We were all in the same ritual circle, knew each other well, and saw each other frequently. As we taught each class, we recruited new student teachers for the next, and so our circle began expanding.

Originally, we were an open collective: anyone could come to meetings, get involved in the work, and participate in decisions. We shortly realized the pitfalls of this openness when we found ourselves dealing with an actively hallucinating psychotic at one meeting, or with people who had strong opinions but no interest in the work. Also, with everyone involved with every decision, meetings were long and often tedious.

We soon shifted to a model of working groups we called 'cells', partly as an ironic reference to Communist cells and partly because the word described what the groups did, namely perform specific functions for an overall body: teaching, putting out a newsletter, planning public rituals, etc. Cells had autonomy over their own affairs. A central, closed collective was formed for coordination and to decide on larger issues.

The collective had a tight mechanism for letting in new people: someone would be proposed, and the whole group would have to reach consensus on their admission. We had no mechanism for getting people out, and that proved to be a problem. Over time, the collective grew insular. People didn't want to let new people in and risk getting stuck with people they didn't like. People stayed in the collective when they were no longer actually doing work, and people who were doing work weren't in the collective. Others who might have been interested in joining were entirely mystified by our selection process and had no idea how to get in.

After about fifteen years of existence, we began a long process of restructuring. We collectively wrote a statement of our Principles of Unity. We created a new body called 'The Wheel,' in which working cells had actual representatives that they chose. The old collective resigned and passed on its power.

In the meantime, however, we had expanded in other ways. For years, we'd been teaching weeklong intensives we called Witchcamps in various parts of the US and Canada and Europe. Each camp had inspired local people to begin to teach and organize classes, rituals, and gatherings. Originally, the San Francisco teachers' cell staffed all the camps or chose all the teachers. But as people in other locations developed their own experience and skills, they began to resent the 'central control' and to ask for a voice in those decisions. We eventually created a spokescouncil structure for the whole web of Witchcamps. The spokescouncil consists of a teacher and an organizer from each camp community. It is not empowered: major decisions must go back to the communities for consensus. It meets once a year face-to-face, and once a year online in an extended e-mail meeting.

In setting up these structures, we've tried to assure maximum freedom, creativity, and autonomy while instituting minimal rules and the least amount of centralized control necessary. We've found that certain informal roles are useful in our organizations, our celebrations, and our actions. We've called them crows, snakes, graces, dragons, and spiders.

The task of the crows is to keep an overview, to keep the groups' direction in mind, to look ahead, and see to the big picture. The task of the snakes is to keep an underview, to notice what's not happening, who is not present, what problems are brewing.

Graces invite people in, make people welcome, expand the group, Dragons watch the boundaries, keeping track of the details and guarding against intrusions. And spiders sit in the center of the web, linking and communicating.

At times these roles are formally designated. At other times, they're roles we can each take on. They are all aspects of empowering leadership. When they are articulated, they can be shared and rotated more clearly.

We've tried to assure maximum freedom, creativity, and autonomy while instituting minimal rules and the least amount of centralized control necessary.

Empowering Leadership in the Web

Power-over – Power-among

Leadership is necessary and valuable even in anti-authoritarian groups. But the empowering leadership needed in such groups is very different from leadership in hierarchical groups. It's not the authority to give orders, issue decrees, make unilateral decisions, or tell people what to do. Rather, empowering leadership is about persuasion, inspiration, and the sharing of power, information, and attention. It's the leadership that steps out in front and says, 'Hey, let's go this way!'

Empowering leadership is not based on power-over, on the ability to control or punish others. It draws on a different sort of power that I call power-among. It's based on respect, on people's assessment that what I'm saying is worth hearing, perhaps because I have more experience or skill or knowledge in a certain area. In most indigenous cultures, elders wield a great deal of power-among because of their greater experience.

Listening to those with greater experience can save a lot of trial and error. If the elder says 'Don't eat that plant, my uncle did and he died in agony', we can save a lot of pain by following that advice. But power-among can also lead to dependency and transmute into power-over. Too much obedience to the words of the elders can prevent experimentation. Maybe Uncle died in agony not from the plant but from something entirely unrelated, and we're passing by a perfectly good food source. In the post-modern world, when situations and constraints change so rapidly, the experience of the past is not always a valid guide to the future. When power-among is recognized and identified, it can be assessed and challenged if need be.

For someone who is moved to take leadership in an empowering manner, power-among is a precious resource, and we do well to think of it as a limited resource. I think of it like I think of the water in my tank in summer that is filled from a spring. Theoretically, it's endlessly renewable. In reality, it fills slowly in August, and it can all too easily be lost if I do something really stupid, like leave a hose on. Once it's gone, it's going to take time for it to recover. If I use too much of it, I diminish the reserves.

Stepping Back as much as Stepping Forward

Empowering leadership means stepping back as much as stepping forward, not doing something you are good at so that someone else has a chance to learn.

Influence in a group is also best used judiciously, and always with respect for others. Never take it for granted. Always listen to the opinions of others with respect. Leave room for others to learn and make mistakes. Overused, influence breeds resentment and dries up.

Empowering leadership means stepping back as much as stepping forward, not doing something you are good at so that someone else has a chance to learn. But stepping back is not empowering if you are sitting silent but are inwardly glowering and criticizing.

George Lakey, a longtime organizer and nonviolence trainer, talks about the value of silently cheering for your students as they practise an exercise. Silent cheering has become one of my ongoing practices as a teacher, trainer, and leader. If I step back and let someone else facilitate a meeting, I consciously cheer them on internally: 'Go, Charles, go – hurray, that was a brilliant move, now, yeah, a home run!' Imagine the difference in atmosphere if I'm sitting there thinking, 'That was stupid – I would have done that better. Oh no – why did you say that? I should be up there, not him!'

Empowering leadership is not just a metaphor. It means literally supporting others energetically and emotionally, and creating an atmosphere in a group in which that energetic support and respectful attention is the norm. In such a group, people are more creative and smarter and make better decisions, and more energy is generated to do the work.

Power-among is best saved for those moments in which skill and experience are vitally necessary. But do use it when it's needed. When the plants in the garden are about to die, water them – that's what the water is for. When a thousand people are gathered for a meeting after the first day of blockading in Seattle and trying to decide what to do the next day while the police are outside tear gassing the street, the group needs the most experienced and skilled facilitator possible. But that person will meet less resentment in a tense situation if she or he has not previously facilitated every other meeting.

Issues Leadership – Process Leadership

There are several types of leadership we might exercise in a directly democratic group. We might call the first one issues leadership, proposing actions, directions, tactics, decisions, raising issues, urging the group to take certain directions. The second we could call process leadership: helping the group find effective ways to make decisions, share skills, and solve problems. Meeting facilitation, training, skills sharing, meditation, and counseling might be some of the ways process leadership is exercised.

In directly democratic groups, when we exercise process leadership we generally try to remain neutral and not exercise leadership around issues. So, if we're facilitating a meeting, we don't argue for a particular proposal. That would concentrate too much power in one voice. If we have a strong action to propose to the group, we don't facilitate that agenda item. If we're embroiled in a conflict, we don't also try to mediate it. When we're training a group, our job is to provide skills and a chance to reflect on experiences that will help people form their own opinions and make their own choices, not to impose our own philosophy or values. Pushing our own agenda would not only be an abuse of our power-among, it would be ineffective and likely cause resentment rather than inspire respect.

Sharing Power in Direct Democracy

Empowering leadership means sharing and expanding skills, passing them on as widely as possible, and making space for others to bring in their own creativity, to take material and make it their own, to do things you wouldn't have thought of, to make their own mistakes but also their own discoveries.

Empowering leadership is not about always having the brilliant idea yourself, but about recognizing and supporting the ideas of others. In ritual, sometimes one person will begin hesitantly humming a new tune or putting words to a chant. A good ritual leader is always listening to the group, ready to join her voice and make that softer melody audible,

Sharing information, sharing skills, supporting the creativity of others, networking, and communicating spread power throughout a group and therefore increase its effectiveness and intelligence.

Through the practice of direct democracy, we can develop forms and models that establish a true contrast to hierarchy and domination. We can learn from our mistakes and experiment, exploring approaches on a small scale that may eventually become a way to organize society on a large scale so that each person has a voice in the decisions that affect us.

For the author's biography, see page 74.

Beatrice Briggs inspires us to see meetings as rituals and to infuse these times of togetherness with respect, meaning and beauty. She calls for us to not waste our time in settling for less!

Meetings as Ritual

Beatrice Briggs

Consider for a moment the possibility that meetings are rituals.

By rituals I do not mean religious rites, although they too are rituals. Nor am I referring to personal routines, such as brushing one's teeth, especially those that are performed unconsciously, out of habit. For the purposes of this reflection, ritual is defined as a repeatable cultural performance, a specific act performed on a specific occasion. Rituals are culturally coded behaviours that give us a heightened sense of identity and meaning. Rituals help define us as a community; they remind us of who we are, how to behave and what is of ultimate value.

The human species has invented itself through ritual. Human cultures are a product of ritual – and ritual is our primary cultural product. Because rituals both shape and mirror cultural evolution, they are a rich source of information about the social order and a powerful tool for its transformation. I am suggesting that meetings are one of the dominant rituals of our times and therefore, properly used, could serve as an effective instrument for social and cultural change.

What if we saw meetings – understood as gatherings to discuss issues of shared importance and to make collective decisions – as a basic human need, like food, sleep or sex? What if meetings were treated not as a boring obligation, but as essential for survival? What if meetings connected us to our psychic depths, to our local community, and to the great mystery? What if meetings reminded us of what is sacred, of what must be treasured and protected? How would meetings be different if we saw them as an opportunity to educate, guide, nourish and heal ourselves? What if we entered into meetings with passion, reverence, and a sense that our participation was of vital importance?

Rituals grow out of myths, the 'big stories' we tell about our role in the evolutionary journey of the universe. They are the narratives that, when joined to ritual, create a web of meaning out of which our individual and collective identity emerges. We are the stories we tell and the rituals we perform. So how can we harness the dual power of myth and ritual to make our meetings more bearable?

Loss of Ritual – Loathing of Meetings

As local cultures all over the planet have been marginalized and even eradicated by the interests of multinational corporations and the governments who serve them, many rituals have lost their connection to the sacred. Most of us no longer celebrate the new moon, the solstice, the harvest or the return of migrating birds. Instead we flock to the shopping mall, pack the sports stadium and go to ugly, boring, embarrassing, oppressive, alienating, and infuriating meetings.

Facilitation

The rituals practised in most meetings produce a specific kind of suffering. Decision-makers who already know what they plan to do are required to pretend to listen to the opinions of others. Participants are obliged to sit through meetings in which it is obvious that their ideas, if expressed at all, will have no real impact on the final decision. People talk too much or not at all. Agendas are too full, poorly organized or non-existent. Discussions meander, priorities are unclear, and the decision-making process swings between despotism and anarchy. And so forth?

Applying the Criteria for Good Ritual to Meetings

Here are some of the lessons we can learn from 'good' rituals, meaning those that inspire and energize us, that might make our meetings more meaningful and effective.

Be clear about the purpose. In general, those who attend a wedding are clear about the purpose of the ritual. They do not confuse it, for example, with a football game. Do we know the true purpose of the Monday morning sales meeting? If we did (and had a choice), would we bother to attend?

Know your role. The godparents at a baptism understand that they are committing themselves to the on-going spiritual education of the child. What is the role of those who attend a condominium meeting? To complain about the neighbours? To listen to committee reports? To advise the board of directors? If their role were clearer, would they behave differently?

Plan ahead. Good rituals require careful preparation. A meeting in which the room is clean and the chairs in place, an agenda has been drafted, the right people are present and the needed materials are at hand sets the stage for an effective session.

Make it special. Rituals transform the ordinary into something special. When we take the trouble to put flowers on the table, bake cookies for the coffee break, or simply greet people with a smile as they arrive, we send a message that beauty, caring and human connection are some of the values that guide our work.

Take time to get centred. The world is full of difficulties and distractions that need to be set aside in order to enter into ritual space. A moment of silence can help get everyone mentally 'in the room' and focused on their intention for being there.

Vary the timing and texture. Rituals can be short or long, formal or impromptu, complex or simple. Meeting formats should vary according to their purpose.

The Facilitator

If meetings are a contemporary ritual, then the facilitator can be viewed as a kind of 'process priest(ess)' who helps set the tone, maintains the focus and guides the group through the various stages of its work. A novice facilitator, like a recently ordained priest, may be a little insecure at first. A more experienced facilitator can handle larger, more complex groups. A seasoned facilitator, who has done his/her own inner work, can serve a more shamanic role, accompanying the group through confusion and confrontation until some resolution is reached. A long or complex meeting, like a 'big' ceremony, calls for an experienced team of facilitators, as well as other process roles, to hold the energy.

Conclusion

If, as suggested at the beginning of this article, meetings are culturally coded performances, then they can be modified to meet the urgencies of the times. We need meetings that invite dialogue, promote understanding, encourage collaboration, stir creativity, and meet our fundamental need for meaning and belonging. We need meetings that engage our hearts and minds and give us an opportunity to make a positive difference in the world. If we settle for less, we are wasting our time.

Beatrice Briggs is the director of the International Institute for Facilitation and Consensus, a professional team of facilitators, trainers and consultants who specialize in participatory decision-making processes. A native of the United States who lives in Mexico, she travels extensively, providing facilitation, training and consulting services. The author of the manual *Introduction to Consensus*, Beatrice has a Master¹s degree from the University of Chicago.

IIFAC, Plaza Corporativa #113, Domingo Diez 1589, Col. El Empleado, Cuernavaca, Morelos 62250, México · (T) +52 777 1022288 · (F) +52 777 1022290 · email@iifac.org · www.iifac.org

The Limits to Participation

Beatrice Briggs

One of the most difficult issues for groups that want to be open, inclusive and participatory is establishing limits to participation in their decision-making processes. Here are four common scenarios that dramatize some of the forms that this dilemma can take:

- *Scenario #1*: A committed group of individuals works hard to establish trust, develop ground rules and an effective process for discussion and deciding key issues. Then new people arrive who are eager to join in, but they lack training in the decision-making method being used, are unclear about the group's vision and mission, and are unfamiliar with the background of the issues being dealt with. How can the group welcome these newcomers without spending a lot of time in meetings reviewing the group's history and procedures?

- *Scenario #2*: A group has defined a process for discussing a specific issue, usually something relatively complex and/or controversial. After several productive meetings in which all available points of view on the issue are considered and a decision is about to be made, a group member who has not participated in the previous meetings shows up, asking many questions that have already been answered or voicing objections based on ignorance of the information previously shared. Should the group take extra time to educate the late arrival about the meetings she missed or make the decision anyway, running the risk that she might block the proposal?

- *Scenario #3*: A friend of one of the members attends a meeting as a visitor. In the course of the meeting, he begins to raise his hand to speak, expressing opinions about the topics under discussion. Should he be allowed to participate?

- *Scenario #4:* A small, overworked committee is organizing an event for a group that has a large, but relatively inactive membership. The committee sends regular reports on its progress to the members and occasionally asks for feedback on specific proposals by email. Suddenly two very upset members of the larger group appear at a committee meeting, demanding time on the agenda to express their views on the committee's work. Should they be given time to speak?

In theory, many groups, not wanting to replicate the exclusionary practices of many traditional, hierarchical organizations, claim to be open to all. When they encounter situations similar to those described above, however, they begin to wonder how to reconcile the ideal of participation with the real difficulties that this implies.

Let's be clear: a participatory process does not always mean that everyone decides everything. Simply showing up at a meeting does not automatically confer the privileges of speaking or voting. Setting limits to participation can be both reasonable and necessary, as long as the intention is to establish a functional process and not to protect a closed inner circle. The challenge is to establish clear criteria for participation and then enforce them in a fair and equitable manner.

Here are my comments regarding the scenarios described above. Obviously, there is no single right way to address these issues.

- In the case of *Group #1*, my recommendation would be that they provide special sessions for prospective new members, perhaps just before the regular meeting and then require that the newcomers observe several meetings in a row before being invited to participate in discussions. The right to vote (or block, in the case of consensus process) is only granted after a person has demonstrated commitment to the group's goals, familiarity with its processes and becomes a full-fledged member.

- In the case of *Group #2*, the ideal solution would have been to establish a requirement at the outset of the process that participation in the discussion meetings is necessary in order to take part in the final decision. Since that was not done, I see no option but to take the time to bring the latecomer up to speed before making the decision, however frustrating that may be for the others.

- For *Group #3*, I would recommend that they establish a clear policy regarding visitor's attendance and participation in meetings. In general, I favour an open meeting policy, at which visitors are welcome, but as observers only.

- *Group #4* has a slightly different problem since an active conflict has erupted in its midst. The committee really has almost no choice but to listen to what the angry members have to say. After all, they may be bringing important perspectives to the committee's attention or providing information that the committee has failed to consider. If the committee itself is weak or torn by internal conflicts, this episode could provoke a crisis. If, on the other hand, the committee has clear authorization from the larger group for the work it is doing and a solid, transparent process that includes establishing clear criteria for the decisions it makes, it will probably be able to absorb the angry members input with equanimity, make any necessary adjustments in their plans, and carry on, strengthened by the experience.

Defining the Limits

The key to dealing with these and similar situations is to openly discuss the limits to participation in your group. Who can participate? Who can decide? Under what circumstances? Talk about what it was like being a newcomer to the group, how easy or hard it was to feel that you belonged. Evaluate how serious a problem disruptive participation really is. Are these people being disruptive because our policies and procedures are oppressive or exclusive? Or do they simply not understand how we work? Figure out a structure and process that is consistent with your group's values, write it down, portray it graphically, explain it to everyone, make future adjustments as necessary. Remember, setting limits to participation is not just a way to keep people out, it is also a way to respect the hard work of those who have been consistently involved in the group's evolutionary process.

For the author's biography, see page 104.

In this text, Giovanni Ciarlo gives us some clear step-by-step advice on the facilitation of group meetings. Since much energy can be unnecessarily lost in this realm, it is certainly worth taking a close look at!

Group Facilitation
A Step-by-Step Guide

Giovanni Ciarlo

When groups gather to create a vision, make decisions, or plan activities, they have options on how to conduct their meeting. One way is to come together, identify what needs to be discussed, and decide how to proceed. Another way is to prepare ahead of time, planning meeting details and proceeding in an orderly and prescribed way. In either case the group has much to gain by using a facilitator.

A facilitator's role is to guide the group through the meeting processes of deliberate dialogue, topic discussions, and decision-making. A facilitator is a skilled questioner who can help equalize participation, elicit wisdom, and clarify the situation at hand.

Facilitation is an art. A good facilitator is patient and levelheaded, has a strong memory, stamina, humor, skills, and the ability to track complex signals and care for the group. A facilitator makes the meeting process easier, more focused and fair; but he/she is not someone who will lead or direct the group. The facilitator's job is to serve the group in a professional and impartial way, and to clearly define his/her role for all clients.

In a sense, the facilitator is in the group, but not of the group. He/she is impartial. The facilitator does not voice an opinion with regard to the content of a group's discussions, does not sponsor agenda items, has no stake in the outcome of discussions, and is unbiased about the subject matter. A facilitator does, however, guide the group through discussions by being aware of and prepared for differences, multiple interpretations, and other forms of conflict. A good facilitator considers the needs of the group as a whole, and finds ways of focusing on those issues that encourage discussion and lead to resolution. Those new to facilitation are encouraged to apprentice with experienced facilitators and should practise whenever possible. Being a group facilitator is an opportunity for personal growth, and a facilitator should always strive for greater personal awareness.

A good facilitator can save a group considerable time and make the meeting a pleasant experience that ensures agreement and resolution. Before working with a group, a facilitator must prepare: Outline an agreement with the clients, clarify the purpose of the meeting, create an agenda, research background information, assess the dynamics of the group, sign contracts, design process formats, select activities, and prepare guidelines. After a meeting, a facilitator is responsible for helping the group reach a conclusion, as well as evaluating the meeting and planning follow-ups.

The following steps should be considered when facilitating.

Plan ahead   A facilitator should participate as much as possible in meeting preparations and agenda planning. Develop close relationships with key participants, including other facilitators, if any. Become informed about the projects and proposals that will be discussed. This will help move the group toward creative solutions and encourage even participation among members. Some meetings require more preparation than others – from several hours or days, to weeks or months. Generally speaking, the facilitator should clarify the terms of his/her involvement two or more weeks before the scheduled meeting. This includes getting any applicable training, identifying the meeting time and location, and clarifying compensation. It is also important for the facilitator to get a sense of the group's decision-making style and obtain background information to better understand group dynamics.

Meet with group members   The facilitator should meet with group members to plan an agenda and consider which processes he/she will employ for discussions and breakthrough items. The facilitator is responsible for planning an appropriate opening and closing activity, and for ensuring that all agenda items have a sponsor and a time limit. He/she should also anticipate potential difficulties and plan resolution strategies.

Plan a site visit   A site visit to meet with those in charge of the space will help the facilitator prepare for the meeting. He/she can plan the setup, which includes devising a seating arrangement, maintaining temperature control, locating the restrooms, identifying breakout areas, etc. The facilitator should be aware of ways to enhance the meeting space, such as using tablecloths, centrepieces, flowers, candles, or other decorative items. He/she should also check with organizers about refreshments, childcare, translation services, etc. It is appropriate to request the provider be as ecological as possible.

The facilitator should also take stock of needed supplies and equipment, like easel paper, markers, tape, name tags, projectors, computers, printers, etc. It is a good idea for the facilitator to have a personal toolkit with some of these essential items, and to check with agenda sponsors to see what equipment they will need.

Be well rested   The facilitator must be alert to maintain good mental agility and keep track of the agenda, ideas, participation, subtle messages, time, and

A good facilitator considers the needs of the group as a whole, and finds ways of focusing on those issues that encourage discussion and lead to resolution.

all other aspects of running the meeting. Have a centering technique, such as deep breathing, prayer or meditation to stay relaxed and focused. Dress appropriately for the meeting – clothes should not attract too much attention or be too different from the group, but project a professional image.

Arrive early   The facilitator should arrive to the meeting with plenty of time to set up. Go over a checklist and make sure that the space is clean, the equipment works, all supplies and refreshments are ready, restrooms are open, etc. Before the meeting begins, the facilitator should write the agenda, ground rules, responsibilities and other relevant information on easel sheets that all can see. If changes or corrections need to be made, write them clearly on the same sheets.

Prepare opening activities   The facilitator must prepare opening activities by giving the group relevant information about the facilitation, the group, the expectations, the purpose and the scope of the meeting. When appropriate, the facilitator leads, or asks someone in the group to lead, an opening ceremony. This is usually followed by a round of introductions, which gives group members a chance to 'break the ice', hear their voices, build familiarity, identify participants, and in general 'warm up' for the meeting. At this point the facilitator clarifies the decision making process, posing questions such as: Who decides? Are visitors and observers allowed to participate? If so, how? Does everyone understand the adopted decision making mechanism? Will it be by consensus? By majority rule? Or by percentage of votes? This is also a good time to identify who will be taking the meeting minutes, and in what format.

Identify ground rules   Before addressing the proposed agenda it is a good idea for the facilitator to review the ground rules for the meeting. These should be clearly posted for easy reference in case the meeting starts to deviate. Groups that have been working with the same agreements over time may skip this step, but new groups or those experimenting with a new meeting process should go over the ground rules. Ground rules might include: Beginning and ending on time, one person speaks at a time, speak only for yourself, no interrupting, everyone gets a chance to speak, seek solutions, turn off cell phones, maintain confidentiality, etc.

Address the agenda   When the group is ready to review the proposed meeting agenda, the facilitator identifies who prepared the agenda and gives ownership to the group. During this time he/she negotiates changes, makes sure that sufficient time is allotted for all agenda items, clarifies the nature of each item (introduction, informational, discussion or decision), creates a contract with the participants, and gives an overview of what the meeting is about and when it will end. Once the agenda revision is finalized, the facilitator should strike the word 'proposed' from the title. Acknowledging that the agenda in front of the group is the working agenda is a powerful tool for avoiding crisis and/or sidetracking during the meeting.

Facilitate the meeting   At this stage the facilitator turns the floor over to the persons sponsoring each of the agenda items. The facilitator introduces an item and facilitates any discussion. During discussion, it is a good idea for the facilitator to clarify what is being said. This is where a clear process is helpful. To keep the group from getting stuck in 'icebergs' (items that don't seem to move forward), help them figure out how to deal with unresolved concerns.

If after discussion an item requires a decision, the facilitator should restate the proposal to make sure it is clearly understood and ask the group if they are ready to decide. If the answer is 'yes' and the group is working with consensus, the facilitator should ask if anyone wants to block the decision. If so, he/she should try to resolve the situation. If there are no blocks, the facilitator should ask if anyone wants to 'stand aside,' then make sure all answers are registered in the meeting minutes. If there are no blocks and not many stand asides, the group has reached agreement on that item and can move on. The facilitator should also ask the minute-taker to read each decision so that everyone can hear and approve them.

Include light items   Throughout the meeting 'light items,' such as announcements should be included to change the pace and give participants a moment to breathe before tackling the next agenda item. If there are several announcements, intersperse them in the agenda or ask participants to submit only written announcements to save time.

Breaks and games are good techniques to alter the meeting pace. It is strongly recommended that the group break every 90 minutes or less to give people a chance to refocus, take care of personal business, go to the bathroom, or make phone calls without disturbing the meeting. The facilitator should tell the group when to reconvene. Generally speaking 15 minutes is a reasonable break time, unless it is lunchtime or the group has been meeting for a long time. Sometimes the energy of the meeting requires that the facilitator introduce a game or other group activity to lighten the atmosphere. It is helpful for the facilitator to develop a repertoire of games for a variety of situations, or to ask someone to lead a game. These are excellent tools for bonding and moving the group forward through difficult topics.

Adopt a stance   The facilitator should stand in front of the group when presenting a topic or calling on participants, and stand to one side during others' presentations. The facilitator should avoid polarizing language, judgments, use of the word 'but,' or assigning ownership of an idea to a specific person. Try to be as neutral as possible, and identify the few main points of the conversation. This can be achieved through nonverbal awareness, presence of mind and the ability to see past the verbiage to

It is helpful for the facilitator to develop a repertoire of games for a variety of situations, or to ask someone to lead a game. These are excellent tools for bonding and moving the group forward through difficult topics.

underlying issues. It also requires that the facilitator be evenhanded, fair and impartial to the issues.

Stay on topic   The main functions of the facilitator are to maintain the speaking order and keep the agenda on track. When many people want to talk at once, create a stacking order. Do not let the group stray off topic or follow discussions that deter from the agenda. Conversely, when there are few interventions the facilitator can allow people to speak at random. When an item takes much longer than anticipated (an 'iceberg'), ask the group if they want to give it more time, and where the time will come from. In some instances the facilitator might recommend sending the item to a committee, or continue discussion at a future meeting.

Save time   There are several techniques for saving the group time, including straw polls, brainstorming, asking for consensus, asking those who haven't spoken for their opinion, assisting someone in formulating a proposal, etc. Remember that the facilitator does not provide answers, but rather is a skilled questioner who can move things along by simply asking the right questions or referring to the ground rules stated earlier. These techniques can equalize participation, elicit wisdom, clarify points, summarize items, support the shy, silence the verbose, handle the 'experts,' or make participation more dynamic.

Cope with stress   The facilitator will undoubtedly encounter stressful situations. During these times, take a moment to refocus or ask for the group's help. Side conversations disrupt meetings and the facilitator can deal with them in a variety of ways. Call attention to side conversations by standing next to the people who are talking. If everyone is talking at once, or if there are emotional outbursts or other distractions call for a 10 to 15 minute break and return to the agenda when the meeting resumes. In all cases the facilitator must protect the group and him/herself from verbal attacks. If this occurs, refer to the ground rules, speak privately with the offender and/ or those offended, and watch for 'power plays' by people looking to get their way.

Include an evaluation   At the end of the meeting the facilitator helps the group find ways to deal with unresolved items, plan the next meeting, implement approved proposals, rewrite proposals that were not approved, collect agenda items for the next meeting, and carry out an evaluation of the current meeting. The evaluation is a critical step and should not be skipped. It is here that the group gets a chance to educate its members on process issues and to speak publicly about the things that were successful, as well as things that needed improvement. An evaluation helps the group get a sense of ending on a constructive and, hopefully, positive note. At this point the facilitator can thank the group, the organizers and particular individuals for their contributions, and give the group a chance to do the same.

Close the meeting   Formally concluding the meeting allows people to make closing remarks and creates a sense of intimacy among participants. The facilitator should lead a closing activity or ask someone in the group to do so. This might be a song, a round of final words, a short silent meditation, a dance, or any other collective and participatory item.

Ask the group to leave the room as it was at the start of the meeting   The facilitator or a participant should collect the easel pages and archive them until the minutes and all matters of the meeting have been finalized. Remind the minute taker to type the minutes in a clean, concise format, and send them to the appropriate person for distribution and approval. Make sure the minutes are kept safe and that the minute taker can be contacted for follow-up if necessary.

Make time to relax   After a meeting the facilitator may feel exhausted and need to recharge. Debrief with a co-facilitator (recommended when facilitating large groups) or another close colleague. Make time to reflect, relax and write in a journal. This is a very important step for personal growth, professional improvement and self-evaluation.

The above information was condensed from *Introduction to Consensus* by Beatrice Briggs.

Giovanni Ciarlo is co-founder of www.huehuecoyotl.org Ecoaldea Huehuecoyotl, a centre for the exploration of the arts and ecology in central Mexico (www.huehuecoyotl.net). He helped form the Ecovillage Network of the Americas (http://ena.ecovillage.org) and serves on the Board of the Global Ecovillage Network (http://gen.ecovillage.org). He is also a professional Arts-In-Education Consultant and a trained group facilitator. He is an associate member of the International Institute for Facilitation and Consensus (www.iifac.org) and leads workshop trainings in Group Facilitation in the US and Mexico. Since 2003 he has co-directed sustainability programs in Mexico in collaboration with Goddard College of Vermont and Living Routes Ecovillage Studies of Massachusetts. He currently divides his time between the US and Mexico, linking community sustainable projects in both countries.

Kosha Joubert looks briefly at the state of affairs in the Ecovillage of Sieben Linden and then goes on to show how the concept of collective intelligence could inspire us to approach meetings in new and fresh ways.

Tapping into Collective Intelligence
The Growing Edge in the Ecovillage of Sieben Linden

Kosha Anja Joubert

> If we wish to survive the social and ecological crisis that we have created we need to get deeply involved in the development of new community structures within our society. LYNN MARGULIS, Evolutionary Biologist

This piece starts by looking at the present state of affairs in the ecovillage of Sieben Linden. I focus on the social dimension, but to give you an idea of how deeply the different dimensions (ecological, financial, worldview and social) are intertwined, I will pay a brief visit to each of them. After all, we need socially sustainable human communities to design ecologically sustainable lifestyles. And we need financially sustainable communities to evolve spiritually. Human creativity unfolds holistically in connection to the whole circle of life.

State of Affairs

The ecovillage of Sieben Linden is an ecovillage in the most classical sense: a green 'island' in the East German countryside, successfully working to regenerate a rich eco-social system in an area of former agro-industry. Founded with the aim of becoming a model village for a new culture of sustainability and a centre for research and education, Sieben Linden is designed to accommodate approximately 300 inhabitants once all the buildings are finished. Today, ten years after the first inhabitants moved to the land, 80 adults and 32 children live here. All around us, high unemployment rates prevail and villages are emptying out. Sieben Linden, on the contrary, is not able to absorb the amount of people that would like to join!

Ecological Design

'Treading softly on the earth' and 'luxurious simplicity' have become our trademarks. We started off with a strong emphasis on the material and ecological aspects of sustainability. Straw bale-buildings with compost toilets, a closed water cycle, feeding of solar energy into the grid, heating with wood from our forest and eating from our gardens are all part of the overall design.

There is a lingering luxury to living in a place that allows us to follow such a wholesome lifestyle. Being a mother with knowledge about the state of our planet, I feel gratitude when I watch my children roam these fields and forests.

Financial Design

We founded a cooperative so that we own our 42 hectares of land and community infrastructure collectively and each person pays 12,300€ to join in. The sharing of ownership and responsibility serves as a solid foundation for building community. Neighbourhood homes are financed through a building cooperative. We are individually responsible for our incomes, with a lot of sharing and mutual support happening.

Together, we run an educational association. People of all ages and walks of life come for shorter or longer periods to learn and share in our way of life, and often leave with fresh inspiration to walk their talk on sustainability in a more consistent way. At the same time, these guests bring valuable financial assets to our small local economic system, which in turn, spurs development in the surrounding region.

Worldview

In Sieben Linden, there is a broad diversity of pathways in the spiritual realm, but all are connected to an underlying process of listening to and reconnecting with nature. Small groups meet for yoga and meditation in the morning, some have moved into deep ecology or follow shamanism, others walk the gardens and watch the night skies for contemplation. We have all taken a step and are willing to change our lifestyles in order to find an expression for our compassion for life on earth.

At the same time, we are all children of a culture that seems bent on destruction. We carry residues of distrust and separation within us. We have been taught that it is safer to assume that nature, other humans, and the universe are hostile, than to meet them unguarded. We have a tendency to experience our way of looking at things as the best way and to feel threatened by other ways. This is part of what we bring to a life in community and need to transform together.

Social Design

Meeting

In the social realm we distinguish between time and space for feeling, for thinking and for organizing. We have:

- Meetings for deep, emotional sharing with the aim of strengthening love, compassion and mutual trust.
- Meetings for sharing of worldviews, spiritual paths and political thinking with the aim of growing in awareness and building a pool of common values.
- Organizational meetings with the aim of realizing our dreams together.

Taking time off for inner processes seems like luxury to many, even though we experienced again and again how it enhances our overall level of trust, joy, creativity and effectiveness as a community!

Whenever we neglect the first two, the third, organizational meetings, become very tedious.

However, it needs a strong focus to hold enough time and space for deep emotional sharing and sharing of worldviews. There is always so much to do! Taking time off for inner processes seems like luxury to many, even though we experienced again and again how it enhances our overall level of trust, joy, creativity and effectiveness as a community! The method we have found to be most helpful in building trust within our diversity is the Forum. (See the article by Dolores Richter.)

In Sieben Linden, we have a strong affinity to diversity and grassroots democracy, springing as we do from a German history that includes Nazism and, more recently, East German communism. We are very cautious of what Irving Janis (1972) called 'Groupthink' (an excessive striving towards group harmony at the cost of a critical assessment of the situation at hand).

One expression of this caution can be found in a culture of communication that places a strong emphasis on reason and critical reflection. While there are many benefits, this sometimes stifles the enthusiasm and juice of new ideas at too early a stage of group discussion. And when people step into discussions with the aim of convincing others of their point of view, taking decisions can become time-consuming and strenuous.

Taking Decisions

Our decision-making procedures are based on consensus, based on the belief that each person holds a piece of the truth and that decisions become durable when supported by all. As our community grew, however, so much was happening in so many areas that we were overwhelmed. We ended up talking so much and doing so little … We redesigned our organizational structures so as to delegate as much decision-making power as trust allowed to subgroups (these work with consensus). Ideally, only more pertinent matters that concern us all now show up in our general meetings.

Initially, we found that many lukewarm frames of mind were hidden in our consensus decisions and we developed a wish for more outspokenness and clarity. Today, a decision needs two-thirds of the inhabitants to stand fully behind it before it can pass. There are four voting options:

- Fully positive.
- Not fully positive, but I'll support it.
- Not in support, but I'll stand aside.
- Veto.

If you have a veto, watch out! It means stepping into deep communication with all the others involved and taking responsibility for finding a better solution!

Taking on Responsibility

Reality also teaches us what Manitonquat describes so well:

> For a while I thought we were doing great without leaders. But then I began to notice that whenever we did something well, there was always a leader – not in title, but someone who quietly took responsibility and did the thinking that was necessary to get the job done, presented proposals, asked for help, inspired and encouraged others.

We have enough responsibility for everyone to take on his or her share! In practice, the boundary between creative and repressive power remains a fine line and one main cause for dispute. The group often looks critically at individuals who hold a lot of responsibility in order to catch signs of manipulative self-interest early. And while we expect our many community-leaders to be able to integrate criticism, at times it wears them out.

Neighbourhoods

Another expression of our care not to end up in 'Groupthink' can be found in Sieben Linden being a community of communities: we designed the ecovillage as subgroups of 15-30 people, called neighbourhoods. The original idea was that each neighbourhood would follow a different approach to sustainability, build together, and offer a home base for its members. The reality has shown many expressions of networks and systems coming into existence instead of the clear-cut neighbourhoods. The overall social fabric that makes up the larger community organism is thus woven together from patchwork pieces – intricate patterns and colourful threads in ways that continually change.

Tensions within the social dimension

Group communication in organizational meetings is often tedious and uses up valuable human resources. After years of intense involvement, individuals tend to loose interest and withdraw from these group activities.

How can we allow for more individual potential to unfold within the group setting?

> We need to ask ourselves whether we are finding consensus on the level of the lowest common denominator or on that of the highest possible level of individual potential in our communities. In visiting different communities I have found a tendency to come together around the lowest possible denominator.
>
> THOMAS HÜBEL, spiritual teacher working with communities in Germany

How can we use diversity to empower unity instead of weakening it? At times, the 10 per cent in which we differ overshadows the 90 per cent in which we are of one mind.

Our Growing Edge – The Way Forward

> No problem can be solved from the same level of consciousness that created it. We must learn to see the world anew.   ALBERT EINSTEIN

In Sieben Linden, as in all humanity, we are in the midst of a paradigm shift from mistrust to trust and from separation to connectedness. The solutions to the questions we are facing can only be found through an evolution of inner awareness. In the following, therefore, though focussing on our growing edge in the social dimension, I will start off with a personal reflection of our way forward in the dimension of worldview.

We are coming to realize that elementary particles, humans and communities are all wholes that are holographically nestled into larger wholes and can be seen as bundles of potential rather than inert matter ...

Worldview

New physics, chaos theory, systems thinking, Gaia theory, and the concept of morphogenetic fields are all infiltrating our consciousness. They are changing the world we see into a more holographic and integral whole. We are coming to realize that elementary particles, humans and communities are all wholes that are holographically nestled into larger wholes and can be seen as bundles of potential rather than inert matter: nothing exists independently from how it is looked on by others. We are finding that we have power in evoking certain qualities within each other and within the world. The community (and the world) we experience is a mirror of our inner experience at any given moment. If we are in a state of trust and joy with life, our community seems to smile back at us. If we are in a state of distrust, it often snarls.

Spiral meeting

Even though new realizations are streaming in, our thinking and our actions are always likely to revert to the separation and distrust that is habitual and especially so when we are in a state of anxiety. As David Bohm (physicist) states: 'Normally, our thoughts have us rather than we having them.' To change our consciousness is an assignment that is not to be underestimated. How can we use our communities to walk this path together? I believe our capacity to think together instead of separately can greatly aid us in speeding up this inner evolution.

Social Design

> What is new in the world of today is that the best and most reachable doorway to deeper spiritual experiences is no longer through individual meditation but through group work.   OTTO SCHARMER

Meaningful conversations have the potential not only to transform human relationships, but to transform human consciousness!

In order to break free from our habitual thought patterns, David Bohm proposed to step into 'Dialogue'. His idea was quite simple: bring 20-40 people together in a room and let them talk freely about any topic. Mix in a few simple, yet challenging instructions like: letting go of inner assumptions, deep listening and authentic self-expression – and you can be sure to start a process that will bring our unconscious worldviews into the open and lead the group to a higher level of congruence and collective understanding.

Many methods with similar aims have been developed and used by different communities, some, like talking stick circles (see *The Way of Council*), for thousands of years. The Forum, Harrison Owens 'Open Space Technology' and the 'World-Café-Movement' (Juanita Brown and David Isaacs) are other methods that come to mind. They all set the stage for tapping into human collective intelligence.

A common starting point is what Francisco Varela called suspension: letting go of our preconceptions and historical ways of making sense, instead of coming to meetings with a clear set of arguments, ready to convince everyone else. Once we stop defending our point of view in a struggle for recognition, we can start communicating *with* instead of *against* each other. We can start having meaningful conversations, where we enhance the contributions of others before adding our own. Prerequisites for suspension seem to be a certain level of trust and a focussing of attention on a common higher goal.

People in groups in all walks of life have had experiences where the whole of a group in conversation suddenly becomes more than the sum of its parts and is able to tap into a new level of wisdom. When a group reaches this kind of level of coherence, a higher level of organizational order comes into play. A group intuition is activated that seems to be directed like an antenna towards where inspiration might be coming from next. The group starts to be creative as a whole. This synergetic phenomenon is called *collective intelligence* and we've probably all experienced it at some point or other. In Sieben Linden we have, but far too seldom. Why should we ever want to revert to lesser levels of communicating?

Realizing that the realities we are facing are too complex for our habitual thought processes and individualized ways of reasoning to grasp, makes this option even more attractive. Sensing the depth of connectedness in outer realities leads to new levels of connectedness in our nervous systems:

Sensing the depth of connectedness in outer realities leads to new levels of connectedness in our nervous systems

The normal human brain comes with potential software-like systems just waiting to be turned on – latent upgrades!   BECK AND COWAN, p. 51

When groups become really good at this, it can lead to very quick decision-making procedures, since we build on our intuition instead of the linear process of reason.   ROBERT KENNY, Organizational Consultant

In these situations we really create something new together. This is what makes it so exciting for us to participate. We birth the next stage of evolutionary consciousness.   JUANITA BROWN

Now, to return to the tensions that presently exist within the social dimension of Sieben Linden, I believe that an awareness of the phenomenon of collective intelligence and a clear intent of tapping into it together pose an answer to the questions posed above ('Tensions within the social dimension').

1. Group communication is often tedious

When we share deeply, tedium does not arise. This happens only in organizational meetings when a clash of opinions instead of mutual inspiration takes place. Holding a clear intention as a group to reach towards a higher level of coherence and synergy in such situations is a necessity if we want more joy and energy to flow! (See Bea Briggs' 'Meetings as Ritual', page 102.)

Helpful steps:

- Take care of Groupspace: punctuality, clear time-frame.
- Start off with an opening exercise that builds intimacy and trust within the group organism.
- Make sure the issue at hand is stated clearly and feels meaningful (connected to a higher goal) to everyone. If not, arrange for a different composition of people (to whom it does feel meaningful) to come back to the issue somewhere else.
- Ask people to become aware of, and suspend, prior judgments.
- Call attention to the quality of collective intelligence and ask people to hold this field in their awareness for the duration of the meeting.
- Invite a time of silence while asking people to open up to inspiration and solutions.
- Ask people to practise deep listening and authentic expression.
- Allow for moments of silence between contributions.
- Trust the group and ask excellent facilitators to support the group.

After a period of years of intense involvement, individuals lose interest and withdraw from group activities.

We can take this as a sure sign that the time is ripe for the group to change and move into a higher level of awareness. One possibility would be to use *Spiral Dynamics* as a model to assess where the group is and what the next step could be.

2. How can we allow for more individual potential to unfold within the group setting?

Collective intelligence implies an interplay of powerful individuals that allows our highest potential to be expressed and directed to a common higher goal. In this kind of team play individuals can tap into a higher level of intelligence and creativity than we could have by ourselves. Paradoxically, once we stop struggling for individual recognition, we can rise above habitual thought patterns and express our individuality with more ease.

Individuality, not individualism, is the cornerstone of community. Individuality is synonymous with uniqueness. This means that a person and his or her unique gifts are irreplaceable. The community loves to see all of its members flourish and function at optimum potential. In fact, a community can flourish and survive only when each member flourishes, living in the full potential of his or her purpose.   MALIDOMA SOMÉ

The whole will become more than the sum of its parts only once every part has found its place within the whole.
Helpful steps:

- Take time to find out about each other's dreams and visions.

- Take time to mirror each other's qualities.

- Step out of the duality of hierarchy and heterarchy. While hierarchy is the power of one over many on a vertical level, heterarchy is the power of the many over the one on a horizontal level. 'Heterarchy by itself is differentiation without integration, a collection of singular parts without a deeper purpose: a heap, not a whole.' (Ken Wilber)

- Instead, create holarchies! The concept of holons, coined by Arthur Koestler, describes the different levels of complexity that our natural world is made up from. Molecules, cells, tissues, organs and organisms, for instance, are all holons (nestled wholes) in a biological holarchy. Information flows vertically and horizontally in all directions. Each level mirrors and influences all others.

- Design and refine a natural holarchy for the whole community that allows for maximum energy flow. Are there systemic levels that we are not integrating consciously? Has our vision of the circles of influence of the community become too narrow? Can we broaden our vision to include the highest potential of all our members?

- Understand that in our holographic reality it does not matter on which level we take on full responsibility (leadership) as long as we do!

3. How can we use diversity to empower unity instead of weakening it?

Rivers and streams don't seem to need to cling to a certain concept of self in order to fulfil their destiny. With sparkling confidence, they flow down crevices and around mountains, becoming a trickle in the dry season and swelling to a mighty stream in the rainy season, never losing their sense of direction. They always end up in the ocean.

We can experience our diverse individual ways of seeing the world as enrichment as we stop competing and open up to our collective intelligence. We can bring more consciousness to the constant process of coming together as a community, then retreating as individuals, then coming back together … It is as if the community organism breathes in and out. Both movements are needed for life to take place.

Helpful steps:

- Sensitivity: Opening up individually to our senses. Listening to life within and around us. Deciding to trust.

- Responsibility for self: Taking on responsibility for our feelings, thoughts and actions.

- Opening up: Reaching out to and valuing the other.

- Dialogue: Speaking my own truth and listening deeply to the truth of others.

- Embracing Diversity: Opening up to a deeper view of reality that encompasses individual viewpoints.

- Alignment: Searching for group alignment in vision and action.

- Evolution: Settling on a common plan for action.

Experiencing the trial runs of our action plans spirals us to a next level of observation, sensitivity and listening to life within and without us. The cycle begins anew.

Conclusion

Even though we live the above 'helpful steps' only in the best of our moments here in Sieben Linden, it's like tasting honey and we keep pushing our edges to go there again.

For the author's biography, see page x.

2   Communication Skills:
Conflict, Facilitation & Decision Making

Communicating for Peace

Alongside the formal methods of communication that can be so helpful in building the social fabric of community, there will always flow the streams of informal communication. Where people meet and chatter, look one another in the eye and connect, have a row in the corridor ... all these are part of creating the glue of community. Gossip constitutes one of these streams.

Gossip as a Group Dynamic

Beatrice Briggs

Gossip is an ancient, universal phenomenon. It evolved with language and is part of the currency of the informal information economy. Like beads and pelts, gossip has been a medium of exchange since time immemorial. We trade it for more gossip – and for a sense of belonging. After all, no one can gossip alone. Gossip happens in every human group. Some try to prohibit or control gossip and others make commendable efforts to break the habit, but gossip persists. What is its social function? How can we explain its staying power? How can we capture the energy contained in gossip and transform it into something more constructive?

Gossip, understood as talk about the personal affairs of others, exchanged in informal conversations – usually when the person in question is absent – can take a variety of forms. It can be well intentioned or malicious, accurate or false, trivial or a matter of life or death, public knowledge or a secret shared by a privileged few. It can be fresh news or the repetition of communal folklore. It can bind a group together or blow it apart.

Groups gossip to define themselves. Outsiders and newcomers can read the visitor's guide, the employee handbook, the bylaws or the newsletter, but only insiders know, understand – or care about – the gossip. Our gossip partners are usually our closest friends. Tell me who you gossip with and what you gossip about and I will tell you where you are in the hierarchy of the group.

Gossip is an underground medium of communication, unofficial, unregulated, unsanctioned – and often untrue. The accuracy of the information is secondary to the sense of emotional connection between the gossipers. Gossipers are not trained journalists, collecting facts in order to present a balanced story. They are ordinary humans trying to figure out what is going on in the bewildering situations in which they find themselves.

For those on the social margins, gossip is a survival tool. Cut off from the banquet of information available to the powerful, those of low rank must scavenge whatever crumbs fall their way. Sharing these gleanings with others is an act of solidarity. That women are often stereotyped as chronic gossipers is a byproduct of their historic oppression. Gathering by the well or the river, our foremothers exchanged information about the things that defined their lives: births, deaths, illnesses and the activities of the men. How else would they know what was going on?

Listening to what people are gossiping about is one way to find out what conflicts are brewing in a group. Gossip serves as a social safety valve and may delay or avert the eruption of an open conflict. Venting feelings such as fear, jealousy, anger, confusion or frustration through gossip does not make the underlying problem go away, but a 'gossip fix' can temporarily relieve the pain. It can also be habit-forming.

Groups often waste their energy complaining and gossiping about each other rather than joining forces to effect positive change. If gossip is the only way a group communicates, trust withers and paranoia spreads. You never know what is being said behind your back.

On both a personal and group level, gossiping can be a dangerous game. Despite being an ancient and apparently universal activity, its rules are unwritten. You learn too late when you have gone too far. A confidence is betrayed, the person you are talking about overhears, the information you pass on proves to be false. You can cause hurt, damage another's reputation, and bring shame on yourself. On a more sinister note, infiltrators wishing to destroy a group can use the gossip network to spread false rumours, defame certain members, and otherwise manipulate popular opinion.

The alternative at the individual level is to use talking to others only as a way to clarify your thoughts and feelings before deciding when and how to speak directly to the person you are gossiping about. The challenge for groups is to create viable alternatives to gossiping: opportunities for honest dialogue, heart sharing, conflict resolution and other processes designed to share information, verify its accuracy, express feelings and decide what to do.

But forget about trying to repress gossip altogether. Like any outlaw, it will always thrive on the margins.

For the author's biography, see page 104.

Forum is a process of group communication that has served communities like Zegg in Germany and Tamera in Portugal so well that more and more communities have started to learn about it.

Forum
A Way of Group-Communication

Dolores Richter

The Goals of Forum

Forum is a group facilitation to build self-awareness, honest communication and trust in communities. It is a creative way to hold personal sharings by providing a stage on which community members can make public their true motivations, deep feelings and ideas to their fellow bodies. Through transparent sharing, questions of daily life can become an invaluable focus and catalyst for individual and community growth.

Forum is designed to work with people who are living or working together, sharing a common vision and who are committed to certain values such as self-responsibility, compassion, solidarity and truth.

In order to understand Forum it is important to know that its main aim is to promote a culture of nonviolence. In the process we search for answers to the question: What mental, spiritual and social conditions are needed so that humans can live together in truth, solidarity and freedom. What is the source of violence – and how can we create conditions for a non-violent world?

Forums wants to support the transformation from a culture of violence to one that cooperates with life and life principles: from a culture of domination to one of partnership; a culture of competition to one of cooperation; a culture of exploitation to one of self-awareness and compassion; a culture of possessiveness to one of contact and intimacy.

This transformation process must happen on both an individual and societal level at the same time and it is this process that Forum was created to serve. It does this by encouraging self-awareness and self-development, witnessed and supported by community colleagues.

Through the personal work of the individuals in Forum and the feedback they receive, the community comes to know itself, to discover its values, to reflect on its experiments, and to refine and evolve its vision.

What is Forum?

Forum is about liberation, understanding and communication *now*. It provides a framework for investigating human nature. Forum is not therapy, nor is it a method in itself; rather, it is a ritualized form of communication designed to enhance transparency, spiritual growth and community.

Forum is a special kind of communication process. It is a creative way for a group with a common vision and value system to create a safe space where members can share with the group in such a way that the consciousness of both the individual and the collective is raised. In the Forum, the personal is transmuted to the universal. This is achieved through the loosening of identification with, and attachment to, emotional states through a light and non-judgmental climate of caring and acceptance.

In part, Forum provides a stage for thoughts and feelings that are ever present in daily life but which lie veiled or suppressed out of fear of rejection or judgment. It is a vehicle designed to bring into group consciousness what has been, until now, only present in the individuals' consciousness. In the course of this process of making the hitherto private public, implications and connections that were only latent may surface. In a single Forum session several individuals may work, in a series of Forums everyone will have worked, and thus over time the Forum becomes a powerful basis for raising the level of awareness of a whole community.

Forum is not, however, a collection of random personal sharings. Because it is informed from the beginning by a set of shared values and long-term goals, what emerges is channeled by the commitment to personal change, honesty and aliveness. When used frequently in an ongoing group Forum ultimately becomes like a school of life, a classroom devoted to the exploration of Life and Truth.

In community it can be useful to separate problem solving and decision-making. When a decision is to be made, it can start with a Forum process designed to make ideas, personal intentions or emotional background transparent. When this has happened, the decision making process can go ahead without being sabotaged by personal agendas.

It is our fear of the insecurity and unpredictability of life that makes us want to dominate.

Sometimes you will be surprised what you say when you step fully into the role of the actor in the centre of the Forum and the process begins to flow. What emerges is the complexity of the human condition: its beauty, potential, paradoxes and violence. In Forum you experience the echoes of human history reflected in the experience of individuals and all these discoveries pave the way for change and development.

How can Forum Promote Nonviolence?

It is our fear of the insecurity and unpredictability of life that makes us want to dominate. We fear that which we cannot control or organize – feelings, longings, loneliness, weakness – or others, who are different from us. The life-force both inside of us and in the world cannot be controlled yet we are not comfortable with letting go and opening up to the constant change that is basic to all life.

To transform the culture of domination we must make friends with all that is inside of us: our feelings, our loneliness, our deep wish for intimacy. Violence happens when we feel disconnected from others, nature, ourselves; nonviolence can happen when we allow real contact to take place.

And real contact can be such a challenge! We long for intimate friendship, for community, yet this longing to be connected brings up many fears for most of us. The sense of 'the other' creates fear of comparison and lack – am I good enough? Too loud? Too small? Do I like him/her; do they like me?

We fear real contact with people because it brings us face to face with the unknown in ourselves.

So we create life-styles that keep people at a distance – by staying securely in our jobs, feeling comfortable with the TV or computer, using hierarchical structures of communication, hiding in workaholic or alcoholic behaviour patterns or living in single apartments. We fear real contact with people because it brings us face to face with the unknown in ourselves. We can discuss ecology, finances, politics, make decisions and still we be hiding from one other. Life wants true community – to know others from within, to be visible and seen at the deepest level – yet this sort of contact can be disturbing and will definitely bring change and upheaval. It also brings a great gift: a person in true contact with others cannot hurt, lie, murder or rape.

Forum wants to be part of this learning to step into real contact with myself – my longings, my highest potential and my shadow – with other people, with nature, with life. What comes to the surface when we begin working in Forum is not always nice. The suppressed and the hidden may emerge into the light of awareness. This can be done playfully, or it can be done seriously, and one way or the other, it helps to create deeper contact.

How Forum Works

The individuals making up a Forum sit in a circle. One person goes into the middle as though going onto a stage while the others form the audience. The presenter or actor has the power and the space to speak and act without being interrupted by the others who initially play the role of observing spectators.

The presenter brings with him/her a longing to communicate and learn through revealing in words and actions thoughts, feelings, values, opinions, emotions and judgments about a situation. The other, the facilitator, focalizes and guides the process by intervening from time to time in the presenter's flow. In this way the presenter and the facilitator stage a kind of extemporaneous play together in the centre of the Forum, while the group in the circle around them form the silent audience until the work is complete.

When the presenter has finished, others can step into the middle to give feedback and express what they perceived. Now the presenter can learn what others think about him/her and what they have to say which supplements, broadens and sharpens the personal issue he/she brought forward. The discovery of what others think and value about us, what perhaps keeps them from loving us, what meaning we have for them provides us with essential social feedback.

After the feedback a new presenter stands and ventures forth into the centre.

The Role of the Facilitator

Each session of Forum, usually lasting about 60–90 minutes, is guided by a facilitator plus a co-facilitator, who remain members of the group but take on the temporary role of facilitating the process. The facilitators are the only ones who can intervene in the presenter's process. They must hold a high level of self-awareness and be able to channel the energies, issues and processes of the Forum. It is a role of service and can be fulfilled in different ways: as a soft moderation which guides just by asking questions that lead to the source of the issue; playfully and artistically; in a strict and directive way – but all forms of facilitation are to serve the presenter who stays fully responsible for the content and style of what is presented.

Facilitators are people who feel drawn to the role and have trained their skills. Forum facilitation is not neutral because Forum supports what is authentic, alive and true, that which comes into the light beyond politeness and the daily games of hiding and disguise. The ideal of Forum is to bring out the beauty of the person, revealing their highest potential. If a person is stuck with a problem the facilitator listens to the facts but also helps the person to detach. The facilitator will encourage the presenter to look at it from a higher perspective and learn from it. Example: if one person envies a quality of another the facilitator may ask him/her to express that quality playfully, to act as if she has the quality herself. In this way, the presenter can find out whether there is a hidden quality in her that wants to emerge – and lead her to embrace and strengthen it by acting it out.

The more knowledge one has about one's own habitual patterns of thinking and behaving the faster one can perceive them in others and intervene in a supportive way. The skilful facilitator possesses a broad human knowledge, a high social consciousness and a deep sense of responsibility. While the facilitator does, to some extent, direct and shape the Forum process, he/she remains in the role of a facilitator, asking questions to illuminate the issue, mirroring the actor in a way that allows exploration, reveals connections, and connects with the bigger picture. From there, solutions may happen.

The more knowledge one has about one's own habitual patterns of thinking and behaving the faster one can perceive them in others and intervene in a supportive way.

The Process of Letting Go

Forum does not primarily aim to solve issues. Rather it aims to make the essence of an issue or person visible. When we see the core essence of a person a feeling of love that transcends personal sympathy wells up. Often Forum is also about sorting out the different factors and feelings that impact a situation. The solution of an issue more often than not turns out to be a letting go. When deeper understanding comes, a releasing of attachment

*Forum wants
to lift the level
of energy and
wants to trigger
the expression of
life force.*

takes place. This letting go seldom happens by attacking the issue directly. It is more likely to occur by taking a playful detour, which at first may seem to lead away from the solution.

Forum wants to lift the level of energy and wants to trigger the expression of life force. When the level of energy can be successfully raised, a change of perspective in body and soul take place. Sometimes this energy shift can be very simple – when the facilitator invites the presenter to move faster, or to exaggerate gestures, or to put a sound to a feeling. When the energy shifts, a new perspective may open up.

We have become so used to hiding our feelings that we often lose touch with them altogether. We laugh when we feel like crying, we say no when we mean to say yes, and yes when we mean to say no. In the Forum we allow different aspects of our being to speak. So you might go to one corner and speak for one aspect, then go to another corner and speak for another, perhaps opposite, aspect. Theatrical suggestions can shift the energy sufficiently enough for a thought buried deep inside to be expressed.

You may discover that being angry with someone is just a surface emotion. At another level you may discover that the deeper wish you didn't dare to express is for a closer connection. As soon as one comes into contact with a deeper need and finds a way to express it and have it heard, the anger disappears.

Theatrically acting out inner dialogues or emotional processes is a step toward disidentification: I come to see that I am not this anger; I am not this fear: I am not this jealousy. This way of reacting is actually only one possibility out of many. To lose identification with these passing states means that I have found an inner position of witnessing what is. I have found my unchanging centre. In that place you find yourself no longer attached to the seemingly so important plans, needs and fears that are present in every moment. This insight allows for a more playful stance. From the perspective of being a witness you stop projecting the experiences of the past into the future and your intelligence is freed up to act.

For example, when your partner or your lover makes plans that do not include you, and you react with fears of abandonment you become identified with this fear of loss. As you express your fear sadness, that very expression brings you back to your own joy and humour of existence. You disidentify from the fear and are able to see that the behaviour of your lover or partner is simply his or her true path at this moment. You can be the detached witness of it.

This kind of work leads us to our core, our inner truth, to expression freed from hiding and pretence. Forum is above all about truth – not truth as a moral category, but the truth that shows itself when we listen deep inside and allow ourselves to trust others, the truth that emerges when it no longer makes sense to maintain walls and wear masks.

Doubtless the path to social consciousness, compassion and contact requires an inner metamorphosis and Forum, because it is simultaneously personal and social, has the power to bring this about in us.

Forum in Practice

The Forum evolved as a way to create essential transparency by embracing and cultivating the authenticity and diversity of its members. At the Zegg community there are large Forums held periodically which the entire community attends; there are smaller Forums held by subgroups such as work departments, special interest groups, the youth; and there are also special training Forums for visitors and guests from other centres and communities. Forum combines well with added tools like Co-Counseling, Non-Violent-Communication or Constellation Work.

For the author's biography, see page 79.

Gill Emslie introduces a Process Work approach to transforming conflict though embracing the skills of deep democracy. She illustrates its application through examples of her work in a grassroots project in Bolivia.

From Conflict to Community
A Deep Democracy & Process Work Approach

Gill Emslie

Process Work is a process orientated, cross-disciplinary approach to individual and collective change. What particularly stands out for me about working in projects in Bolivia and in other very different settings in Europe, is that the skills outlined below can be applied in any context, and while the language and metaphor used may need to be adapted to a specific situation, the underlying whole systems approach and compassionate attitude needed towards human experience is the same, whether it be within grassroots organizations in the global south, the global ecovillage network or in corporate Europe.

Through these experiences it has been humbling to realize how similar we all are. The myriad of common threads that can be found in all of these settings has deepened my understanding of the systemic and interconnected nature of the world we live in, giving me hope that increasing our skills and awareness in this area can make a difference and lead to major and lasting change.

Process Work

Process Work has been pioneered and developed over the last 25 years by Drs Arnold and Amy Mindell and their colleagues. Process Work started as therapeutic work and then developed into group work, and organizational and leadership development work. Arnold Mindell, initially a physicist, subsequently studied psychology at the Jungian Institute in Zurich. Process Work theory and practice draws on Jungian psychology, physics, Quantum theory, shamanic traditions and Taoism.

Process Work seeks to increase awareness and in so doing supports the individual, group or organization concerned to access a broader base of insight from which to make choices. Obstacles, disturbances and even conflicts are seen as an attempt to bring new information to a person, group or organization and even to help them to realize their full potential. Process Work assumes that each soul, individual or collective, has a drive towards wholeness, which creates an underlying motivation to seek meaning in life.

Deep Democracy

For organizations, communities and nations to succeed today and survive tomorrow, they must be deeply democratic – that is, everyone and every feeling must be represented. Deep democracy is awareness of the diversity of people, roles, and feelings about issues. When we are asked to become aware of and value our deepest inner experiences, almost any group or world situation becomes immediately different and manageable (Mindell, 2002).

Deep Democracy is one of the pillars of Process Work. It links one's attitudes and belief systems with one's external experience, offering an approach that supports a deeper understanding of the interconnected relationship between our 'inner' and 'outer' realities. Cultivating this approach on an organizational or group level leads to a more deeply felt sense of resolution and congruence in all aspects of organizational or group life, leading to a shift in atmosphere in the workplace which allows more individual and collective creative expression. This leads to enhanced performance and focus.

Three Levels of Awareness

In Process Work there are three levels that the facilitator will be aware of in the process of facilitating conflict. These levels can appear simultaneously or at different times and skill and fluidity is required by the facilitator to stay very present with the signals that are present in any conflict which will indicate at what level the conflict needs to be facilitated.

1. Consensus Reality

Here we deal with 'real' events, problems, and issues connected with the development of individuals, couples or groups. Facts and feelings are used to describe conflicts, issues or problems. The dynamics of rank, power and privilege are apparent here.

2. The Dreaming Level

Here what emerges are dreams, deep feelings, the unspoken truths, 'double' or unintentional signals and ghost roles (unrepresented figures) as well as the zeitgeists (spirits of our times) that often unconsciously influence the 'field' of our groups or communities.

3. The Nondualistic or 'Essence Level'

At the deepest nondualistic or 'essence' level, Process Work deals with the sensing of tendencies which move us, but which are not easily expressed yet in words. This area of human life is sometimes like a subtle atmosphere around people and events.

Deep Democracy recognizes the simultaneous importance of the three levels of experience. Everyday reality and its problems are as important as those figures reflected in the dream level, and are as important as a spiritual experience at the essence level of reality where rank no longer exists.

Rank Power and Privilege

Owning and acknowledging one's rank helps to create a more congruent and authentic atmosphere.

Mindell defines rank as 'the sum of a person's privileges. A conscious or unconscious social or personal ability or power arising from culture, community support, personal psychology and/or spiritual power. Whether you earned or inherited your rank, it organizes much of your communication behavior, especially at edges and hot spots.' (Mindell, 1995)

When facilitating individuals or groups it is helpful to support the areas of strength in each person and how they can use this for the benefit of the whole. Many of us have difficulty doing this, but the effects of rank are felt anyway. Owning and acknowledging one's rank helps to create a more congruent and authentic atmosphere. When rank is not acknowledged, it will communicate itself through unintentional or double signals, where the body language, content and tone of what is being said do not match. We often tend to react to these signals and because the other person or group, does not identify with them, conflict often ensues.

There are four aspects of rank:

- **Social rank**: derives from the privilege and power that comes from money, class, gender, race, education, age, health, and physical appearance and other values held in high esteem by the mainstream.
- **Psychological rank**: comes from feeling secure and cared for, or from surviving suffering and becoming stronger and more compassionate.
- **Spiritual rank**: comes from a connection with something sacred that keeps one centred during difficult times.
- **Contextual rank**: comes from the power and privilege that is derived from a position or role in a particular context.

Working with Rank Awareness in Bolivia

Ana Rhodes (a friend and colleague from Findhorn) and I were invited to work with a group of largely indigenous farmers in Caranavi, a small frontier town on the edge of the rainforest in the Las Yungas in Bolivia. The farmers were representatives of an agricultural producers network aiming to produce organic fairtrade products. We had been told that the group suffered from apathy and a lack of engagement and that our brief was to teach conflict facilitation skills and motivation.

The Cultural Context

Bolivia is an extremely beautiful country. Nestling amidst the Andes in South America, its capital city, La Paz, sits at 3,800 metres above Sea level.

Stretching from the majestic icebound peaks of the Cordillera Real and bleak high altitude deserts of the Andes to the lush rainforests and vast savannahs of the Amazon basin, Bolivia is a rich resource of biodiversity. The beauty and variety of this landscape are matched by the ethnic and cultural diversity of the country's population, the majority of whom are of indigenous decent. The languages of Imara and Quechua, amongst others, are still spoken as the first language of many. One of the 'poorest' countries in the world, the country's underdevelopment has been, perhaps, a blessing in disguise for the environment, allowing vast wilderness areas to survive in near-pristine condition.

Unfortunately, although the country is incredibly rich in natural resources, growing pressure from the North and globalized 'free trade' agreements' mean that national markets find it increasingly difficult to protect local interests. In the last 30–40 years over 40 per cent of the country's population of five million has followed global trends, moving to the rapidly increasing urban slum areas of La Paz.

Spinning wool

The Training

On the second day of the training we worked with the concept that conflict is not just something that happens outside of ourselves. We are part of the system within which the conflict is happening and consequently affect and are affected by the conflict. We then introduced the dynamics of rank, power and privilege and encouraged the group to find areas of rank that they could celebrate.

At the end of this exercise one of the participants, Victor, stood up suddenly and began addressing the room in his native language of Imara. His presence and posture had changed dramatically. From being relatively quiet and somewhat deferential in nature, his posture, tone of voice and presence changed completely, unexpectedly commanding the attention of all present. It seemed as if it was no longer just Victor speaking, but something greater that was pouring through him. There was a tangible sense that he

Cochabamba women

was speaking, not only on behalf of himself, his family and community but also for all proud indigenous people of Incan descent, and perhaps for the spirit of all peoples who have been marginalized over the centuries, finding his and their voice. The power of their presence was palpable.

When Victor stood up we were very touched, and especially when he went on to share how he had lost confidence in himself after years of being humiliated for being indigenous. We saw how the 'symptom' of apathy that we had been asked to address in the training, was directly related to a lack of confidence because of the voices of humiliation and criticism that he and his people had internalized over the centuries.

As Victor picked up his rank, finding the inspiration and courage to speak out, the atmosphere in the room changed completely. A sense of passion and commitment to taking a stance filled the room. This was exactly the energy that the group needed to confront the conflict that they were facing in their local area in which a very large company was pressuring the local communities to sell their land, loose their autonomy and become employees. The community leaders' response up to that point had been mostly to shout at the company representatives and walk out of negotiations, leaving the more vulnerable members of the community to be won over by false promises. As Victor accessed the sense of inherent wisdom, dignity and entitlement within himself and in the group, their right, and ability to stand for autonomy and sustainable livelihood became stronger.

This example shows how important the understanding of the dynamics of rank and power are for any group or organization. When rank is used without awareness it can lead to abuse, which can happen both when the hierarchical structure of a group or organization is clear, and in groups that identify with equality where often there are hidden power structures that lead to conflict.

Working with Open Forums

An Open Forum is the application of Process Work principles to large scale interactions. It is a method of working with groups that facilitates conflict or difficulty as it arises in the atmosphere, or 'field'.

This approach involves

- Identifying the issues or themes that are currently 'up' in the group.
- Reaching agreement or consensus on which theme to work with.
- Identifying the roles, voices or differing points of view that are represented, or that may not be represented but are none the less felt by all concerned.
- Facilitating an interactive discussion or unfolding of the theme, including the less tangible or obvious aspects of the dynamic.
- Noticing temporary resolutions or shifts in atmosphere, as well as points of tension and group 'edges'.

An atmosphere, or 'field', includes not only the individuals concerned but also the entire organization or culture of which the group is a part. It consists of the more familiar or overt aspects of group life like agenda items, identified roles and rational discussion as well as the less obvious and more difficult aspects of any group. Such as the minority views, shadows or 'elephants in the room', cultural influences that reflect the belief systems and 'spirits' of the time, as well as 'ghosts' which are the points of view or opinions that are not identified with or easily expressed in the group and yet strongly influence the field. Often when these 'ghosts' are voiced and interacted with there is a sense of relief and resolution.

Addressing the content and structure of concerns is important in groups. However, if the underlying issues or feelings in the background are not addressed it is unlikely that a deeply felt resolution will be reached.

Applying Open Forum in the training

On the third day we began to teach an open forum approach to working with large group conflict. The theme that the group chose to explore was the conflict between their cooperatives and the large company on their doorstep that was pressurizing them to sell all the raw coffee beans. There was a sense of urgency in the group because they had to make this decision within two months. The alternative was to take the risk of strengthening and organizing their own cooperatives, advocating for the right to trade freely and activate the local government support that they would need to do this.

Although there was a clear wish to do the latter, there was also a sense of apathy or hopelessness in the atmosphere that we had begun to address the previous day with Victor. In the group of 26 participants there were two people who already worked for the company and were able to represent their point of view. This was very helpful in terms of having all the sides of the conflict represented.

We facilitated the open forum by inviting people to take positions or 'roles' that represented the various points of view. After airing many points of view and feelings, those in the group began to express some of the despair, and anger that they felt, and as we worked with these roles, encouraging people to inhabit different sides of the dialogue and to experience 'the other side' the atmosphere began to change. The sense of absolute entitlement and clarity that they experienced as so oppressive from the big company representatives became an ally, as they were able to access that state within themselves.

... he was so impressed by the next steps that had emerged from the open forum that he offered his support to take the dialogue to the next level ...

A renewed sense of resolve, solidarity and commitment to strengthen the cooperatives and to look for solutions that would enable them to become more effective in all areas of coffee production began to emerge. Rather than just focusing on fighting the company, they could then use that energy to build alliances, improve the internal practices of their own organizations, and find ways to be more inclusive of other producers.

We ended the training with a decision making process that supported the group to come up with clear next steps which they could take, in order to really ground their intention and to strengthen themselves as cooperatives.

The president of the coffee cooperatives arrived unexpectedly to hear the outcomes of the workshop and he was so impressed by the next steps that had emerged from the open forum that he offered his support to take the dialogue to the next level needed with the local government.

The Role of the Facilitator

This chapter provides an outline of some ideas drawn from Process Work that we have applied in our work in the last few years. Because Process Work is not a prescriptive approach, but one based on unfolding the signals as they appear in the moment, it is a creative, alive and intuitive process. This requires the full engagement of the facilitator and willingness to work on increasing her own levels of awareness, particularly in the area of belief systems and bias, so as to be facilitating from as clear a space as possible. As she forms part of the field, the facilitator's inner attitudes will be communicated either directly, when they are held with awareness, or through double signals if they are not consciously identified with. This is why the ability to reflect internally, or to do 'inner work', is an important part of the facilitator's skill set. Being fully congruent is what instills confidence and generates trust. It is what will help to build the quality of relationship between the facilitator and the group that is necessary for working at the deep levels required for organizational transformation.

In Bolivia we also ran trainings in Leadership and confidence building for women and organizational development and we will be returning to run training for trainers programmes over the next few years so that the local people themselves may incorporate these tools, along with others into their own training programmes.

I would like to thank my colleagues and teachers who over the years have provided, and continue to provide, huge amounts of inspiration and support and without whom I would not able to do this work.

Gill Emslie, Dip. PW has many years of experience working as an international facilitator, trainer, and psychotherapist. She was a member of the management committee of the Findhorn Foundation for five years from 1995–2000, where she was responsible for human resources, internal training, supervision and conflict facilitation within the organization. During this time she also introduced supervision skills and internal organizational support structures which continue to serve the organization to function more effectively. She is a founding member of the Findhorn Consultancy Service, which was founded in 1999.

Her training and experience in transpersonal psychology, and organizational develop-ment provide the framework for her to work as a coach and trainer in the areas of organizational development, leadership, personal and professional development, staff training, Process Work, supervision, conflict facilitation, specific skills for women in leadership, confidence building and a holistic approach to intentional design, monitoring and evaluation (Outcome Mapping).

Gill currently works within the corporate and voluntary sectors both in Europe and Latin America and is an affiliate of the International Institute of Facilitation and Consensus (IIFAC), and the Research Society for Process Orientated Psychology UK (RSPOPUK).

gemslie@findhorn.org · www.findhornconsultancy.org · +44 (0)1309 691880 or +44 (0)7812 704 035

Azriel Cohen shares his experience of working to build bridges between people from different religions and Israelis and Palestinians – in the Dalai Lama's village in India, in a Buddhist community in France, and in Jerusalem. His article challenges us to think about how our inner realities and our relationship to our bodies impacts our work for peace.

Towards a Holistic Model of Conflict Resolution

From Israelis & Palestinians to our Relationship with Animals

Azriel Cohen

Only in my mid-20s did I realize that deep goodness was to be found among people from backgrounds different than the world I grew up in. This is everyone's story: believing the unfamiliar 'other' is not good, and one of the dynamics underlying war. This realization spurred me onto a 15-year journey of transformative encounters with 'others' which has led to deep meetings with peoples and cultures I had negative ideas about. Most recently it includes exploring my relationship with animals and plants. My own transformation led to specializing in designing non-threatening environments that facilitate transformative encounters between peoples from differing backgrounds.

I will share some of what I learned along the way that may useful for people interested in conflict resolution and work with diversity.

Peacemaker, Heal Thyself

I grew up in a kind, gentle and pious close-knit Orthodox Jewish community in Toronto. There was so much meaning and depth within our world that I never gave much thought to how I viewed people outside my community. The turning point was one summer during a lunch break at the Ontario College of Art. I always sat alone after lunch to recite my after-meal prayers because I wanted no one to know what I was doing. One day a student who I really did not like because of his strange appearance – long hair and unfamiliar clothes – did not leave when the meal was done. Hesitantly I told him I was going to pray silently for a few minutes. He asked me about my spiritual practice in a way that took me by surprise. He was curious, sincere and respectful and knew so much about my tradition. I was shaken. What a wonderful person. How many other people do I perceive with wrong ideas? My journey began.

Since then I have studied various models of conflict resolution and community building and engaged in encounters and deep friendships with individuals and communities from groups I believed I was not allowed to get close to. This includes non-Orthodox Jews, Christians, Muslims, Hindus, Buddhists, Germans and Arabs.

To work for peace you do not need to fly to a country where there is war. It begins with your self. Here is an exercise everyone can do to contribute to peace and healing of conflict: make an inventory of who in your life you judge negatively and consider 'other'. Think about all the people who you encounter, including family, friends, neighbours and co-workers.

Most people don't experience a positive change towards the 'other' by having a gun put to their head. Often a moment of 'aha' – that the 'other' is experienced differently than ever before – occurs when there is safety and the opportunity to interact with the 'other' around something that has nothing to do with the topic of conflict. So be creative and gentle as you work towards healing your relationship with others. Put on some inspiring music, light a candle, allow yourself to daydream about how you might engage with these 'others', record your thoughts with a pen and let your intuition guide you.

Bridging between Religions in the Dalai Lama's Village

In 1997, minutes from the Dalai Lama's village in India I created the Ohr Olam Project, an experiment in creating community between people normally seen as not getting along. Dharamshala, at the foothills of the Himalayas, attracts thousands of spiritual seekers from all over the world. Though far away from any existing Jewish community, there is always a critical mass of hundreds of Jews from greatly varied backgrounds from around the world, especially post-military Israelis. The local community is Tibetan Buddhist, Hindu and Muslim. Distanced from the politics of the Jewish world we dreamt of a community that nurtured transformative encounters between different kinds of Jews and between Jews and people from other faiths.

The Dalai Lama's deep respect for all the world's religions, something that tends to elude the big three monotheistic religions, was one of the main reasons for choosing Dharamshala. We met the Dalai Lama privately and he wholeheartedly endorsed creating the project, "However", he said, "I am older than you and I know that such work of healing conflict will not be finished in your lifetime. It will take generations. Yet, if your work affects one person it will have been worth it. If it impacts ten people that will be wonderful, and if it impacts one hundred even more so." We spoke to the Dalai Lama about building bridges between groups in conflict and he shared with us a multi-level program he and Bishop Tutu had outlined. The outline included:

- Programmes that enable leaders to meet each other simply as people, not just in the role of leader.

- Intellectual forums.
- Meetings between laypeople.
- Service projects where the two parties in conflict serve a third party in need.

The Ohr Olam Model

The program created an environment that attracted people from all walks of life, spanning the range of Jewish beliefs and practices as well as people from many other religions. The Ohr Olam model included:

- Appropriate staff – friends walking a path of personal transformation who get along with people from very diverse backgrounds.
- Multi-layered program – that meets the needs of as many different kinds of people as possible. The program included ritual – a huge Passover Seder, prayer services, classes and workshops on Jewish mysticism, social and musical programs, and interfaith dialogues.
- Dropping expectations of changing anyone, and a clear intention to make everyone feel welcome – no matter what their background.

The program ran for almost five years and over 2,500 people participated. It was highly successful, deeply impacted many people's lives and attracted significant interest in the media.

Encountering Counterforces to Peace

I thought about the historical pattern of peacemakers getting assassinated and wondered if I was really ready for this work.

I was not adequately prepared for the inevitable – steps forward in peace-making provoke counterattacks by forces committed to perpetuating war and conflict. A messianic fundamentalist Jewish group, split off from the Hasidic Lubavitch movement, who found the idea of Jews sincerely respecting people of other faiths to be evil, came to save the Jews. They aggressively spread misinformation about our project and tore down our posters. Lubavitch headquarters wrote to me, asking me to turn to the local Indian police. I decided to take a step back from the project, thought about the historical pattern of peacemakers getting assassinated and wondered if I was really ready for this work.

Bringing Israelis & Palestinians to Plum Village

In the spring of 2001, I co-initiated a project called Peace Begins With Myself, a program that brought delegations of Israelis and Palestinians to Thich Naht Hanh's Plum Village in France. In the spirit of the Buddhist tradition, Thich Naht Hanh teaches that making peace always comes back to transformation of the individual, and it relates to all aspects of life. Making peace between groups in conflict is part of a greater holistic process that relates to every element of our lives, including even how we breathe, eat and walk. In a humble way it happens one person, and one step at a time.

Such a transformation will take much longer than we may be comfortable with. My first lessons in Plum Village were about patience. There was conflict within the group and some participants were not following Thich Naht Hanh's guidance. I asked for a private conversation with Sister Gina, the facilitator of our group. I shared with her my distress. She told me that at the beginning of her time in Plum Village, Thay ('teacher', as he is commonly known to his followers) would share a vision and she would feel responsible to make it happen, but it did not manifest as quickly as she expected and she would get frustrated. "Thay shares visions with us, and we rush to realize them, yet he seems to have all the patience in the world," she said. "He speaks to us about processes. What I did not understand then, which I do now, is that he sometimes sees processes that can take three hundred years."

My first lessons in Plum Village were about patience.

Buddhist Wisdom: Mindfulness

In Plum Village I learned about the power of reducing how much we do while increasing our 'mindfulness'. Doing less, but doing it with more presence actually improves our effectiveness, contrary to the perception of most Westerners. For example, as a painter, I am learning that it is better to reduce the number of hours I spend creating, and when I do paint, to do so with a sense of inner centeredness. There is a quality of self-restraint in this path because it means that sometimes holding back from the impulse to create. To be mindful is to approach life with a broadened sense of being, attending with care to how we sleep, eat and speak, how we use our time and even how we walk. The practice of mindfulness shifts us towards quality rather than quantity. Its essence is to simplify and slow down. Mindful eating refers to only eating when we eat, focusing of our awareness on 'I am eating' and being mindful, both in thought and physical sensation of the process of eating. Being mindful in all aspects of living affects how I paint, and in Plum Village I learned how it affects how we make peace.

A most potent practice in making peace is mindful listening. My first glimpse of the power of this practice was after mindfully listening to a member of the Israeli delegation in Plum Village for twenty minutes. I not only remembered every word that was spoken – I also had an uncanny experience of the images and sensations behind the words. Mindful listening is an experience of moment-to-moment listening. It is quite simple and you can try it with a friend. Ask you friend to share something with you. While they speak sit as relaxed and alert as you can, perhaps in a meditation pose. Sit with an awareness of your body and focus your attention on how your breath moves in and out. Let your only thoughts be 'I am sitting here present for you.' Do not respond to the other person. Simply stay with your breath and this thought 'I am sitting here present for you.' Let the person's words move through you without attempting to process or remember what they are saying. Notice how different this feels from how you normally listen. Then switch roles and notice how it feels to be listened to this way.

Through mindful listening both Israelis and Palestinians discovered that for the first time they not only heard but also felt one another. Some Israeli veteran peacemakers, with close to fifteen years experience said they did not hear anything new but somehow they were able to feel the Palestinian experience with an unfamiliar depth.

Stability

We sat together and were asked to 'water each other's flowers' – to share what we saw that is beautiful in one another. This practice creates a stable foundation of goodness in the relationship between people …

Another central theme of the program at Plum Village was stability. During the first few days we did not discuss the conflict but rather were engaged in a process of learning how to sit, walk, eat, speak and listen mindfully, attuning to nature and being immersed in the international community. The aim was to be stable enough to engage with the energy of conflict. We engaged in a practice which Thich Naht Hanh calls Watering the Flowers which is based on an ancient Buddhist monastic practice, as a way to maintain community and work through conflict. We sat together and were asked to 'water each other's flowers' – to share what we saw that is beautiful in one another. This practice creates a stable foundation of goodness in the relationship between people, a foundation that is necessary to contain that which is painful and difficult. Thich Naht Hanh said often groups fail because they get into painful issues before establishing stability.

The listening sessions at Plum Village were contained both by time – generally not more than two hours a day – and by people. We saw how knowledge of group dynamics and conflict resolution theory needs is not enough. The facilitators of our group were the top monks and nuns in Plum Village, people who had many years of practise transforming their own suffering and conflict.

Energetic fields of healing spaces and war zones

It was during the second delegation in November 2001 that I began to think about the cultural relevance of a Buddhist environment to the Middle East conflict. Plum Village was filled with rules about such things as silence, interaction between the sexes and alcohol. The Palestinians from Nablus had been trapped in their city for over a year, unable to leave because of military closure. When they arrived in France they were frustrated by the structure and especially with rules about when to speak and where to smoke. More than anything they wanted to walk around, smoke, talk, experience the open fields of southern France and visit Paris. This was more important to the program, and the Buddhist rituals and Vietnamese culture were unfamiliar. There was a curious moment when a Jewish participant – a religious Jewish settler who had served as a military officer in Gaza – and the Palestinians stood aside laughing at the strange bell the Buddhists were using to get everyone to be quiet. They violated the quiet and enjoyed it together. I laughed to myself and thought 'Israeli and Palestinians have joined as friends now that they shared a common enemy – the oppressive Vietnamese monks'.

The second delegation returned from Plum Village and the Intifada intensified. There were actual or foiled terrorist bombings almost every day, and though many people around the world were touched by what we were doing, it was unclear how our efforts could counteract the forces of war. At best I felt we were gaining tools to simply help us from drowning. The group lived with a split personality. In Plum Village, everyone was embraced as integral to the group and the energy was generally contained, held by the Plum Village environment. Back in Israel, clashes between members of the group were not dealt with using the techniques from Plum Village and some people were pushed out of the sangha (community) because of personal agendas. Everyone was trying so hard, but something was not working. It seemed that there was some kind of invisible field that we were fighting against.

Learning from Animals

I began to sense something was happening to me just by living in this field of violence and fear. I had a physical sensation like some kind of poison was leaking into my system.

I decided to take time away from Israel and went into retreat at the ecovillage Findhorn in Scotland, sensing there was something to learn about peace by retreating from not just a war zone but from cities. I wanted to tune into the wisdom of the body and the healing frequency of nature and Findhorn was an ideal starting point. Healers guided me to learn about the physical sensations of being safe and how those sensations can be nourished regardless of our surroundings. During long walks in nature I explored aligning my movement, relaxing my breath and listening to silence until I was in an unfamiliar but incredibly peaceful frequency. A week after Findhorn, I was walking in the countryside tuning into this frequency and saw a young deer about 150 metres away from me. Very conscious of my movements, breath, thoughts and even how I used my eyes I witnessed the deer get closer to me until it came right up to me to smell me then licked my clothes. I began to walk and the deer followed by my side for about thirty minutes. Animals seemed to hold a key to healing and I began to wonder if wild animals run away from people because humans generally exude a frequency of violence.

I began to walk and the deer followed by my side for about thirty minutes.

Trauma, Violence and the Nervous System

A few months later in the US, I was introduced to Somatic Experiencing (S.E.), and suddenly a lot of puzzling things made sense. S.E. is a system of trauma healing rooted in the observation that wild animals, though constantly in danger, almost never exhibit symptoms of trauma. I learned how trauma is stored in the body, that contemporary neurological research has found that the brain is affected by unresolved trauma, and that resolution of trauma in the nervous system can break cycles of violence. S.E. refers to 'trauma vortexes' and 'healing vortexes'. Each vortex has a magnetic pull on people and affects or infects them. A place like Findhorn is a healing vortex and a terrorism filled area is a trauma vortex. Simply being in these spaces can heal or traumatize the nervous system.

The collective dynamics of both Israeli and Palestinian societies can be mapped onto models used to understand the impact of trauma in the individual. Societies that have been traumatized can get stuck in flight, fight or freeze responses. If there is a physiology to the cycles of war and violence then dialogues and encounter groups are not enough – healing of the body must also be addressed.

Reprogramming with Creativity

Creativity is a wonderful vehicle for both personal transformation of conflict and sharing that transformation to inspire others. Living again in Jerusalem, my response to the second Intifada was to create 'The Travelling Jerusalem Café', a multi-media art installation about café culture in East and West Jerusalem. Terrorists targeted Cafés in Israeli West-Jerusalem and most Jews considered Palestinian East Jerusalem very dangerous. The exhibit depicts what is beautiful and even mundane in places associated with fear with the intention of reclaiming the ability to experience safety where there is a sense of danger. When the exhibit travels overseas, it includes storytelling about my experiences in the coffee shops. In Israel, the exhibition includes sample tastes from various cafes and invites Jews and Arabs to interact in the same space around a shared pleasure-café culture. One participant referred to the exhibit as 'living peace' because when there is no conflict, people just do regular things together.

Shalom and Salaam

Healing conflict between humans is a holistic matter, relating to the collective, individual, the mind, body, soul and our relationship to the other-than-human world around us. Various theories of conflict resolution and healing can be seen as expressing different facets on a large crystal. As we are able to go beyond our tendency to compare which approach is better and surrender to the possibility that multiple realities coexist, we may be able to perceive a whole shape that we never knew before. 'Shalom' in Hebrew means peace and is related to the word that means whole. 'Salaam' meaning peace in Arabic is related to the word for surrender. Peace is a process of surrender and revealing harmony between all parts.

Those of all wanting to work on healing conflict between people are invited to take a holistic approach. Numerous theories exist about how to heal conflict and war and countless individuals and organizations are working towards this goal. Some relate to healing conflict between groups, some to healing within the individual and others to healing between humans, other life forms and Earth. Healing conflict between people is a holistic matter and should include input from various models of conflict resolution, mind-body healing within the individual and healing between humans and other life forms.

You can try a simple experiment with animals: note where there is tension in your body, allow your muscles to relax and straighten your posture. Feel all of your body and notice your breath, allowing it to become calm and deep. Walk as gently as you can while thinking only positive thoughts towards the animal such as 'I am safe'. Approach an animal. See if they allow you to get closer than usual and try to sense how you experience each other. Currently I am using photography to deepen my exploration of my relationship with other-than-human life forms in a process I call Interspecies Conflict Resolution.

I also continue to explore my relationship with individuals who at first I experience discomfort around, and those who annoy me.

Azriel Cohen, MFA, is a painter, photographer, inter-cultural facilitator and public speaker. His passions include improvisational dance, music and ecology. Having grown up in an insular Orthodox Jewish community with very specific notions about the outside world, he conducts research on what happens when we meet unfamiliar and even threatening 'other' cultures. His deeply personal explorations pay attention to cognitive, emotional and even bodily reactions. His findings translate into multimedia art installations and creative social projects that bridge between cultures, and he specializes in interfaith and Israeli-Palestinian relations. He has experienced over 30 countries and founded programs in Dharamshala, India – home-in-exile of the Dalai Lama, Thich Naht's Hanh's Plum Village in France, the U.S. and Israel. He also works also as a creative consultant to develop cultural and environmental projects. He lives in Israel.

azrielcohen@gmail.com • www.azrielcohen.com • +972 54 203 4270

Marshal Rosenberg outlines the core principles of Non-violent Communication – a practice that enables openhearted connection between people and groups. NVC moves us beyond judgement and a win-lose paradigm, to one where our deeper feelings and needs are articulated and strategies are developed that enable us to reconnect with the natural joy of giving to another.

Bringing Peace to the World
Excerpts from 'Speak Peace'

Marshall B Rosenberg
compiled by Kosha Anja Joubert

> We need a more peaceful world, growing out of more peaceful families and neighbourhoods and communities. To secure and cultivate such peace, we must love others, even our enemies as well as our friends.
>
> HOWARD W HUNTER

In this article we will look at creating peace by connecting to life at three levels:

- First, within ourselves, how we can connect to the life within ourselves so we can learn from our limitations without blaming and punishing ourselves. If we can't do that, I'm not too optimistic how we're going to relate peacefully out in the world.
- Second, how to create life-enriching connections with other people that allows compassionate giving to take place naturally.
- Third, how to transform the structures we've created – corporate, judicial, governmental, and others – that don't support peaceful, life-enriching connections between us.

Speaking peace is communicating without violence. Speaking peace is a way of connecting with others that allows our natural compassion to flourish. I've found no more effective means of reaching a peaceful resolution of conflict.

I started looking at new forms of communication because of a couple of questions that had been in my mind since childhood. What is it that gets into people that makes them want to harm people? How come there are people who seem to enjoy contributing to the wellbeing of other people and at the same time other human beings who want to do violence to one another?

The primary purpose of Nonviolent Communication is to connect with other people in a way that enables giving to take place: compassionate giving. It's compassionate in that our giving comes willingly from the heart. We are giving service to others and ourselves – not out of duty or obligation, not out of fear of punishment or hope for a reward, not out of guilt or shame, but for what I consider part of our nature. It's in our nature to enjoy giving to one another.

If that is so, then how come the violence? I believe that the violence comes because of how we were educated, not because of our nature. I believe that it started long ago with myths about human nature that framed humans as basically evil and selfish – and that the good life is heroic forces crushing evil forces. We've been living under this destructive mythology for a long time, and it comes complete with a language that dehumanizes people and turns them into objects.

We have learned to think in terms of moralistic judgments of one another. We have words in our consciousness like right, wrong, good, bad, selfish, unselfish, terrorists, freedom fighters. And connected to these judgments is a concept of justice based on what we 'deserve.' If you do bad things, you deserve to be punished. If you do good things, you deserve to be rewarded. Unfortunately, we have been subjected to this consciousness, this faulty education, for a long, long time. I think that's the core of violence on our planet.

Peace Within Ourselves

For most of us the process of bringing about peaceful change begins with working on our own mindsets, on the way we view ourselves and others, on the way we get our needs met. This basic work is in many ways the most challenging aspect of speaking peace because it requires great honesty and openness, developing a certain literacy of expression, and overcoming deeply ingrained learning that emphasizes judgment, fear, obligation, duty, punishment and reward, and shame. It may not be easy, but the results are worth the effort.

Nonviolent Communication keeps our attention focused on two critical questions:

- What's alive in us?
- What can we do to make life more wonderful?

What's alive in us?

To tell people what's alive in us we need to be able to tell them what they're doing that is supporting life in us, as well as what they're doing that isn't supporting life in us. But it's very important to learn how to say that to people without mixing in any evaluation. This involves *observation literacy*. Any words we use that imply the wrongness of others are tragic, suicidal expressions of what's alive in us. They're tragic and suicidal because they don't lead to people enjoying contributing to our well-being. They provoke defensiveness and counter-aggression. Labeling people leads to self-fulfilling prophecies. It's ineffective.

It's important to have a vocabulary of feelings that really does just describe what's alive in us and that in no way involves interpretations of other people.

We want to go inside of ourselves and tell people what's alive in us when they do what they do. This involves *feeling literacy* and *need literacy*. To say clearly what's alive in us at any given moment we have to be clear about what we feel and what we need. We have feelings every moment. The problem is we haven't been educated to be conscious of what's alive in us. There are different ways we might express our feelings, depending on what culture we grow up in, but it's important to have a vocabulary of feelings that really does just describe what's alive in us and that in no way involves interpretations of other people. Sadly, very few people have much of a feelings vocabulary.

Feelings can be used in a destructive way if we try to imply that other people's behaviour is the cause of our feelings. The cause of our feelings is not other people's behaviour, it's our needs. Their behaviour is a *stimulus* for your feelings, not the *cause* of your feelings. I'm sure most of us knew this at one time. It's not what other people do that can hurt you; it's how you take it.

It's very important that when we do express our feelings we follow that expression with a statement that makes it clear that the cause of our feelings is our needs. When we can connect at the need level, it's amazing how conflicts that seem unsolvable start to become solvable.

What can we do to make life more wonderful?

Now, let's turn to the other basic question: What can be done to make life more wonderful? To respond to this second basic question, you're going to make a specific, clear request. Your language is positive in the sense that it requests what you *do want* the other person to do, rather than what you *don't want* or what you *want them to stop doing*.

Now, once we have made this clear request, we need to make sure it's not heard as a demand. Earlier we talked about criticism – how anything that implies wrongness is a kind of communication that's not going to get our needs met. Another form of communication that's very destructive in human relationships is a *demand*. What determines the difference between a request and a demand is how we treat people when they don't respond to our request. In order for them to trust that it's a request, they need to know that they can disagree and be understood. Be able to empathize with dissent in a way that makes it safe for people to disagree. When you have that, you will come to agreements everybody will respect.

When our objective is to get somebody to stop something, punishment looks like an effective strategy. But if we ask ourselves two questions, we would never use punishment again:

- What do we want the other person to do?

- What do we want the other person's reasons to be for doing what we want them to do?

As I've mentioned, the purpose of Nonviolent Communication is to create connections so people give to one another out of compassion – not out of fear of punishment, not out of hope for rewards, but because of the natural joy we feel of contributing to one another's well-being.

Now, some people don't believe you can have order in your home, business, organization, or government unless you make demands and force people to do things. Yet, when we do things that don't come out of this divine energy that makes compassionate giving natural, when we come out of this culturally learned pattern of doing things because we *should/have to/must* get rewards or out of guilt, shame, duty, or obligation … well, then everybody pays for it. Everybody.

One distinction we need to be clear about is the concept of 'power over' versus 'power with'. Power over others gets things done by making people submit. Research shows that companies, families, or schools that use power-over tactics pay for it indirectly through morale problems, violence, and subtle actions against the system.

Power *with* is getting people to do things willingly, because they see how it's going to enrich everybody's well-being by doing it. That's Nonviolent Communication. One of the most powerful ways we've found of creating power *with* people is the degree to which we show them we're just as interested in their needs as our own. We create more power *with* people to the degree that we evaluate honestly and vulnerably without criticism. People are much more concerned about our well-being when we share power than when we tell them what's wrong with them.

How to Change

> He that lacks time to mourn, lacks time to mend.
>
> Sir Henry Taylor

We want people to change because they see better ways of meeting their needs at less cost, not because of fear that we're going to punish them, or 'guilt' them if they don't. First, we'll look at how that change can occur within ourselves, then with other people whose behaviour is not in harmony with our values

First, ourselves: Think of a mistake you made recently, something you did that you wish you hadn't done. Then think, *How do I educate myself when I've done something I wish I hadn't done?* That is, what do you tell yourself at the moment you regret what you've done?

Many people educate themselves in a way people educated us when we did things that authorities didn't like. They blamed us and punished us, and we internalized it. How do we know that we are educating ourselves in a violent way? Three feelings will tell us: depression, guilt, and shame. We need to learn, but without hating ourselves. Learning that occurs through guilt or shame is costly learning.

Look behind these judgments to the need at the root of them. That is to say, what need of yours wasn't met by the behaviour? When we get in touch with needs of ours that weren't met by our behaviour, I call that mourning – mourning our actions. But it's mourning without blame, mourning without thinking there's something wrong with us for doing what we did. When I help people get to that connection, they often describe the pain almost like a sweet pain compared with the depression we feel when we are educating ourselves through blame and judgments.

A very important part of Nonviolent Communication is recognition of choice at every moment, that every moment we choose to do what we do ...

Look at the good reasons why you did what you did. I don't think any human being does anything except for good reasons. And what are those good reasons: to meet a need. *Everything* we do is in the service of needs. Often it's not easy to empathically connect with that need. If we look inside and say what was going on in us when we did that, very often we say things to ourselves like 'I had to do it; I had no choice'. That's never true! We always have a choice. We don't do anything we didn't choose to do. We chose to behave that way to meet a need. A very important part of Nonviolent Communication is this recognition of choice at every moment, that every moment we choose to do what we do, and we don't do anything that isn't coming out of choice. What's more, every choice we make is in the service of a need.

Many people have a great deal of pain surrounding things they've done or experienced in their lives. In helping people address the source of their pain, the first thing we do is get them to be conscious of the things they're telling themselves about what creates their pain. If we're not able to empathize with ourselves, it's going to be very hard to do it with other people. If we still think when we make a mistake that there's something wrong with us, then how are we not going to think there's something wrong with other people for doing what they do?

Life-enriching Connections with Others

The other half of Nonviolent Communication shows us how to make empathic connection with *what's alive in the other person* and *what would make life more wonderful for them*.

Empathic connection has a very specific meaning and purpose. Empathic connection is an understanding of the heart in which we see the beauty in the other person, the divine energy in the other person, the life that's alive in them. We connect with it. The goal isn't to intellectually understand it, the goal is empathically connecting with it. It doesn't mean we have to feel the same feelings as the other person. That's sympathy, when we feel sad that another person is upset. It means we are *with* the other person. This quality of understanding requires one of the most precious gifts one human being can give to another: our presence in the moment.

Let me show you what choices you have with every difficult message coming at you from another person:

- You can take it personally. I suggest that you never, never, never listen to what other people think about you. I predict you'll live longer and enjoy life more if you never hear what people think about you. And never take it personally.

- You can judge the other person for what they said to us. We could either think or say aloud, *That's not fair*, *That's stupid*, or whatever. I wouldn't recommend that.

- The recommendation I have is to learn to connect empathically with any message coming at us from other people. To do that you have to see what's alive in them.

When we teach people to empathize with people from other cultures who are behaving in ways we don't like, we find ways of resolving our differences peacefully. It's good to realize that, at the core of our humanity, we all have the same needs.

When we try to sense what the other person feels and needs, we could be wrong. But even if we're wrong, if we are sincerely trying to connect with the divine energy in another human being – their feelings, their needs at that moment – that shows the other person that no matter how they communicate with us, we care about what's alive in them. When a person trusts that, we're well on our way to making a connection in which everybody's needs can get met.

When a person can trust that we sincerely care about what they are feeling, what they are needing, they can start to hear you. Notice this doesn't require that we agree with the other person. It doesn't mean we have to like what they're saying. It means that we give them this precious gift of our presence.

Now, when we put this all together, it looks like this:

- We may start a dialogue with the other person by telling them what's alive in us and what we would like them to do to make life more wonderful for us.

- No matter how they respond, we try to connect with what's alive in them and what would make life more wonderful for them.

- We keep this flow of communication going until we find strategies to meet everybody's need.

Once people don't have to defend themselves against our single-mindedness of purpose to change them, once they feel understood for what they're doing, it's much easier for them to be open to other possibilities.

Social Change

In our training we want people not only to come out with awareness of how Nonviolent Communication can be used to transform our inner world, we want people to see how it can be used to create the world outside that we want to live in. We can show we do have the power, we do have the energy, or at least we can get it. How do we do that?

Domination Structures

According to people like historical theologian Walter Wink, about eight to ten thousand years ago a myth developed that the good life was good people punishing and conquering bad people. This myth seemed to support living under authoritarian regimes. And these *domination societies* excel at programming people to think in ways that make nice, dead people out of them. They'll do what people tell them.

Nonviolent Communication offers people caught up in domination systems a way of thinking and communicating that I'm sure would make their life much more wonderful.

At the same time we developed this way of thinking, of judging one another in ways that imply that reward is justified and punishment is justified. We created judicial systems based on *retributive* instead of *restorative* justice and so reinforced the idea that reward and punishment are deserved. I believe that this way of thinking and behaving is at the core of violence on our planet.

We still have a domination society, except that we have substituted an oligarchy for a king. We have what I call a *gang* dominating us rather than an individual. In many of our social-change efforts, we are seemingly concerned with the actions of groups of people rather than individual behaviors. In my way of thinking, gangs are groups that behave in ways we don't like. Some gangs call themselves street gangs. They're not the ones that scare me the most. Other gangs call themselves multinational corporations. Some gangs call themselves governments.

I don't think the people caught up in domination systems are bad people overtly trying to manipulate the masses. Rather, they have developed the structure, they believe that they are blessed with being somehow closer to higher authority, and they're doing this to preserve this higher authority's presence on the earth. Nonviolent Communication offers people caught up in domination systems a way of thinking and communicating that I'm sure would make their life much more wonderful. We can show them a game that's much more fun to play than dominating other people and creating wars!

Despair work

Despair work is Joanna Macy's concept. She's a person working in social change whom I admire very much. She points out how important it is to do despair work, noting that spirituality and social change go together. If we have a good, powerful spirituality, we are much more likely to reach our social-change objectives.

Despair work in Nonviolent Communication may take this form: I get together with my colleagues the night before an important meeting and say to them, 'It's going to be hard for me to see this man as a human being tomorrow when we go in there. I've got so much rage inside that I need to do some work on myself.' My team listens empathically to what is going on in me. I have this wonderful opportunity to express my pain and be understood. They can hear the rage I feel – and then, behind the rage, my fear about my hopelessness that we could ever get such people to connect with us in a way that would be good for everyone.

It may take a long time to do all this work, if I have deep pain and a lot of despair. For part of that time I may say, 'Those of you who have seen him communicate, could we do a little role-playing? I want to try to see his humanness through the way he usually speaks.' I had never seen the man, but they had, and they showed me how he communicated. I worked hard the night before to see his humanness so I wouldn't see him as an enemy.

Communicating with 'gangs'

> Out beyond ideas of rightdoing and wrongdoing there is a field:
> I'll meet you there.   RUMI

First, we need to liberate ourselves from *enemy* images, the thinking that says there is something wrong with the people who are part of these gangs. Once both sides get over the enemy image and recognize each other's needs, it's amazing how the next part, which is looking for strategies to meet everyone's needs, becomes pretty easy by comparison. It's getting people to see that you can't benefit at other people's expense.

The most common elements I've found in the conflicts I've been asked to mediate are that people – instead of knowing how to say clearly what their needs and requests are – are quite eloquent in diagnosing other people's pathology: what's wrong with them for behaving as they do. Whether it's two individuals, two groups, or two countries that have conflicts, they begin the discussion with enemy images, telling the other person what's wrong with them. The divorce courts – and the bombs – are never far away. Every time we go up into our head and make a judgment of others instead of going into our heart and seeing the needs, we decrease the likelihood that other people will enjoy giving to us.

Conclusion

Peace requires something far more difficult than revenge or merely turning the other cheek; it requires empathizing with the fears and unmet needs that provide the impetus for people to attack each other. Being aware of these feelings and needs, people lose their desire to attack back because they can see the human ignorance leading to these attacks; instead, their goal becomes providing the empathic connection and education that will enable them to transcend their violence and engage in cooperative relationships.

Nonviolent Communication shows us how to have the courage to face the power and the beauty that is within each of us.

I believe, as did Teilhard de Chardin, that a peaceful world is not only possible, it's inevitable.

Some Basic Needs We All Have

Autonomy: choosing dreams/goals/values; and choosing plans for their fulfilment

Celebration: celebrate the creation of life and dreams fulfilled; celebrate losses: loved ones, dreams

Integrity: authenticity; creativity; meaning, self-worth

Interdependence: acceptance; appreciation; closeness; community; consideration; contribution; emotional safety; empathy; honesty; love, reassurance; respect, support; trust; understanding

Physical nurturance: air; food; movement; protection; rest; sexual expression; shelter; touch; water

Play: fun; laughter

Spiritual communion: beauty; harmony; inspiration; order; peace

Source: *Speak Peace in a World of Conflict* by Dr Marshall B Rosenberg, 2005 – published by PuddleDancer Press (for more information visit www.CNVC. org and www.NonviolentCommunication).

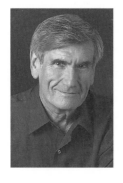

Marshall B Rosenberg, PhD is the founder and director of educational services for the Center for Nonviolent Communication, an international peacemaking and training organization. He is the author of *Speak Peace in a World of Conflict*, and the bestselling *Nonviolent Communication: A Language of Life*. Dr Rosenberg is the 2006 recipient of the Global Village Foundation's Bridge of Peace Award, and the Association of Unity Churches International 2006 Light of God Expressing Award. Rosenberg spends more than 250 days each year traveling the globe, teaching Nonviolent Communication (NVC) in hundreds of local communities, at national conferences, and in some of the most impoverished, war-torn states of the world. Growing up in a turbulent Detroit neighbourhood, Dr Rosenberg developed a keen interest in new forms of communication that would provide peaceful alternatives to the violence he encountered. Dr Rosenberg first used the NVC process in federally funded school integration projects to provide mediation and communication skills training during the 1960s.

3   Personal Empowerment & Leadership Skills

Personal Empowerment

Integral Leadership

In this speech, Wangari Maathai speaks particularly to the women of Africa, and through them to all of us, reminding us of our power to step into action and make a difference.

Nobel Peace Laureate Speech 2004

Wangari Maathai

Your Majesties
Your Royal Highnesses
Honourable Members of the Norwegian Nobel Committee
Excellencies
Ladies and Gentlemen

I stand before you and the world humbled by this recognition and uplifted by the honor of being the 2004 Nobel Peace Laureate.

As the first African woman to receive this prize, I accept it on behalf of the people of Kenya and Africa, and indeed the world. I am especially mindful of women and the girl child. I hope it will encourage them to raise their voices and take more space for leadership. I know the honour also gives a deep sense of pride to our men, both old and young. As a mother, I appreciate the inspiration this brings to the youth and urge them to use it to pursue their dreams.

Although this prize comes to me, it acknowledges the work of countless individuals and groups across the globe. They work quietly and often without recognition to protect the environment, promote democracy, defend human rights and ensure equality between women and men. By so doing, they plant seeds of peace. I know they, too, are proud today. To all who feel represented by this prize I say use it to advance your mission and meet the high expectations the world will place on us.

This honour is also for my family, friends, partners and supporters throughout the world. All of them helped shape the vision and sustain our work, which was often accomplished under hostile conditions. I am also grateful to the people of Kenya – who remained stubbornly hopeful that democracy could be realized and their environment managed sustainably. Because of this support, I am here today to accept this great honour.

I am immensely privileged to join my fellow African Peace laureates, Presidents Nelson Mandela and F W de Clerk, Archbishop Desmond Tutu, the late Chief Albert Luthuli, the late Anwar el-Sadat and the UN Secretary General, Kofi Annan.

I know that African people everywhere are encouraged by this news. My fellow Africans, as we embrace this recognition, let us use it to intensify our commitment to our people, to reduce conflicts and poverty and thereby improve their quality of life. Let us embrace democratic governance, protect human rights and protect our environment. I am confident that we shall rise to the occasion. I have always believed that solutions to most of our problems must come from us.

In this year's prize, the Norwegian Nobel Committee has placed the critical issue of environment and its linkage to democracy and peace before the world. For their visionary action, I am profoundly grateful. Recognizing that sustainable development, democracy and peace are indivisible is an idea whose time has come. Our work over the past 30 years has always appreciated and engaged these linkages.

My inspiration partly comes from my childhood experiences and observations of Nature in rural Kenya. It has been influenced and nurtured by the formal education I was privileged to receive in Kenya, the United States and Germany. As I was growing up, I witnessed forests being cleared and replaced by commercial plantations, which destroyed local biodiversity and the capacity of the forests to conserve water.

In 1977, when we started the Green Belt Movement, I was partly responding to needs identified by rural women, namely lack of firewood, clean drinking water, balanced diets, shelter and income.

Throughout Africa, women are the primary caretakers, holding significant responsibility for tilling the land and feeding their families. As a result, they are often the first to become aware of environmental damage as resources become scarce and incapable of sustaining their families.

The women we worked with recounted that unlike in the past, they were unable to meet their basic needs. This was due to the degradation of their immediate environment as well as the introduction of commercial farming, which replaced the growing of household food crops. But international trade controlled the price of the exports from these small-scale farmers and a reasonable and just income could not be guaranteed. I came to understand that when the environment is destroyed, plundered or mismanaged, we undermine our quality of life and that of future generations.

Tree planting became a natural choice to address some of the initial basic needs identified by women. Also, tree planting is simple, attainable and guarantees quick, successful results within a reasonable amount time. This sustains interest and commitment.

So, together, we have planted over 30 million trees that provide fuel, food, shelter, and income to support their children's education and household needs. The activity also creates employment and improves soils and watersheds. Through their involvement, women gain some degree of power over their lives, especially their social and economic position and relevance in the family. This work continues.

... work was difficult because historically our people have been persuaded to believe that because they are poor, they lack not only capital, but also knowledge and skills ...

Initially, the work was difficult because historically our people have been persuaded to believe that because they are poor, they lack not only capital, but also knowledge and skills to address their challenges. Instead they are conditioned to believe that solutions to their problems must come from 'outside'. Further, women did not realize that meeting their needs depended on their environment being healthy and well managed. They were also unaware that a degraded environment leads to a scramble for scarce resources and may culminate in poverty and even conflict. They were also unaware of the injustices of international economic arrangements.

In order to assist communities to understand these linkages, we developed a citizen education program, during which people identify their problems, the causes and possible solutions. They then make connections between their own personal actions and the problems they witness in the environment and in society. They learn that our world is confronted with a litany of woes: corruption, violence against women and children, disruption and breakdown of families, and disintegration of cultures and communities. They also identify the abuse of drugs and chemical substances, especially among young people. There are also devastating diseases that are defying cures or occurring in epidemic proportions. Of particular concern are HIV/ AIDS, malaria and diseases associated with malnutrition.

On the environment front, they are exposed to many human activities that are devastating to the environment and societies. These include widespread destruction of ecosystems, especially through deforestation, climatic instability, and contamination in the soils and waters that all contribute to excruciating poverty.

In the process, the participants discover that they must be part of the solutions. They realize their hidden potential and are empowered to overcome inertia and take action. They come to recognize that they are the primary custodians and beneficiaries of the environment that sustains them.

Entire communities also come to understand that while it is necessary to hold their governments accountable, it is equally important that in their own relationships with each other, they exemplify the leadership values they wish to see in their own leaders, namely justice, integrity and trust.

Although initially the Green Belt Movement's tree planting activities did not address issues of democracy and peace, it soon became clear that responsible governance of the environment was impossible without democratic space. Therefore, the tree became a symbol for the democratic struggle in Kenya. Citizens were mobilized to challenge widespread abuses of power, corruption and environmental mismanagement. In Nairobi's Uhuru Park, at Freedom Corner, and in many parts of the country, trees of peace were planted to demand the release of prisoners of conscience and a peaceful transition to democracy.

Through the Green Belt Movement, thousands of ordinary citizens were mobilized and empowered to take action and effect change. They learned to overcome fear and a sense of helplessness and moved to defend democratic rights.

In time, the tree also became a symbol for peace and conflict resolution, especially during ethnic conflicts in Kenya when the Green Belt Movement used peace trees to reconcile disputing communities. During the ongoing re-writing of the Kenyan constitution, similar trees of peace were planted in many parts of the country to promote a culture of peace. Using trees as a symbol of peace is in keeping with a widespread African tradition. For example, the elders of the Kikuyu carried a staff from the thigi tree that, when placed between two disputing sides, caused them to stop fighting and seek reconciliation. Many communities in Africa have these traditions.

Such practices are part of an extensive cultural heritage, which contributes both to the conservation of habitats and to cultures of peace. With the destruction of these cultures and the introduction of new values, local biodiversity is no longer valued or protected and as a result, it is quickly degraded and disappears. For this reason, The Green Belt Movement explores the concept of cultural biodiversity, especially with respect to indigenous seeds and medicinal plants.

As we progressively understood the causes of environmental degradation, we saw the need for good governance. Indeed, the state of any county's environment is a reflection of the kind of governance in place, and without good governance there can be no peace. Many countries, which have poor governance systems, are also likely to have conflicts and poor laws protecting the environment.

In 2002, the courage, resilience, patience and commitment of members of the Green Belt Movement, other civil society organizations, and the Kenyan public culminated in the peaceful transition to a democratic government and laid the foundation for a more stable society.

It is 30 years since we started this work. Activities that devastate the environment and societies continue unabated. Today we are faced with a challenge that calls for a shift in our thinking, so that humanity stops threatening its life-support system. We are called to assist the Earth to heal her wounds and in the process heal our own – indeed, to embrace the whole creation in all its diversity, beauty and wonder. This will happen if we see the need to revive our sense of belonging to a larger family of life, with which we have shared our evolutionary process.

In the course of history, there comes a time when humanity is called to shift to a new level of consciousness, to reach a higher moral ground. A time when we have to shed our fear and give hope to each other.

That time is now.

The Norwegian Nobel Committee has challenged the world to broaden the understanding of peace: there can be no peace without equitable development; and there can be no development without sustainable management of the environment in a democratic and peaceful space. This shift is an idea whose time has come.

I call on leaders, especially from Africa, to expand democratic space and build fair and just societies that allow the creativity and energy of their citizens to flourish.

We are called to assist the Earth to heal her wounds and in the process heal our own – indeed, to embrace the whole creation in all its diversity, beauty and wonder. This will happen if we see the need to revive our sense of belonging to a larger family of life …

Those of us who have been privileged to receive education, skills, and experiences and even power must be role models for the next generation of leadership. In this regard, I would also like to appeal for the freedom of my fellow laureate Aung San Suu Kyi so that she can continue her work for peace and democracy for the people of Burma and the world at large.

Culture plays a central role in the political, economic and social life of communities. Indeed, culture may be the missing link in the development of Africa. Culture is dynamic and evolves over time, consciously discarding retrogressive traditions, like female genital mutilation (FGM), and embracing aspects that are good and useful.

Africans, especially, should re-discover positive aspects of their culture. In accepting them, they would give themselves a sense of belonging, identity and self-confidence.

There is also need to galvanize civil society and grassroots movements to catalyse change. I call upon governments to recognize the role of these social movements in building a critical mass of responsible citizens, who help maintain checks and balances in society. On their part, civil society should embrace not only their rights but also their responsibilities.

Further, industry and global institutions must appreciate that ensuring economic justice, equity and ecological integrity are of greater value than profits at any cost.

To the young people I say, you are a gift to your communities and indeed the world. You are our hope and our future.

The extreme global inequities and prevailing consumption patterns continue at the expense of the environment and peaceful co-existence. The choice is ours.

I would like to call on young people to commit themselves to activities that contribute toward achieving their long-term dreams. They have the energy and creativity to shape a sustainable future. To the young people I say, you are a gift to your communities and indeed the world. You are our hope and our future.

The holistic approach to development, as exemplified by the Green Belt Movement, could be embraced and replicated in more parts of Africa and beyond. It is for this reason that I have established the Wangari Maathai Foundation to ensure the continuation and expansion of these activities. Although a lot has been achieved, much remains to be done.

As I conclude I reflect on my childhood experience when I would visit a stream next to our home to fetch water for my mother. I would drink water straight from the stream. Playing among the arrowroot leaves I tried in vain to pick up the strands of frogs' eggs, believing they were beads. But every time I put my little fingers under them they would break. Later, I saw thousands of tadpoles: black, energetic and wriggling through the clear water against the background of the brown earth. This is the world I inherited from my parents.

Today, over 50 years later, the stream has dried up, women walk long distances for water, which is not always clean, and children will never know what they have lost. The challenge is to restore the home of the tadpoles and give back to our children a world of beauty and wonder.

Thank you very much.

Wangari Maathai faced enormous obstacles in life, not the least of which was that in Kenyan tradition women are seen as the submissive property of men. Nevertheless, she stubbornly pursued an education and eventually became a professor of veterinary medicine. Soon after that, she entered a traditional marriage and had three children. But because of her growing activism, her husband called her 'too educated, too strong, too successful, too stubborn, and too hard to control' and divorced her. The President of Kenya labelled her 'a mad woman who is a threat to the order and security of the country'. Threatened with death, and in hiding during much of her long years of activism for human rights, women's rights, and environmentalism, Ms Maathai has been courageously steadfast. Among her many accomplishments is the founding of the Green Belt Movement, an organization that concentrates on environmental conservation and community development by planting trees to protect the soil. It was through this organization that she became known throughout the world, and in 2004, she became the first African woman to receive the Nobel Prize 'for aiding democracy and attempting to save Africa's forests'.

Fredrick Onyango Demosh

Scilla Elworthy calls upon us to connect across continents in order to help create peace in our world. She shows how networks of human support and community do not stop at borders, but spread out to change the structures of violence into networks of nonviolence.

The Power of Nonviolence

Scilla Elworthy

The Status Quo

In his report *A Secure Europe in a Better World* (2004), Xavier Solana, EU High Representative for Common Foreign Policy, wrote as follows:

> Almost 3 billion people, half this world's population, live on less than 2 Euros a day [... roughly £1.30 or $2.50]. 45 million continue to die every year out of hunger and malnutrition. Sub-Sahara Africa is poorer now than it was 10 years ago. In many cases, the failure of economic growth has been linked to political problems and violent conflict. In some parts of the world, notably Sub-Sahara Africa, a cycle of insecurity has come into being. Since 1990, almost 4 million people have died in wars, 90% of them civilians. Over 18 million people have left their homes or their countries as a result of conflict.

More and more economists are coming to the conclusion that the deeper causes of this situation lie in global rather than local policies: governmental support for a massive worldwide trade in weapons, encouragement of an obsession with consuming, and economic policies that penalize poorer countries. If we look deeply, we discover that ultimately these policies are causing conflict.

Ordinary Heroes

And yet, ordinary people all over the world are doing something about these huge problems. In our research (Oxford Research Group) into more than 200 conflicts worldwide, we found that in every conflict, there are people brave enough to take the difficult and dangerous path of peace-building, rather than pick up an AK 47. It is a privilege for me to tell you about some of them.

Fifteen years after her father was killed in the bombing of the British Conservative Party Conference in 1984, **Jo Berry** decided to go and meet

Patrick Magee, the man who planted the bomb. She had the courage to reconcile with him. Now they work together to build bridges between those who have suffered in the troubles in Northern Ireland – the victims and the perpetrators.

Dr Sima Semar, Afghanistan, is now Head of the Independent Human Rights Commission in Iraq. She is not only a woman, but also from the Hazara Tribe, a persecuted minority. She has fought discrimination against women from a young age. She received her Doctor Title in Kabul 1982. She later had to flee to Pakistan, where she established the first hospital for women. Today, from this model, 12 clinics, four hospitals and 60 schools (with 37,000 students) for women have developed.

Maria Mangte, India, lost her parents, husband and two children to inter-tribal warfare in Manipur (Northeast India). In the fight over the freedom Manipur state, in spite of political differences, she found she could be neutral between the two sides and became a mediator. Eventually, in 1996, she was appointed Secretary General of the Indian Confederation of Indigenous and Tribal Peoples.

Peace Direct

As we speak, there are groups of people in the midst of the violence in Afghanistan, in DR Congo, even in Iraq, who are risking their lives to prevent other people from getting killed. They are mediating, building bridges between communities, confiscating guns, resolving disputes and protecting the vulnerable. The trouble is, most of these people are completely unsupported and are in danger of giving up through lack of resources.

At the same time, there are all over the world many people who are fed up with war as a way of sorting out conflict, who want peaceful solutions, but don't know what they can do to help. We have set up Peace Direct to offer people a 'bite-sized' piece of the problem of war, by putting them directly in touch with a group of peacemakers in a certain area of conflict. These 'twinned groups' can learn from each other: those in the west can offer backing in the form of getting media coverage for their 'unarmed hero' friends, sourcing resources (such as mobile phones, or a video camera to record atrocities), helping to change the policies of our own government, or simply sending a weekly postcard of support:

- **Peace Direct** has linked conflict resolution workers in the most violent areas of DR Congo with an individual in London who has helped to raise funds towards a conflict resolution centre in DR Congo.

- We brought Mr Ghandi, Principal of the Lucknow Montessori School, with two students and a colleague, to the UK. They told the story of how, when Northern India was aflame with communal violence after the Ayodhya mosque was destroyed in 1992, the school acted with others to ensure peace prevailed in Lucknow, just 80 miles from the seat of the violence in Ayodha. We had meetings in 6 locations across England, and opportunities to exchange experiences of building peaceful communities with schools, youth groups, interfaith groups and universities.

- We have connected up a website designer in Wales with a network of conflict resolution practitioners in Africa to enable them to build and develop their website, thereby facilitating the sharing of their experience and skills.

- Sami Veglioglu is a British Iraqi who was impelled to return to his home city Kirkuk to set up a Humanitarian Liaison Centre, in which individuals who have suffered wrongs as a result of the conflict in Iraq can have their story heard and be helped to find redress. 'I have to reach people before they pick up a gun and take matters into their own hands' says Sami. Through Peace Direct people in Bristol have been funding the centre since it opened in July 2004, sending regular messages of support, and helping Sami find other sources of funding.

- The Centre Resolution Conflits was established in the Democratic Republic of Congo in 1993 and became a formal organization in 1997. In the beginning training in alternatives to violence started with training community elders, church and non-governmental organizations and political leaders. In 2000 the emphasis shifted to training young people. The Centre has twice been destroyed. Each time the leaders have relocated, the second time with financial support from a woman in Oxford through **Peace Direct**, and carried on with their work.

Opting for Nonviolence

In combat you may risk your life to kill others; in nonviolence you may risk your life so that no one else will be killed. This requires rigorous training and deep conviction; the effect it has on violent, cruel or angry people is *more powerful than more violence*. It affects them at a profound level. It is the force of **Satyagraha**, developed by Gandhi and entirely successful in driving the British out of India. The practitioner renounces the use of force, voluntarily and on principle, and replaces it with determination combined with compassion, combined with courage.

This is the power Martin Luther King taught and used to vast effect in de-segregating the deep South. It is what Aung San Suu Khi used when she walked unarmed straight up to the machine guns of Burmese soldiers who had been ordered to shoot the demonstrators she led. It is what Nelson Mandela developed during 27 years in jail and used to prevent a civil war in South Africa on his release. It was the power behind the 'Velvet Revolution', which brought down the Iron Curtain. It was the power that deposed President Marcos in the Philippines, General Pinochet in Chile and Slobodan Milosevic in Serbia.

Nonviolence requires an extraordinary commitment of those who practise it, from whatever religious or cultural background they may come. It requires serious learning, which is now available, it requires practise, and devotion; most of all it requires the transformation of ourselves. We have to look deeply into our own anger, our aggressiveness and our fear. It's as hard as training for the Olympics. And the results are no less rewarding. When you meet real peace-makers, they are radiant. They radiate an inner spaciousness, a joy and a power that is greater than any weapon.

Professor Michael Nagler, founder of the University of California Peace and Conflict Studies programme, estimates that nearly one third of the world's people have practised some form of nonviolence, or 'life force', for the redress of grievances:

> This is the concept of 'people power'. The idea is that the power of an aroused populace is greater than the power of the state, since the state depends on the consent and the cooperation of its citizens. And when citizens rise up, as they notoriously did in the Philippines twice in recent memory, the state is powerless to stop them. But people power is only the tip of the iceberg. The real nonviolence, in my understanding, is person power. That is, the power of the single individual.

That's you. I know that you've been born into a tough world. But you also have fantastic opportunities: to talk and to understand the world from another person's point of view. Practise stepping for a moment or two into another person's shoes, and see the world as they see it. This way you bring about change. This way you'll be a change-maker. This way you'll refuse to do what the media and the main culture want you to do, which is to do what you're told and live in fear and learn to hate. This way you'll become what we call an 'Unarmed Hero'. This way you will make the world a safer and happier and better place than the world you were born into.

Dr Scilla Elworthy founded the Oxford Research Group in 1982 and was Executive Director until December 2003. It is for this work that she was awarded the Niwano Peace Prize in 2003 and nominated three times for the Nobel Peace Prize. She then founded Peace Direct, which grew out of O.R.G.'s conflict prevention work, became an independent NGO with charitable status during 2004, and was named 'Best New Charity' at the Charity Awards 2005.

Peace Direct, 56 Leonard St, London EC2A 4JX,UK • (T) +44 (0)845 456 9714 • (F) +44(0)20 7794 2489 • info@peacedirect.org • www.peacedirect.org.

Hide Enomoto outlines the philosophy and practice of Co-Active Coaching – a tool for personal empowerment that can also help ecovillages to fulfil their purpose in the world.

How Can We Support Each Other to Step into our Power?

Hide Enomoto

What is Coaching?

There are countless models in the field of coaching, but most of them originate from the world of sport. It is said that the word 'coach' first appeared in the Middle Ages in Eastern Europe to mean a horse-led carriage. This is why the word is still used sometimes to describe a bus or an airplane in the modern world. It carries people to where they want to go. In a similar way, a coach supports athletes to achieve their goals. However, the way they support the athletes has mostly been through telling them what they should do, often with the use of reward and punishment.

In the late '70s, some coaches began to doubt the effectiveness of this kind of method and instead tried a different approach. They preferred to ask questions about what athletes were noticing while they were engaged in their activity. To use an example from tennis: a coach would ask questions like 'Where is your focus of attention when you hit the ball?' or 'How did your body feel when you swung your racket?' whereas a traditional coach might say something like 'Don't take your eyes off the ball!' or 'You must keep the face of your racket square to the ground when you hit the ball.' What is the effect on the athlete? When a coach tells the athlete what he should do, he has no choice other than to follow, especially if it comes with the voice of authority. The athlete's own will is irrelevant here. However, when a coach asks the athlete questions, her/his awareness is raised. If the coach follows up with another question like 'What do you want to keep in mind next time around?' the athlete has choice and can exercise their free will. These kinds of coaches use an 'ask-and-empower' approach as opposed to the traditional 'command-and-control' approach. They have found that athletes who have been supported in this way often have higher motivation and achieve better results in the long run.

Another benefit of this ask-and-empower approach is that the coach does not have to be an 'expert' in a given sport. Normally, what happens in a command-and-control approach is that the athletes who have enjoyed high performance over the course of their career become coaches. They are expected to impart and to transfer their expertise to those they train. This is possible and valid if the focus is on performance and results. However, this approach misses the aspect of personal human development. Instead, the ask-and-empower approach has its emphasis on developing the athletes as human beings that extend far beyond their sports career. Anyone who knows how to empower others can actually coach no matter what sports the athletes are engaged in. In fact, it was found that coaching does not even have to be about sports at all because anyone can benefit from it in order to live an empowered life. This is how coaching became much more than just training athletes in the world of sports.

In the '90s, coaching found its way into the personal realm, giving rise to Personal or Life Coaches. It became a trend in the US and then in other industrialized countries. I came across coaching in the US in 1995 when I was taking a course in graduate studies and quickly realized its power and potential to change people's lives. I will describe a coaching model called Co-Active Coaching, which has been developed by CTI (The Coaches Training Institute based in San Rafael, California), one of the pioneering organizations in the field.

Coaching has also found its way into the corporate realm. It is often seen as one of the most important competencies that people in management positions have to develop in order to empower those they are supervising. Corporate / Business Coaching tends to put more emphasis on performance, compared to its counterpart in the personal realm.

Philosophy of Coaching

On one level, coaching is a set of communication skills and processes designed to empower those with whom we are communicating. However, there is another level that relates to the philosophy of coaching. In Co-Active Coaching, this philosophy takes the form of the 'Four Cornerstones':

- Coach holds the client as naturally creative, resourceful and whole.
- Coach addresses the client's whole life.
- Coach holds the client's agenda.
- Coach dances in the moment with the client.

In a professional context, the client normally pays the coach to receive her/his service on a regular basis. However, in this article, I am talking about coaching in a wider context. So, even if I use the term 'client' for the sake of simplicity, it can be anybody. It can be your spouse, your child, your colleague, your friend or your neighbour. Given that, I would like to explain what each of these cornerstones means in more detail.

Coach holds the client as naturally creative, resourceful and whole

In order to truly empower others, we have to first see them as whole human beings and not as 'problems to be solved.' We have a tendency to approach others with a mindset of 'what's wrong with this person?' But, in coaching, we stand firmly in the belief that there is nothing wrong with anybody. Of course, we all fail and make mistakes every now and then, but that doesn't mean that we are wrong. In fact, one of the greatest obstacles to living an empowered life comes from judging others or ourselves as wrong. We learn best when we make mistakes. It's obvious when you look at how babies learn to walk. But as we grow older, we become afraid of failing. How can we manifest our highest potential if we do not risk making mistakes? We need to encourage each other to fail if we are to live our lives fully.

Another aspect of this cornerstone is the premise that we have all the answers we need within us. Many of us are trained and educated to believe that answers lie in the hands of authorities or experts: parents, teachers, managers, consultants and so on. We look outwards instead of inwards to search for an answer. But the truth is that there is no definite answer especially in response to a question regarding your own life. Yes, it's unsettling and sometimes tough when an unanswered question is hanging over your head nagging to be answered. But the questions themselves can be much more powerful catalysts for growth than 'easy' answers that come from outside. And when an answer finally does arise from inside, it is often accompanied by a feeling of invigoration because it is YOUR answer, not anyone else's. That's why in coaching we ask questions instead of giving advice. Knowing that we have all the answers we need within ourselves and actually finding those answers from within is the key to personal empowerment.

Coach addresses the client's whole life

In Co-Active Coaching, we focus our attention on the person, not on circumstance because as long as you focus on circumstance, the person will not learn anything ...

Let's say that a client is talking about his dissatisfaction with the current job. If you were to coach this person, where would your focus be? The natural tendency would probably be to focus on his job. You might ask questions like 'What kind of job do you do?' or 'What's the problem with your job?' Or you might even ask, 'What other jobs are available to you?' or 'What can you do to change your job?' As you can see, all of these questions are focused on his job and not on the person. In Co-Active Coaching, we focus our attention on the person, not on circumstance because as long as you focus on circumstance, the person will not learn anything about him/herself. Let me elaborate this a little further. If the person tries to change his job without changing himself, you can be sure that a similar dynamic will show up again somewhere in his life. For example, if his dissatisfaction with the current job is coming from the fact that his boss is asking him to take on more tasks all the time, what might be necessary is to learn how to say no. And it is highly probable that this person is facing similar challenges in other areas of his life; maybe in his family life or community life or in his relationships with friends. So, rather than focusing on circumstance – in this case, the job – it serves this person best if you keep his whole life in perspective.

In Co-Active Coaching, we also have Three Principles:

- Fulfilment
- Balance
- Process

These principles provide coaches with guidance as to where they should put their focus while coaching. **Fulfilment** is about what makes you alive. The key word here is 'values' because you become alive when you honour your values. **Balance** is about making powerful choices. The key word here is 'perspective' because you can see that you have numerous choices when you expand your perspectives. **Process** is about being where you are and fully experiencing life in the moment. The key word here is 'feeling' because people feel the richness of their lives when they are in touch with their feelings. With these principles in mind, the coach can address the client's whole life without being distracted by the presenting circumstances.

Coach holds the client's agenda

In coaching, the agenda always comes from the person you are coaching. This means that the topic of coaching is chosen and will be brought to the table by those who want to be coached. It's not you, the coach, who gets to decide what to talk about or even how to proceed. Coaching is a particular kind of relationship consciously designed by both the coach and the client with the sole intention to empower the client. This is what sets coaching apart from any other type of communication. It is especially important to remember this if you coach a spouse, a family member, a colleague or a friend.

If you have agreed to coach someone for half an hour, your job is to keep your own agenda out of the conversation during that time. Whatever the agenda, the coach will hold that agenda as long as it comes from the client. It might also be useful to bear in mind that there is an agenda and an Agenda. The small 'a' agenda is the particular topic the client brings to the table, whereas the big 'A' Agenda is something that is always there for the coach to hold i.e. the Three Principles. The coach is always looking for the client's **fulfilment**, **balance** and **process** no matter what the client's particular agenda is. Everyone wishes to live according to their values, to make powerful choices, to move forward, and to experience the fullness of life.

Coach dances in the moment with the client

In coaching, or in almost any interaction with another person for that matter, you can rarely predict what will happen next, let alone where it will end up. Life is full of surprises. However, we don't necessarily do well with uncertainties and tend to want to minimize them by projecting into the future. This can be useful in avoiding risks but, at the same time, the very act of projection or prediction itself brings about different risks if we get attached to them. As soon as we make a prediction, we shut out other possibilities. Especially in coaching, the client changes moment by moment and, if you try to predict, you will lose the connection with your client. Your prediction becomes more important than the client and becomes your own agenda. To refrain from this, the coach has to be present with the client at all times. It's as if you are engaged in a social dance. If you are not present while dancing, you will probably step on your partner's feet. You must be very attentive and ready to match your partner's movement. It is the same in coaching. Never predict. Stay present so that you can dance in the moment with your client. This will enable clients to enjoy the dance of their life.

Stay present so that you can dance in the moment with your client.

The Five Key Components of Coaching

Now, let's move on to what makes coaching work. In other words, how do we actually empower the person we are coaching? In Co-Active Coaching, there are five key components that are crucial to coach your clients in an effective way:

- Curiosity
- Listening
- Intuition
- Self-management
- Action/learning

Curiosity

I've already mentioned that one of the key characteristics of coaching is to ask questions. But, where do questions originally come from? They come from a place of curiosity. We can't actually ask questions without being curious about the other person. Yes, there are people who ask questions without being curious; they already have answers to the question before they ask. Most of these questions take the form of 'yes-no questions' – the kind of questions that can be answered by either yes or no. On the other hand, the more curious questions take the form of 'open-ended questions' – the kind of questions that cannot be answered by yes or no. When you ask an open-ended question, you never know what the answer might be. And it is always better if your clients cannot answer right away because that means that they have to go deep inside themselves to find an answer. The coach's curiosity is what allows the clients to explore their inner world which, in turn, leads to self-discovery.

Listening

This model describes three levels of listening. Level 1 is when your attention is on yourself. It is an Internal Listening of your own thoughts and feelings.

This is a perfect place for the client to be, but not for the coach. You cannot listen to your client fully when you are at Level 1. Level 2 is when your attention is focused on the client like a laser beam. It is a Focused Listening toward the client's verbal and non-verbal communication. When two people are engaged with each other at this level, nothing else exists. You can witness this when a mother is holding her baby in her arms or when two lovers are staring at each other romantically. Level 3 is when your attention is on everything else. It is a Global Listening to the environment within which the coaching is taking place. It is surprising when you realize how much influence the environment has on the coaching. For coaching, the ideal is to listen at Levels 2 and 3.

Intuition

Listening at Levels 2 and 3, coupled with curiosity, will usually provide the coach with enough clues as to what to do next during the coaching session, but there is one more component: intuition. We inherently have access to our intuition, but are rarely encouraged to use it in this modern world where logic and reason have more precedence. But intuition can be a very powerful tool to move a coaching session forward as long as we do not get attached to it. When we get attached to our intuition, it becomes an opinion. If you express your intuition without any attachment, then your client has more freedom to choose how to make use of that intuition. So that means you need to be prepared for a 'no.' And the great thing about offering your intuition to your client is that you'll get the right answer even if your intuition was wrong. You say, 'I had a hunch that it's this' and your client would say, 'No, it's not that. It's this.' There you are – you've just contributed to your client finding out what's true for him/her.

We inherently have access to our intuition, but are rarely encouraged to use it in this modern world where logic and reason have more precedence.

Self-management

One of the challenges you face as a coach is how to become 'invisible.' In order for your clients to really focus on themselves and thus find the answers that lie within them, you have to get out of their way. This means that you need to refrain from bringing your own agenda onto the table to the best of your ability. In other words, when you notice yourself listening at Level 1, you gently shift your awareness back to your client and the surrounding environment. You don't have to blame yourself for going to Level 1. It's natural for us to do that. Just simply notice what has happened. All you have to do then is to get curious 'over there' and allow your intuition to guide you.

Action/Learning

The final component is Action/Learning. To be more exact, this component is made up of two parts: 'forwarding the action' and 'deepening the learning'.

Both are necessary. If you just keep forwarding the action of your client without deepening the learning, it will eventually lead to burnout. On the other hand, if you just keep deepening the learning without forwarding the action of your client, there will be no movement and therefore no change. It is this component that distinguishes coaching from other interventions such as counselling or therapy. In counselling and therapy, the focus is mostly on healing, whereas in coaching, the focus is mostly on personal empowerment through self-discovery and decisive actions.

How Coaching can be Applied in Ecovillages

Now that we've seen what coaching is and how it works, I would like to dedicate the last part of this article to talking about how coaching can be applied in ecovillages and how it can contribute to social change.

In ecovillages, democracy and diversity among the members is generally honoured. This naturally gives rise to more of a 'non-hierarchical' structure compared to other social organizations such as governments, corporations and religious institutions. Even when there is hierarchy, there is more flexibility in who gets to play which role. For example, 'rotating leadership' is a common practice in many communities, so that power belongs to the role, not to the person. In order for this kind of structure to work, members of the community need to have a strong sense of responsibility, i.e. the ability to choose and act out of one's free will.

If members don't have this kind of responsibility, the community will default back to the traditional hierarchical structure where the leader/

follower relationship is more static. This is the major reason why I think personal empowerment is such an important element in designing and developing ecovillages. It has to be embedded in the culture of communities so that empowerment is happening in all directions all the time. Coaching can be a powerful medium through which an 'empowerment culture' is created and nurtured.

One of the ways I see coaching being applied in ecovillages is to have trained coaches offering this service to teams and individuals in the community Such people could also provide training for community members, especially for those who are newly assigned to, or volunteer to take on, a leadership role. This would create the opportunity for as many community members as possible to receive coaching, so that it starts to seep into the culture.

There is another reason for ecovillages to incorporate coaching into their own culture. Since many ecovillages aim to be a model for a way of living which is in harmony with nature and the world, it requires its members to be active not only within the community but also outside the community. An ecovillage cannot be a 'closed system' where there is no input or output from/toward the outside world. Rather, it is an 'open system' which impacts, and also is impacted by, what happens 'out there.' This means that any ecovillage which tries to fulfil its purpose, needs to empower its members to engage actively with the outside world and get their message across. To put it in another way, designing and developing an ecovillage is an act of social change and therefore requires its members to take on responsibility. It takes conscious and powerful actions and visions on the part of people in ecovillages to stay focused on their purpose and stand strong within the dominant force of modern societies. Coaching, if practised regularly in ecovillages, can ignite the fire among its members to be actively engaged in the world and to bring about the social change which is in accordance with their purpose. And that, I believe, will enable people to be responsible not only for their own life, but also for the world at large.

Hide Enomoto has been a Life Coach since 1996 and also has been training coaching skills in many different countries over the past decade including Japan, US, Canada, UK, Norway, Sweden, Turkey, Spain and UAE. He is a senior Certified Trainer with CTI (The Coaches Training Institute), one of the pioneering coach training institutes in the world, and also the founder of CTI Japan. He is also the author of *Stretch Your People by Coaching* (PHP Institute, 1999), which became the best-selling book in the field of coaching in Japan. He has been involved in Ecovillage movement since 2004 and currently lives in Scotland near Findhorn.

3   Personal Empowerment & Leadership Skills

Personal Empowerment

Integral Leadership

Manitonquat doesn't allow us to hide behind feelings of unworthiness. Instead, he teaches us to bring our talents into the open and become a leader. The world needs us now.

Leadership in Circles

Manitonquat
compiled by Kosha Anja Joubert

A world of beauty, a society of love, a life of abundance and joy are not mere fantasies. They are totally possible, assured, in fact, if the human race lasts long enough for everyone to learn the information we are sharing together here. Such a paradise is what Creation was meant to be, and all it requires is for us to apply what we already know. But we have to get going and move humanity quickly in that direction, because the threat of extinction on this planet is very real and very imminent. The purification prophesied by many of our old ones is inevitable. The only question is whether it means that we change or that we are obliterated.

Most people are aware of this crisis on some level. A few people are teaching and organizing to avert at least some part of it. Some have just decided to get what they can for themselves and let what happens happen. 'Eat, drink, and be merry'. I suspect that most people are terrified deep inside, but have shut off that terror because it seems hopeless and too painful. They are paralyzed and cannot even think of solutions. They feel it's all too big and complicated for one person to have any effect. The forces of destruction are too powerful and too entrenched.

Because of this there is a great void in effective human leadership, and this world of ours drifts on an unheeded course towards extinction. Look around your world. In your community, in your town, in your state or nation, on the international scene, where do you see the leaders who, in the hearts of their constituents, inspire change – change in the directions of peace, justice, love, cooperation, beauty and all the things we know are right?

I am going to suggest that your leadership abilities have not yet been uncovered. They are still under wraps, hidden even from you. If your full natural leadership were being exercised, if your true potential were in full force, I would know about you. You would be a shining light and a beacon to the world. Similarly, if I had developed all the potential that is my birthright as a human being I would have changed the world long ere now. I am working on it – seeing to my own circles quite well now, and expanding them all the time. Perhaps if we work together on this we can help each other.

Everyone is a Potential Leader

The fact is that everyone is a potential leader, and a good one. It is part of being human, part of our Original Instructions to be caretakers of the earth. Not to be dominators, hut caretakers, custodians. But almost nobody is living up to her potential as an effective human leader. Why is that? Well, what gets in your way?

Perhaps, like myself, you developed a resistance to the whole idea of leadership on account of bad experiences with leaders and authorities. We have been quite correct in being suspicious and questioning authority, given the history of civilization and where it has led so far. It is really hard for me to explain my concept of leadership in Germany, for example. In their language the word for leader is *führer*, the title adopted by Adolf Hitler. That's enough to make anyone shy of leadership.

But that was not human leadership. That was distressed leadership. Remember, there are two basic human emotions, love and fear. Hitler acted completely out of fear, and as a result created devotion in those who had the same fears and evoked terror and rage in all the rest of the world. If he had had the opportunity to express and heal his own terror and rage at an early age, he could have been an effective, loving, human leader.

This resistance to leadership made me look for groups that expressed opposition to leaders. For a while I thought we were doing great without leaders. But then I began to notice that whenever we did something well, there was always a leader – not in title, but someone who quietly took responsibility and did the thinking that was necessary to get the job done, presented proposals, asked for help, inspired and encouraged others.

I noticed that different people were drawn to coordinate different projects, and that they trained others to do what they had done and rotated into other jobs. Whether or not anyone carries the designation of leader, every project needs to have one person thinking about what is needed and coordinating, inspiring, and organizing. It's good if everyone in the group is thinking as a leader, but it is essential that at least one person do that. It is a good idea for any leader to encourage the leadership of everyone in her group. The more people thinking and inspiring others, the better.

So I would like you to put aside all resistance you may have had and admit that deep inside you are a leader. The world needs you. I need you. We need your support in changing the world, and we also need you to train other leaders. We have a lot of work to do, and we need to get moving.

It's your world. You are the centre of your universe. Creation put you there to take charge of it. It's in your nature to be a leader. It's time for you to take responsibility. For how much? For all of it! What? The whole universe? Right. It's your universe. You are responsible for it all. Your responsibility has no limits.

*If you dedicate
your life to
keeping one
place beautiful
and helping
a handful
of people to
realize their
full potentials,
you will be as
powerful and
as effective
as any leader
who influences
millions of
people directly.*

'Wait a minute,' you say, 'I can't handle all that – and anyway,' you may think, 'it's not in my hands … Only God can be in charge of it all.' Listen. Creation developed *your* mind, *your* heart and *your* will to take charge. No, you don't own the place, but you are the custodian.

The job is not as vast as it might seem. First you take care of yourself. Get yourself warm and fed and rested enough to have all your energy intact. Then you naturally look around for something more to do. You take care of your environment and the people you live with. If you never leave home, your influence will spread from there across the universe. If you dedicate your life to keeping one place beautiful and helping a handful of people to realize their full potentials, you will be as powerful and as effective as any leader who influences millions of people directly. But if you choose to go beyond that, by winning allies and supporters, there are no limits to what you can create in the world.

'I'm just not cut out to be a leader'

So now what gets in your way? A lot of people say 'I'm just not cut out to be a leader'. That's buying the notion that some people are born leaders and some aren't. The fact is, we were all born leaders, only something happened to us, and we lost it. What happened is that we got hurt as children when we received messages that we were inadequate in one way or another. Then we saw a lot of people becoming leaders for the wrong reasons: to get love, attention, to escape, to get admiration and appreciation. Some of us were told our thinking and ideas were stupid and wrong. Some of us were told we were lazy or selfish or greedy. Even when those voices were gone we carried them with us, believing them, believing we were inadequate, not smart enough, not good enough. We are afraid of responsibility because we might make a mistake and get blamed and humiliated the way we did when we were young.

If you have such ideas about yourself still, you need to understand they are all wrong, and they are holding you back. It's not easy to throw off a life-time habit of self-doubt in an instant, but if you understand how wrong those self-doubting thoughts are, you are on the way. You can commit yourself to stepping boldly forth as a leader. All your old terror will come up, but step forth anyway, shaking and laughing and telling everyone you are scared to death but you are taking charge. You will find many to support you, and your scorned fear will begin to loosen its hold on you.

You already have all the resources you need to be a good human leader. Your first resource is your understanding that Creation is good and is working through you to be better and better. That's evolution. The people who share this world are also basically good and are potential allies for you when you break through their barriers of distress and isolation. Your intelligence is a major resource available to you. You can always think. And your ability to make a decision will keep you from ever being stuck.

Training People to Take Charge of their Lives & the World

In my workshops, training people to take charge of their lives and the world, to become healers and teachers and leaders, I have a game I introduce as a tribal dance. Do you remember the children's game 'Follow the leader'? That is what we do as a dance with a hat. I tell everyone they must dance in imitation of whoever is wearing the hat. When each person gets the hat she moves and plays and watches everyone else being her until she has explored her own creativity in movement enough and passes the hat on to someone else who hasn't yet had it. I always love to watch this dance. I see people who have the idea they can't dance become outstandingly creative under the attention of others. I see people who are shy, who never talk, who retreat from any leadership, suddenly become new people under the hat and the respectful observation of their peers. They leap boldly out and delight in having everyone do graceful, expressive, funny, and wildly impossible movements. It's a wonderful game, showing that leadership can be fun. I offer it for your next gathering of friends. Watch the natural leadership in people surge to the fore.

Please realize that you are a powerful person. Where does your power reside? It resides in the fact that at every moment in your life there are a multitude of options, and you are completely free to choose any of them. Whenever you feel stuck, when things seem hopeless, remember you are free right then to choose a new point of view, one that serves you better, that makes you more powerful, more loving, more relaxed, more enthusiastic, more creative, or whatever you want to be.

Maybe you don't want to be a leader because you have held leadership responsibility before, and it wasn't any fun. You worried about everything, had to fight to maintain your authority, got cut down or blamed by others, or you had to do everything yourself if you wanted it done right. It's exhausting. I can understand. Leadership that way is hard.

But we don't have to set it up that way. You don't have to be a martyr or a tyrant or a workaholic to be a leader. Good leaders know how to pace themselves, to vary their work and to enjoy what they do, to play heartily, to rest deeply, and to get the help and support they need. Good human leadership is refreshing.

Thinking about a group beyond yourself is refreshing. It empowers your creativity. If you inspire others with your confidence and enthusiasm, you can delegate the work to others. People don't like to be ordered around, hut they do appreciate being asked for help. People are naturally cooperative. When they are not under stress, they are natural allies for you and for each other.

What Does an Effective Human Leader Do?

First, a leader inspires. She shows confidence and inspires confidence in others. She can communicate the value of the work to be done and the ability of the people to do it. She has integrity. Her words and her actions are consistent with each other. Her information is correct. She is committed to the group and to the task at hand. She is decisive and courageous and has stamina, but is also flexible and open-minded. She encourages the leadership of the others in the group. Above all, a leader loves not only the group, but each person it in, and she shows it. She breaks through the isolation, which accompanies all our distress. She holds the highest expectation for each member, knowing how capable and brilliant they are. She appreciates them in public, and she helps each one with getting rid of whatever is getting in her way. She inspires love with her love.

I know that's not what a lot of people who are supposedly experts in business and government think leadership is, but when I see really effective human leadership in operation, and it's fairly rare, that's what it is. Those experts still have a lot to learn. The new teachers of management skills are now stressing the values of cooperation, of paying attention to and eliciting the best thinking from all the workers. This has led to increased efficiency and output. I haven't heard of any teacher daring enough yet, however, to suggest that managers should actually love their workers!

What are the Tools You Need to be an Effective Human Leader?

Maybe the most important is listening. You can't think for a group of people, so you need to hear their thinking. You may be the one to organize and coordinate their activities, but most often they will have a good idea of what is needed in their department of the task. A variety of insights always gives you a broader picture, but there is another important reason why learning to listen, listen, listen is all-important: everyone is walking around with a lot of unexpressed feelings that they are eager to share with anyone who will pay attention to them for a few minutes. Even men who find it impossible to show their feelings can easily be encouraged to talk about something in which they are very interested and into which they have feelings invested. People have a natural intuition that expressing these feelings is healing for them, but, outside of therapists and clerics, there are few people willing to listen. Everyone is trying to tell you their problems. Successful hairdressers, bartenders, and cabdrivers have learned the value of listening, and people really let out all their problems on them.

There are two important reasons for you to listen to the feelings of people in your group. The first is that unexpressed feelings dominate people's consciousness and keep them from their best thinking. The second is that it is an act of love and caring, and you will be highly regarded and sought after as a friend and counselor, which makes your work as leader that much easier.

Another important leadership tool is the art of communication. A leader can articulate her concepts and ideas clearly, express goals in a way that excites and inspires, and encourage confidence, cooperation and affection in the group and for each individual.

Perhaps the most important tool is you yourself. Your own confidence, your own willingness to tackle the job, your enthusiasm for the work, your affection and respect for your co-workers, your courage and good humor, these all help set the tone of the group and the work. You also need an awareness of the past history of the group, a good grasp of the present situation, what is required now, and an inspiring vision of the future – an exciting and worthwhile goal.

Good human leadership means encouraging and bringing out the leadership potential in others, having the highest expectations for all that they can be. It means thinking well, not only of the group, but of each individual in the group, finding what's getting in their way, and helping them grow into their full potential as leaders. A good leader will welcome a bright, new, potential leader. If someone looks like she is out for your job, you will rejoice! That's just what you have been looking for. You want to train someone as soon as possible to take over for you, so you can move on and create new, more challenging and interesting work for yourself in the world, and teach her to do the same.

A good leader will take responsibility to change any feelings of powerlessness she may have, realizing it is completely in her power to choose her point of view, including that of being capable of handling any task worth doing. She will not blame any external conditions for her impotence. She will not wait for someone else to do it, someone who 'knows better' or 'whose job it is' or 'who has more power'. She will eliminate any dependency she may have on others, which stems from feelings of powerlessness. This includes dependencies on lovers, systems, government, and God Herself. However, a good leader will make allies for herself and for her group among other groups and other leaders.

She will take responsible leadership in every area of her life – at home, at work, in relationships, in community, nations and in the world. And she will decide to enjoy it all, to live every moment well and have fun.

As a teacher and a leader you yourself will begin to learn and to grow at a faster rate. Thinking of a group, of other people, of expanded possibilities makes your life richer and more interesting. Your understanding and creativity grow apace. In these days of crisis for our world, I am less interested in simply healing individuals so they can function well, and more interested in training people to be teachers and leaders who will teach others to be teachers and leaders and quickly bring an end to all violence, hunger, poverty, oppression, and injustice in the world.

As a teacher and a leader you yourself will begin to learn and to grow at a faster rate.

Does that Sound like a Task Worthy of You?

If it does, I am with you. I commit myself to be your ally and supporter in leading your universe to be the human paradise we all want it to be. Remembering that real power is not power over but power drawn from harmony with the Creation, let us walk together in a sacred manner upon a path of Beauty.

I can't guarantee that you won't make mistakes, and that it will all be easy. I can guarantee it will be the most interesting and challenging game you could find to play for the precious time of your life. Walking a Path of Beauty, the beauty and the power of your human essence will radiate from you, and others will want to know what it is you know and what you do to make you the way you are. If you have a circle, they will want to participate, and they will learn and grow from that, and perhaps want to start their own circles, which will create other circles in turn.

I am completely confident that together we will change the world. Together there is nothing we cannot do.

Manitonquat is an elder of the Assonet Band of the Wampanoag Nation. He has published five books so far. He is a former editor of Akwesasne Notes and Heritage, a native journal, and publishes an annual newsletter which is displayed on his website www.circleway. org. He is a director of The Nature School in New Hampshire and of the Mettanokit Native Prison Program that serves seven prisons in New England (a booklet about this program is downloadable free on the Internet).

In the summer months, with his wife Ellika, a Swedish actress and playwright, he presents workshops and international camps in seven European countries to give people an experience of living in the way his books propose. He has recorded six CDs of storytelling and poetry. A list of CDs and books, including his latest, *Changing the World*, can also be found on the website. All earnings from sales and travels are used to support the school and prison program.

Robin Alfred shares with us three principles that form the foundation for holistic leadership: the application of will, the practice of inner listening, and harnessing the deep wisdom of working in ways that are derived from nature and natural systems. This triangle is mirrored by the need to balance task, process and relationship in any endeavour.

Holistic Leadership

Robin Alfred

We face challenging times ahead. Climate change, international insecurity, and something approaching a crisis of meaning in our lives (the Word Health Organization estimates depression will soon be the second most prevalent and debilitating illness in the world, after HIV/AIDS). Living in community, and creating ecovillages, are two responses to this challenge, and when outer circumstances seem to conspire to make life increasingly demanding we also need to see whether we have created 'inner ' realities that sustain us.

This paper will suggest that the development of 'holistic leadership', i.e. leadership that seeks to develop sustainable processes and authentic relationships is one way ahead.

Background

Near to Findhorn, a traditional fishing village in northern Scotland, located at the point of meeting of the Moray Firth and Findhorn Bay, a quiet experiment has been underway for the past 44 years.

This experiment, started by Peter and Eileen Caddy and their friend, Dorothy MacLean, and aided and abetted by three children and the confines of an old caravan, was one of co-creation. Co-creating a life based on co-operation between the human, natural and spiritual realms.

This experiment led initially to the evolution of an 'unintentional' community and now to the creation of an ecovillage – a model for sustainable human settlements based on ecological, economic, social, cultural and spiritual criteria. Starting from nothing except one old caravan, and much faith and positive thinking, the community now has some £4 million worth of assets, 120 staff, and is supported and surrounded by a wider community of some 400-500. It is visited by over 10,000 guests each year, a significant proportion of who take part in residential workshops. In 1998, the Foundation's ecovillage project was accorded NGO status with the UN where it contributes to dialogues about sustainability, values and spirituality.

In the same year, it was awarded Best Practice designation from the United Nations Centre for Human Settlements (Habitat). Most recently, it has gained designation as one of only twelve UN centres in the world focussed on training planners, developers and politicians in sustainable development.

Key to all of this development has been the practice of Holistic Leadership, as embodied and exemplified by the three founders, Peter Caddy, Eileen Caddy and Dorothy McLean.

Holistic Leadership – three principals ans three

While Peter was a man of action and will, of strong intuitive sense, never hesitating to act on what he knew to be right, his wife Eileen was a meditator, someone who listened within and shared with Peter and the community the advice and guidance she received. They were complemented in these pioneering days, by their friend, Dorothy McLean, whose expertise lay in understanding nature's innate intelligence and acting in ways that acknowledged and enhanced this.

Diagrammatically, these three principles, of the application of will, the practice of inner listening, and harnessing the deep wisdom of working in ways that are derived from nature and natural systems are represented in Fig. 1.

Fig 1   Model of Holistic Leadership

'Masculine' Principle
Will
Task

(Peter Caddy)

'Feminine' Principle   Co-creation with Nature
Inner listening   Deep wisdom
Process   Relationship

(Eileen Caddy)   (Dorothy Mclean)

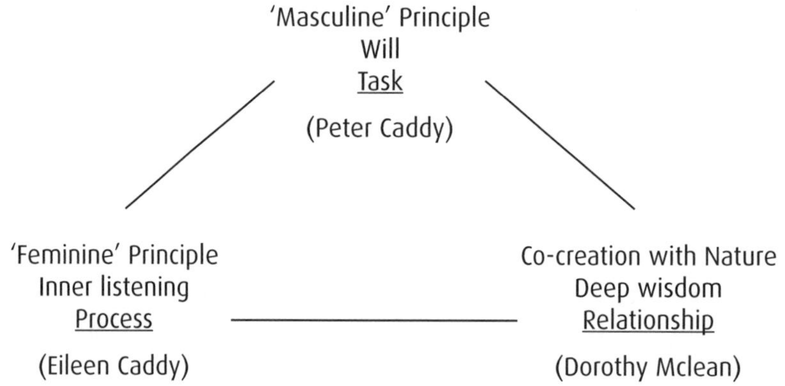

From this, we can see that not only does holistic leadership require a balance between the 'masculine', outwardly focussed will; the more receptive, 'feminine' inner listening; and working with, not against, nature; but that these three 'archetypes' can be translated into a more organizational language by focussing on the need to balance three aspects in any endeavour:

- Task
- Process
- Relationship

Fig 2   Model of Integral Leadership

Task	Process	Relationship
Vision	Decision-Making	Membership
Purpose	Meeting methods	Group dynamics
Product	Communication	Conflict facilitation
Goals	Supervision	Networks
Strategy	Feedback loops	Environment

It is to these we now turn.

Task

Of the three aspects of holistic leadership, task is probably the one we know most about. We are familiar with leadership that focuses attention and energy on the achievement of the task – on clarifying the vision and purpose of the community or organization, on developing the best quality 'product', on creating and reviewing goals and targets, and on developing strategies. This is invaluable. But on its own it is not enough. And this becomes particularly, and painfully, obvious when the circumstances that surround the community become challenging and difficult. At such times, we see the need to pay attention to the processes that are used within the organization, and to the quality of relationships (both internal and external) that are being developed.

Process

A leader who pays attention to the process will be interested in answering questions like these:

- **Decision-making**   Are the right people making the right kind of decisions, and how are they made? Are decisions made according to clear criteria? Do co-workers feel involved? Is their contribution welcomed and valued? How are decisions communicated?

- **Meeting methods**   How are meetings conducted? Are they well facilitated? Do they maximize the contributions of all those present? Do they create or sap energy? Are the 'hidden agendas' spoken to? Are the views of the shy or introverted sought out? Can everyone speak freely?

- **Communication**   How is information communicated through the organization? Do co-workers feel informed and up to date? Does everyone have the information they need to do their job effectively? Are the communication needs of minority groups taken into account? Does the community generally feel 'transparent' or 'secretive'?

- **Supervision**   How are staff supported, and supervized, in their work? Do staff feel valued through the provision of regular supervision?

- **Feedback loops**   Can everyone contribute their thoughts and feelings about what is happening in the organization, and how it is being led and managed? Are leaders skilled in giving clear and helpful feedback to co-workers about their work? Are co-workers free to offer constructive feedback to their leaders? What systems and structures are in place to facilitate open, clear 360-degree feedback?

Relationship

The development of high quality relationships, both within and without the organization, will serve both to make it a place of enjoyment and nourishment, and to enable it to be sustained through the inevitable challenges. The morale, motivation and good heart of its staff counts for so much.

- **Membership**   Is there clarity about who is a member and what their rights and responsibilities are? Clear boundaries and well-delineated roles are key to the development of healthy and productive relationships.

- **Group dynamics**   How does the group function? Does the Chair, group leader or facilitator pay attention to issues of power, roles, gender etc.? Are they able and willing to look at the issues below the surface, the things that everyone knows and gossips about but no one dares to voice?

- **Conflict facilitation**   Where there are conflicts between people in a team or within the wider organization, are these aired openly, seen as inevitable and healthy, and facilitated in such a way as to turn them into creative opportunities for learning and growth? Or are they seen as signs of failure and inadequacy, difficult and disturbing, and ignored or brushed under the carpet?

- **Networks**   What types of networks are being developed inside and outside the organization? Are they founded on the desire for gain and a competitive mindset, or are they founded on goodwill and collaboration? How much trust underpins these networks and how can this be developed and enhanced?

- **Environment**   Does the community seek to work in ways that protect and support the natural environment that sustains it? Is the environment valued as a fragile and vital living entity, or rather as a resource to be used and exploited? Do we relate to the environment as stewards and caretakers, or as people passing through who will take as much as we can? Are we aware of the environmental crisis we are in? What is our individual and collective response to that?

The willingness to face such questions is one of the many facets of holistic leadership. The leader does not need to answer them all, and certainly not at once. Her/his responsibility is to take the lead in creating a culture where such questions are alive, where co-workers can seek and practise the answers, and where the community is seen and experienced as a living, learning classroom.

Now, let's take a look at one example of this, and at the structures and principles that underpin the practice of holistic leadership in the Findhorn Foundation.

Structure

The Findhorn Foundation's organizational structure is quite common and traditional.

Fig 3   Organizational Structure of the Findhorn Foundation

As a charity it is formally run by a self-selecting Board of Trustees that delegates the day-to-day running of the business to the Management Committee.

What may be less common are some of the principles that underlie the structures. Here I highlight three:

- Method of appointment: Members of the Management Committee, who are the managers of their respective Areas/Departments, are all selected by those they manage. This helps to establish a degree of trust and common purpose from the outset. It is a principle that also applies, to some degree, to the appointment of Trustees, where nominations are sought from the staff as well as from within the body of Trustees itself.

When I applied for the post of Chair of Management, part of the appointment process involved my being 'interviewed' by some 60 staff members, at the end of which people were asked to indicate whether or not they supported my appointment. The fact that they unanimously did so was both extremely gratifying, and very helpful when we faced difficult issues in the months ahead. Whatever else were happening, the legitimacy of, and support for, my appointment was never in question.

- Duration of appointment: All appointments are for a fixed period, at the end of which the incumbent may seek to be reappointed. This aims to ensure that staff are not just initially appointed to the right job but that this continues to be the case throughout their period of tenure.

- Review and feedback: Appointments to key staff are reviewed, on an annual basis, by those they manage. Feedback is sought and the incumbent continues in post aware of how their work is being received. They may choose to adapt or not, but at least they are aware, and the staff have been able to voice directly their personal experience. Where the feedback is particularly negative, it is unlikely that the person will choose to continue in the post, knowing they do not enjoy the confidence of those they seek to lead.

Before leaving the question of structure, I want to pay attention to the role of one particular, work area, the **Spiritual and Personal Development Area**, highlighting the following:

- Training
- Supervision – individual and group
- Self-evaluation (focus on relationship between inner reality and outer task
- Conflict facilitation
- Values and ethics

Training

Much of this is 'preventative', i.e. designed to equip staff with the skills needed both to do the job effectively and to build the relationships that will support themselves as people and their ability to do the job well. All staff receive, for example, training in supervision skills (whether they are to be supervisors or supervisees) and in conflict facilitation.

Supervision

This covers both the provision of training (see above) and the provision of skilled 'external' (i.e. outside the line management structure) supervisors who may offer facilitation to a work group during times of difficulty and challenge.

Self-evaluation

Every staff member is offered an annual (and in the early days of their employment, more frequent) self-evaluation interview. While the work department will conduct more task-focussed appraisals, the Spiritual and Personal Development Area offers the individual the space to reflect on how their inner world (values, motivation, life purpose …) is or is not being reflected in their outer reality (in this case, their job). The staff member may or may not choose to then discuss this with their line manager but the organization as a whole is aware of the person's deeper journey, and this aspect of the person is seen and experienced as being of value and importance.

Conflict facilitation

As with 'supervision' this is both provided within the context of staff training, and offered to groups and/or individuals where conflict is being experienced. One of the values that everyone signs up to is a willingness to work on, and hopefully resolve, conflicts as and when they emerge.

Values and ethics

Beyond elaborating statements of values, the Foundation has evolved both a statement that sets out how we all aspire to live and work together (*Common Ground*) and an understanding that working with values requires more than the creation of lists of nice words.

Values

So, how do we make our values live?

Fig 5   Working with Values 1

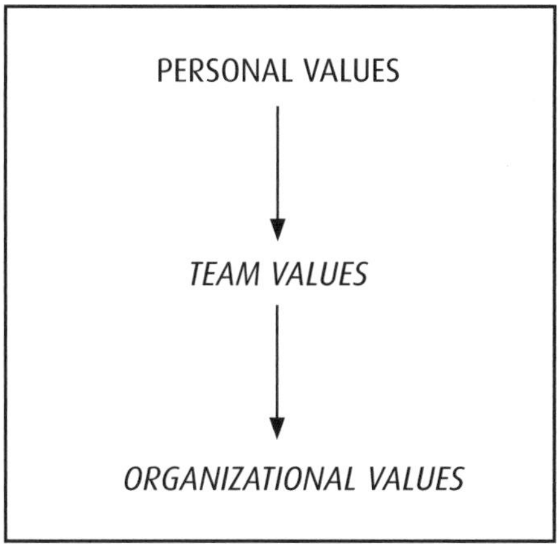

PERSONAL VALUES

↓

TEAM VALUES

↓

ORGANIZATIONAL VALUES

This diagram, or something similar may well be familiar. Many organizations use sophisticated tools to elaborate individual, team and organizational values. These tools may be sufficiently complex to enable both *aspired* and *actualized* values to be made visible, and even for levels of values to be seen (often based on Maslow's hierarchy of needs).

However, for values to be lived there needs to be an awareness of an alternative sequence:

Fig 6   Working with Values 2

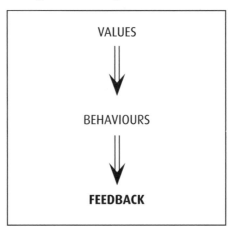

First, we need to translate the words into **behaviours**:

> *OK – integrity is a core value in this community. What does that look like? What are three examples of things we would expect to see in this community if the value of 'integrity' is being lived out? What are three examples of things we would not expect to see here if the value of 'integrity' is alive here?*

and then we need to ensure that mechanisms, and a culture, exist where effective **feedback** can be given and received on how the community's espoused values are actually being experienced.

Such feedback may be sought from within the organization (either through formal, planned reviews and consultations or through the creation of a climate where it is freely offered and received) and/or from other stakeholders through some form of social auditing and stakeholder review.

The creation of a culture where feedback is freely, regularly and openly given and received, will, in turn, require that attention is paid to:

- Rank
- Power
- Culture
- Communication skills
- Feedback skills

The role of holistic leadership in establishing this should, by now, be clear.

Conclusion

The practice of holistic leadership pays equal attention to task, processes and relationships; it understands and practises the appropriate use of will, the necessity of inner listening, and has the ability and awareness to harness natural wisdom; it gives an organization or community a foundation on which its dreams can be built and manifested.

The practice of holistic leadership … will raise questions of how much the individual and collective soul is alive.

The practice of holistic leadership will also, inevitably, promote the questioning of the community's purpose, of how it lives and embodies its values, of how much creativity and inspiration people can express in their daily work – in a word it will raise questions of how much the individual and collective soul is alive.

Holistic leadership makes space for the soul, both of the organization and of the individuals within it. Ultimately, this must lead to orienting at least part of the organization's purpose towards addressing the most pressing needs of humanity – to expanding its focus so that economic sustainability (Task) sits next to social responsibility (Process) and care for the environment (Relationship) and each aspect is seen as equally important, and each is integrated within the other. Such a practice will ensure not only that people are inspired, creative and valued in their work, but that leadership is appropriate to the times we are in, and will help to maximize the chance of survival, and even of flourishing, in the challenging times ahead.

For the author's biography, see page x.

4   Health & Healing ■

Dr Cornelia Featherstone, long-term member of the Findhorn Foundation Community, outlines how diet, exercise, work, spiritual practice, care, focus on life transitions, and even participation in decision-making and governance, all contribute to holistic health and its expression in community. She enjoins us to take full personal responsibility for our health and wellbeing.

Healthy Living in Community

Cornelia Featherstone

I have lived in the Findhorn Foundation Community for over 18 years and as a doctor have had many opportunities to reflect on the role of health in community. For me healthy living is one of the crucial elements of the ecovillage concept.

Beyond the personal benefit of healthy living there is the relationship it has with planet Earth. A healthy planet can foster the health of people and, equally, healthy people want to nurture and heal the planet as they are connected with their environment and can't separate their health from the health of the Earth.

What is Health?

It is easy to take health for granted as we go through our daily lives. Often we consider it only when it fails, when we experience disease or when our energy and life quality is not at a level that we want. To describe health positively is quite a challenge and medical school had certainly not prepared me for it.

The closest I came to an understanding of it was when reading about the Peckham Experiment[*] I grasped that health can be described as 'the ability to respond to all life situations in a way that increases capability, responsibility, autonomy, spontaneity and joy'.[†] With this definition I have a yardstick that allows me to assess where any action or decision made will take me on the spectrum of health – closer to health or further away from it. Qualities like self-empowerment and happiness become important outcome measures to assess facilities and care provided to the community.

Self-responsibility of the Individual

At the core of this approach to healthcare is self-responsibility of the individual. Only with self-responsibility comes empowerment and freedom. The individual can move beyond the state of a victim in a hostile universe

[*] The Peckham Experiment was an inspiring and innovative research project, located in Peckham, London, into the conditions that foster human health. Between 1926 and 1952 two medical doctors and their staff created a family club where many social and sports facilities were on offer to the members, alongside regular medical examinations which assessed the state of health in the individuals and the family as a whole. They created an environment that in their assessment nurtured health: a community with intergenerational contact and a great variety of opportunities for the individual to engage, learn, grow and make their own unique contribution.

[†] Innes Pearse, *The Quality of Life – the Peckham Approach to Human Ethology*, Scottish Academic Press, 1979.

where disease strikes and pending catastrophes have to prevented with drastic and often damaging measures, where life is determined by outside factors and death is the final defeat.

Self-care is a positive and nurturing aspect that brings healthcare into daily life. To counteract the stresses of modern life we can choose to have

- Simple, organic, wholesome foods in season
- An active lifestyle which keeps the body fit
- Time connecting with nature
- Meditation or contemplation for our own inner work
- Nurturing friendships and family relationships
- Massages or healings for touch and balance
- A clear purpose for life and an appreciation of our own contributions

It is the strength of the ecovillage concept that it can provide the individual with all of these.

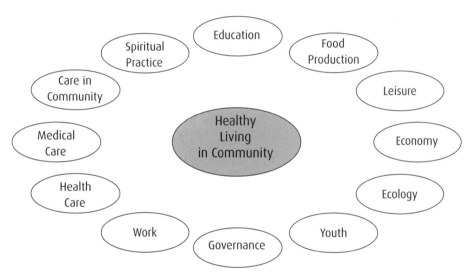

Healthy Living in the Findhorn Community

A day in the life of an ecovillage dweller – not everybody will do all these things every day – but the choice is ours – and the opportunities are there for me to make use of.

Connecting with spirit   Early morning meditation in the sanctuary allows me to connect with Spirit, with my own small voice within, that tells me that God is there in all for me to behold, that the intelligence of nature and other manifestations of consciousness are accessible to me – I just have to ask. Or I can go to Taize singing in the Nature Sanctuary to raise my voice in joy and devotion. Later in the day I can join group meditations or use the sanctuaries, special nature spots or wherever I am at that moment to re-connect and practise mindfulness, compassion or contemplation.

Exercise   A walk to the beach, some of us swim in the bracing Moray Firth every day from May through to November (!), or joining one of the exercise classes on offer. There is much choice: from yoga, tai chi, to dancing (modern, 5 Rhythms, sacred dance or belly dancing), to aerobics – at various times throughout the day. Some are classes, others are groups of friends getting together to support each other and have fun.

Food   A wholesome organic breakfast in a peaceful setting with my family, friends or by myself gives me sustenance to go into the day. Much of my food comes from the gardens and Earthshare (our Community Supported Agriculture project) – it is organic, local, in season, grown with love and with no food miles that cost the Earth. What the gardens or Earthshare cannot provide I find in the Phoenix shop – our community store which offers everything from the whole range of food to herbs, remedies, body care products to arts and crafts and books. My purchases support a local business that gives employment and brings wealth to the collective.

Work   My work inspires and fulfils me – I can express my care for my fellow human beings and for the Earth in a constructive way. I have the option of sharing about my inspiration, my concerns, visions or questions either in the work department or when meeting others. I know that my contribution is only one of many that make the whole community what it is and contribute to its work in the world.

Leisure   Arts, crafts and culture create a rich tapestry of joy, colour and social networking. We are blessed with several very active arts centres – the Universal Hall for the performing arts, the Findhorn Pottery, the Arts Centre dedicated to create beauty, the Weaving Studio. There is a crafts group supporting a regular crafts fair. Many different opportunities to make music, in different choirs, ensembles and bands or just *ad hoc* when taking part in 'community sharings' (evenings or mixed performances in the Hall) or in the 'Open Mike' on a Sunday night, when we can let the performer in us off the lead. Many community members use 'spare time' for volunteer work. In our money driven society it is healing to the individual to be giving freely without counting the return. It can be for the joy of doing things with others, or for the sake of the task at hand – serving people or the environment, or just to experience the joy of giving generously, willingly – as an expression of service or abundance.

Governance   The empowerment gained from having a say in the wider context of our lives is an integral aspect of our community. Sometimes we may groan about the number of meetings and presentations to attend but they offer us a choice to be involved, to have our voice heard, to shape the life of the ecovillage.

Health care and medical care In the ongoing process of change, health is not a static condition. There are many things we can do to enhance our present state of health. To bring positive change it is important to identify the small, manageable next steps we can realistically take to improve our health, be that a change in diet, activity levels or relationship patterns. The next step is to make a commitment to that change and establish a support and review structure that will allow it to become anchored in the daily routine.

Community support is essential for this – not only the infrastructure that offers a broad range of opportunities but also the social support to sustain the change. The community offers a wide range of alternative medicine that can support the quest for improved life style and better health. Alternative medicine is relevant for the treatment of minor ailments to reduce the use of chemical medicine that not only pollutes our bodies but also the environment (both in production and waste disposal). It also plays a significant role in the management of chronic illness for a lot of patients.

In a survey of patients attending their NHS health centres I have found that 71 per cent had experienced some form of alternative medicine, and 38 per cent had used some alternative remedy or seen a practitioner in the last month.[*] This percentage is much higher amongst members of the Findhorn Foundation Community. In a survey of 'elderberries', those over 60 years old, 100 per cent had used alternative medicine at one time and many were using it on a regular basis.[†] Many community members express a strong wish that the medical care provided by their family doctor take into consideration their health beliefs and that they may want to use alternative approaches to manage their health. This was reflected in a series of conferences we held in the 1990s that led to the formulation of the concept of Medical Marriage. Medical Marriage is a model for the new partnership between orthodox and complementary medicine where different specialists, coordinated by their family doctor, contribute to a patient's care.[‡]

Care in the Community

When I arrived in 1988 I found a community dedicated to work and service where everybody was 'pulling their weight'. A down side of that was that people no longer able to contribute felt that they might become a burden and left to go back to their family, or 'out into the world' where they were provided for. This applied to folks getting too old, too ill or young families. I personally felt this removed important aspects of life from the community experience and it was certainly not in line with a holistic lifestyle as I envisioned it. Fortunately I was not on my own with this vision and over the next 10 years I was involved with many aspects of care in the community which expanded the scope of living choices within the Findhorn Foundation Community and allowed it to blossom into a much richer fabric that we can enjoy today and perhaps even take for granted at times.

In 1992 I invited Ina-May Gaskin from The Farm to a conference and she issued the following challenge:

* Cornelia Featherstone, David Godden, Caroline Gault, Margaret Emslie and Marc Took-Zozaya, 'Prevalence study of concurrent use of complementary and alternative medicine in patients attending primary care services in Scotland', *American Journal of Public Health*, 2003; 93 (7), 1080-2.

† Cornelia Featherstone, Peter M Foster, 'The health needs of elders within an intentional community', *Community, Work & Family, 2000*, 3; (1), 103-9.

‡ Cornelia Featherstone, Lori Forsyth, *Medical Marriage – The New Partnership Between Orthodox and Complementary Medicine*, Findhorn Press, 1997. Available as e-book from www.findhornpress. com/ebooks/medmar

Only once a community has reclaimed birth and death can it realize the potential of self-determination and sovereignty.

Over the next 10 years we reclaimed birth and death in a very rewarding and enriching journey:

Natural birth and breastfeeding   My son, Kevin, was one of many who came into this world cradled in the love and care of this community. In 1994 there were four of us pregnant at the same time. We did yoga together and discussed both antenatal care as well as our birth plans. We ordered a birthing tub and crossed our fingers that we all would be able use it. And indeed the babies chose to come nicely one after the other so that we all could use the pool. When I went into labour it was on a cold February morning, in the middle of the community's internal conference. The call went out for hot water to fill the birthing tub and neighbours carried big buckets of hot water to our house. Loving thoughts and prayers were matched by much practical help throughout the day – food brought from the community centre, back massages for both myself and my partner, my 'birth bard' singing to me endlessly throughout the next 14 hours, keeping the pool at the right temperature and making a video of this magical event which Kevin enjoys to watch again and again. Homebirth has become a real option here in the community and many of us have chosen it over the years.

Loving thoughts and prayers were matched by much practical help throughout the day …

The support I received from more experienced mothers allowed me to establish a good breastfeeding pattern which was most rewarding for us parents and for Kevin. In a country where breastfeeding rates are still appallingly low the kids in this community benefit from the great gift of mother's milk for much longer than the kids in the rest of Scotland. It is not always easy but the support is there and women find themselves able to establish and maintain breastfeeding much better than the mums I meet in my NHS practice.

'Elderberries'   Looking after the needs of an ageing community has raised issues of inclusion and validation, sustainability, care at home and disabled facilities. We have several longstanding community members who had given many years of service to the Findhorn Foundation that may have meant low income and insufficient pension provision leaving the individual vulnerable. The Findhorn Foundation has ensured that there was no financial hardship by providing board and accommodation to supplement the individual's personal finance and pension income. Voluntary care as well as care/ funding provided by the Scottish social services has enabled each one to make their own choices within the resources available to them. For those living independently who feel vulnerable at times our Community Helpline, a volunteer service that coordinates neighbourhood help, is a source of reassurance and support. Several community members work as professional carers, allowing them to earn a living whilst looking after those requiring care. We realize the importance of making this community attractive to young people and finding ways for them to stay here to keep the flame of this community burning brightly. With a healthy age spread we ensure a more reliable provision for old age than financial pension plans (even though they are important as well). True human sustainability means a community can hold its vulnerable members and treasure the wisdom and beauty that they bring to any collective. Was it Henry Thoreau who said a measure of a society is the care it takes of those unable to care for themselves? It is a worthwhile measure to apply to an ecovillage. Not to demand of ourselves things that we cannot deliver but to have a yardstick for our maturity as a collective.

Death and Dying   Before 1996 death and dying were not an area where we felt particularly confident as a collective. The few deaths that had happened previously were mainly through sudden events such as accidents. We established a pattern of holding meditations to accompany the soul and create celebrations of life for those who had passed on. In 1996 the best friend of Eileen, one of the community founders, became very frail and required ongoing nursing care. We decided to try and hold her here in the community. With much volunteer help from community members in addition to support from a nursing agency we managed to fully care for Joannie for three months prior to her death. We then handed the body over to the undertaker as was done anywhere else and as we did previously. However there was a sense of incompleteness in not going the whole way with the process. When the next death occurred only five months later the next of kin who also lived in the community asked whether we could keep the body here and hold a wake. On a steep learning curve we found out what was involved in fulfilling the role of undertaker and managed to do it all ourselves. Following that, we organized a conference on 'Conscious Living, Conscious Dying' in 1998. We realized that there was a national movement* and learned a whole lot more about natural funerals with cardboard coffins and green burials. Since then we have had many opportunities to use our experiences in different ways. Sad as each occasion may be, being able to arrange the care, the rituals and celebrations as appropriate for each individual is a healing and empowering experience for all involved.

Summary

The resources, mutual support and holistic ecovillage concept allow the individual to move towards greater health for themselves. This will have effects on the collective as well as on the environment and therefore create a health-enhancing spiral. Health is as much a state of consciousness and mindfulness as of rightful action. All aspects of ecovillage life relate to health in one way or another – it is up to the individual to partake in whatever extent they choose.

* The Natural Death Centre, www.ac026.dial. pipex.com/naturaldeath publishes the *Natural Death Handbook.*

Cornelia Featherstone trained and qualified as GP in Germany. In the search for a more holistic, spirituality based lifestyle she came to the Findhorn Community in 1988. From 1989-98 she focalized initially the community's health department which then became an independent charity. In 1999 she decided to take up a part-time post as a GP in the National Health Service. She continues to be involved in the Findhorn community, she is the medical director of HealthWorks, a holistic health centre in Forres, co-author of *Medical Marriage – The New Partnership between Orthodox and Complementary Medicine* and has researched the nature and extent of use of complementary medicine by patients attending six Scottish NHS health centres.

The Cycle of Life
Birth and Death in Community

Liz Walker

A Blessing Way

We are holding a 'Blessing Way' to honour Poppy and Alison before they give birth. The two women are round and full and due within two days of each other. Poppy is very tall and dark-haired – a beautiful woman with great presence. At 42 she already has one daughter, who is 20. An artist, Poppy has her own part-time business, creating a beautifully designed line of organic cotton bedding.

Alison is in her 30s. Like Poppy, she also has one daughter, who is three. Alison has a beautiful smile that lights her face from within. She practises Buddhist meditation and offers tremendous support, wisdom, and love to those around her.

I am struck by the beauty of the two women – one tall, one shorter – as they sit side by side, both beaming, both with ripe bellies as round as watermelons. Wreaths of wildflowers gathered and woven by Sara encircle their heads. The white and pink flowers against their dark hair make them look like goddesses.

The rest of us, 12 women in all, sit on pillows around a special dark red cloth that is sprinkled with flowers and the images of strong women. Laura and Sara, who have organized the ceremony, begin by leading us in a ritual. We call in the spirits of the four directions and light candles for East, South, West, North, and centre. Special music that was played during another friend's Blessing Way and labour fills the room. I look over at this friend and see that her eyes are wet.

One by one, as we go around the circle, we offer a blessing for the expectant mothers and string a special bead on a necklace for each of them. I have brought two shells from a white sand beach in Costa Rica, and memories of a day of complete relaxation.

One shell is large and convex. It reminds me of Poppy and her round belly. 'It is big, bold, and beautiful. Just like you,' I tell her.

Jim Bosjolie

Alison and Poppy

Alison's shell is a lovely spiral, with an intricate gold and white pattern. "This represents your spirit," I tell her. I hope the women will carry the same sense of peace and calm into the days ahead that I felt on the day I picked up the shells from the beach in Costa Rica.

After the blessings we bathe the expectant mothers' feet in rosewater and massage their heads, shoulders, hands, and feet – six caring women to each woman. "This is like heaven," Poppy sighs.

One woman starts crying. "I wish I had had something like this when I was pregnant," she weeps.

I know that her experience – especially her first birth, which was a miscarriage – has been traumatic. The hospital staff had not allowed any friends to come into her room, and the baby's father was long-gone. She had laboured alone, knowing that her child was already dead in her womb. And to add to the tragedy, her recovery room was right across from the maternity ward, where smiling mothers rested with their healthy new babies.

"This Blessing Way is for all of us, for all women," I say, and the others agree.

We are touching something primal, recreating the art of women supporting women. We could be in ancient Egypt or a traditional village in Russia or a Native American longhouse. And our newly created necklaces – with their special beads, shells, and tiny dancing women made of clay – connect us to our ancestors, stretching back over thousands of years. We have stepped into the healing waters of Mother Earth to celebrate the creation of new life, as women have done since the beginning of time. We open the circle, and release the four directions as we chant, "Blessed be".

Birth

I am delighted when Poppy invites me to be with her during her baby's home birth. "So many times I've seen you think creatively and lovingly when someone is having a hard time. I'd like you to be part of my support team," she tells me.

Poppy's labour and delivery is a long-anticipated event. Alison gave birth five days after her due date, and Poppy is now nine days overdue on hers. She is restless and becoming increasingly annoyed by people's teasing, "Hey Poppy, haven't you popped yet?"

Sara calls. "The midwives say to come over, but please don't come into the room until Poppy asks for you." Sara is an obstetrical RN training to be a midwife and will be at the birth, too.

I hurry over and creep up the stairs, trying to be quiet and unobtrusive. I sit by the low wall of the kitchen and look into the living room where

Poppy is labouring. Two midwives, Sara, Poppy's husband Matthew, and their daughter all hover around her.

Time blurs. Poppy grunts and makes deep primal sounds through the contractions. And my body remembers the intense sensations of birthing my own two sons. I watch and wait and breathe along with her, supporting her even though I am across the room. I am tied to thousands of years of births and to the thousands of women who bring life into the world through this everyday, seemingly impossible miracle. For how else can birth be described?

Rain pours down outside, and Poppy's contractions surge through her in wave after enormous wave of effort. Between contractions she manages to climb into the birthing tub and sink into its warm water. We all sigh and wait for the next wave to take over her body. And take over it does. She pushes and pushes as hard as she can, but still the baby does not emerge.

Matthew holds his wife so that she can remain squatting position, but Poppy is obviously uncomfortable. She gets out of the tub, tries other positions. And although Matthew is young and strong, he is labouring, too as he holds up his six-foot-tall wife.

I decide that I can help by holding Matthew while he supports Poppy in a deep squat. The shift seems to work. Gradually the cervical lip that has been slowing things down disappears and Poppy starts to push again. But we can't sustain our positions for long. So Matthew moves against the wall, with Poppy leaning up against him.

The baby's dark head appears, draws back, and appears again. The room is electric with Poppy's effort and the imminent birth. One of the midwives holds a mirror so that Mathew and Poppy can see what's happening. It becomes clear that Poppy needs to move again – she is squatting too close to the floor, and there is no room to deliver the baby. Matthew, another friend, and I grab Poppy under her arms and heave her up. It takes all my strength to help hold her. But then I look down over her belly.

A powerful contraction grips Poppy's body, and the baby's head emerges, swollen and dark purple. Moments later the rest of the baby slips out, curled in a fetal position and still attached by its blue, unearthly umbilical cord. Poppy slips down onto the floor and cradles her newborn, exhausted and suffused with joy at the same time.

Watching them I can't quite believe that this live, complete human being has really arrived. I marvel at the little purple toes that gradually change to pink and the squinched-up face that has worked so hard to be born.

Birth, like death, connects us to both our animal natures and our spiritual selves. Yet our culture shields us from these gateways of human experience.

I have been reflecting on how privileged I am to have witnessed the birth of Poppy's baby. Birth, like death, connects us to both our animal natures and our spiritual selves. Yet our culture shields us from these gateways of human experience. What if we could all see children being born and the labour of the women who birth them? What if we could reclaim this human passage and bring it home to the community? What a gift that would be. I believe it would help reconnect us to the natural cycles that are such an essential part of our existence and return us to a wholeness that we long for.

The same holds true for death. While birth is a time of great rejoicing, death brings cause for mourning. But the process of dying can itself be a way to profoundly affirm life. Pamela Carson, the only community member to die thus far, taught us how it is possible to live and die with dignity, openness, and courage.

Death

Pamela was diagnosed with terminal stomach cancer shortly after she moved to our community. Stomach cancer is usually a swift killer, cutting down its victims in six months to a year. But Pamela fought long and hard. She had her stomach surgically removed, went through several rounds of chemotherapy, and managed to live for three years after she was first diagnosed.

The community stepped in to help Pamela all along the way. In fact, she often said, "I'm alive today because I live in this community." When chemotherapy nauseated her and she couldn't eat much (causing drastic weight loss), Seagull cooked tasty meals each day to tempt her. Marcie, a professional folksinger, serenaded her during her chemo treatments (amazing the nurses!). Sandra provided weekly Reiki treatments, and Suzanne gave massages. Many others visited, helped with transportation or shopping, or just looked in to make sure she was all right. And I met with her once a week for a delightful hour-and-a-half of creative writing.

Pamela was taking a women's writing class in Ithaca but often couldn't attend. So the instructor sent assignments home. We wrote for an hour or so and then read to each other from our work. It was a great way to get to know each other better. And I got to see a bawdy, zestful side of her that was not otherwise apparent.

For someone who was dying, Pamela packed a lot of punch. When she knew her hair would fall out from the chemo, she decided to cut it all off. But she did so in the best Zen Buddhist tradition, following the custom of head shaving practised by Buddhist monks. We were all invited to the ceremony.

Hair-cutting

It was summer, and the yard was decked out with colorful Tibetan prayer flags. A dignified Pamela sat facing us in a wicker chair that stood behind a low table covered in flowers. The ceremony began with some Buddhist chants. And then Pamela handed the scissors to a close friend of hers from the Zen monastery in Rochester. As Karen snipped off

Pamela's beautiful curly white hair, I felt grief, knowing that my friend did not have long to live. But I was also very moved by the beauty of the event.

Pamela was turning a deep loss into a devotional act. She was letting go, releasing her attachment to her looks as a sort of precursor to letting go of her physical body entirely. She was also modeling a way to maintain her center through her frightening illness and reclaim her power to be fully alive and alert while facing her imminent death.

Pamela did not confine herself to a private event, either. She believed in making the most of publicity if it meant that what she had to teach would reach a broader audience. So it was that a report of her strikingly original ceremony made the front page of the local paper, complete with an article and accompanying photo.

Pamela believed in making the most of publicity if it meant that what she had to teach would reach a broader audience.

A few weeks before Pamela's death, her friends organized a living memorial for her in the Common House. The whole community showed up, although Pamela herself was too ill to attend. People brought their favorite foods and dressed up in elegant clothes for the occasion. Her sister Gail, a former opera singer, sang beautifully. Someone brought a video camera and interviewed people about Pamela's special qualities. Once dinner was over we gathered in a circle to share stories, some light-hearted and some serious.

It was a poignant evening, knowing that we were gathering together our memories of Pamela and celebrating her life while she was still alive. And that, like Huck Finn, our friend could watch her own memorial. In fact, Gail took the video home and reported that Pamela enjoyed watching it many times.

By October Pamela was close to death, and I went to visit her at her home one last time. She was no longer conscious, and a thin line of spittle ran down her chin. Her breath rasped in and out of a body that looked white and waxy. She looked like she had aged 20 years. Tears coursed down my cheeks as I held her hand and whispered my last goodbye. Her eyelids flickered, and I hoped that she could still hear me.

How many of us ever see someone as they are dying? Even in her last hours, Pamela was modeling tremendous openness, giving us the gift of witnessing her death. I left and went for a walk on the land, feeling fully alive and in tune with the world. As I walked I was thinking, This is a good day to die. A few hours later Pamela was gone.

But that was not the end of the story. Pamela, organizer that she was, had planned her own elaborate memorial service. She had arranged for the church, pre-printed programs, chosen people to speak, and picked the songs she wanted sung. The service was held several weeks after she died.

Pamela's memorial was beautiful. And, as usual, her capacity to do the right thing extended even to this final act of her life. Her service gave the whole community a chance to come to closure over her passing.

For the author's biography, see page 64.

*Patch Adams, clown, doctor and social
innovator, argues that the use of humour,
and designing spaces in community
that promote fun and laughter, can help
prevent and de-escalate conflict while
strengthening the glue of community.*

Using Humour to Heal

Patch Adams

Laughter is the Best Medicine

Humour is one of the most important tools in social intercourse. There are no areas of human endeavour that are not improved upon with a healthy use of humour. It is commonly said that 'laughter is the best medicine'. I would like to suggest further that humour is also potent medicine for a healthy community.

Whether one's conflicts are with oneself or others, humour can soften conflict and help move the dialogue along. A humourless person can put a great damper on conflict resolution. If we are unable to laugh at ourselves, many unnecessary conflicts will rise and fester. A common theatre trick, and great social tool, comic relief is there to speed resolution in the most profound of situations. (One never says 'love relief' or 'wonder relief'. The word relief is reserved for humour, the great worker for peace.)

That it is often called disarming implies humour's potential to wage peace. I recall Monty Python's great comic skit about the joke so funny that whoever heard it laughed to death. The military got hold of it and war stopped.

Laughter has been called infectious, implying it spreads rampantly in its environment, another useful characteristic for a conflict resolution tool. There are laughers that can turn whole rooms of people into a laugh-along. When people are laughing they are physically and emotionally vulnerable – maybe even to new ideas, and thus the resolution of conflict.

Humour has been seen as so important in human relations that for centuries in the west, ruling courts had fools and jesters to break tensions and create certain moods. The fool was the person privileged to be honest and confront royalty.

Clowning for Peace

I have been an intentional clown for over thirty years. I live in clown clothes on a day-to-day basis. Selfishly, I want to create a context of humour, fun and play around me, for the raw fun that grows out of such behaviour. However, the commitment to daily clowning publicly grew out of my life as a social change artist. Once I saw the social potential of joy and laughter and how it helps people relax, become more talkative, and softens the tension of strangers, I decided to *be* joy and fun as a political act to help prevent conflict and speed the germination of community.

Good communication is often a behaviour learned after many horrendous mistakes.

I have this theory that public playfulness prevents violence. In over thirty years, every time I have seen an adult and a child fighting in public, slipping into my clown self usually stops the fight instantly. I know my playfulness has stopped fighting in rough bars and protest marches. I think we also see this pacifying effect of fun and laughter at places like Disneyland where people tolerate endless lines with glee; and at Mardi Gras where even though many are drinking heavily and are tightly packed, violence rarely breaks out.

The first thing I would like to emphasize about the value of humour in conflict resolution is its role in the prevention of conflict. Human relationships are very complicated and we get little to no education in growing up on how to do human relations well. Good communication is often a behaviour learned after many horrendous mistakes. It rarely occurs without precious intent. Conflict arises out of misunderstanding, fear, or mistrust. It is best handled in a context of close human intimacy -friendship where one has a vested interest in the wellbeing of the other. When long-term marriages and friendships have been studied to see what factors help keep them together and vital, a sense of humour has been found at the top of the list, before love and security.

The Gesundheit! Institute

I lived communally for 25 years. I started the community and in the mission statement, one of our seven principles was that all activity would be infused with fun. Ours was a very intense, crowded community that was also a hospital for its first 12 years. I knew, especially since we charged no fees, that to prevent burnout and keep my staff, I had to make the life in the community more fun than the alternatives.

Out of this grew the first silly hospital in history. Huge ridiculous events, often centered around staff birthdays, were staged as rituals to bind the community together. Everything was fodder for fan. There were meals served out of pig troughs, silly dances in the gardens. We enjoyed rooms filled to the ceiling with balloons; a wedding where gender roles were reversed and the groom wore a bridal gown. The human relations grew very intimate and I am sure this intimacy is at the core of why these relationships still thrive 25 years later. I know the fun has been what has kept me thrillingly involved.

In every job that must be done, there is an element of fun, you find that fun
and snap, the job's a game …

MARY POPPINS

Patch Adams making new friends in China

Of course, humour is very individual. There is no universal humour. Each group must find their own sense of humour and play, and then do it. Ideally the group would see the value and allocate time and funds for the raw pleasure of play for its members. Ideally, each group would value this equally with the work of the community. Work done in a context of fan moves more smoothly and can be sustained longer. A certain amount of caution and rigidity must be abandoned in order to play and laugh; this relaxation can make for softer conflicts. One can hope that each group has several funny people to see to it that humour comes to every meeting and conflict. Other options are to take very sensitive subjects and make playful games, skits, etc. around them. Jokes play this role in our society where the most frequent jokes are about our most sensitive areas.

Our communal home was a hospital and many who stayed with us had some mental illness. Profoundly unusual behaviours peppered our group life. It was our wish to deal with these problems without medication. We let very anxious, even disturbed (dangerous) people stay in our home in large numbers. Some of our most creative medical work was done in these situations. By relentless compassion, humour and vulnerability, we often saw horrible conflicts resolved. We made it fun to work with people that most of the society shuns.

We found humour was appropriate to life's greatest turning points, toughest conflicts. It was not unlike me to go into a dying patient's room dressed as an angel with a harp and wings and say 'Coming attractions!'

I've done field research on conflict resolution and humour. For 13 years I've taken an annual tour of 30 people (ages 12-80) to Russia to clown. In two weeks of 10-16-hour days, we visit hospitals, orphanages, prisons and public places. No clowning experience is required. I take 30 strangers and put them in a new and potentially stressful situation: very long hours with profoundly sick and dying youngsters, and heart-rending exchanges with children saying 'please take me home'. Yet humour turns painful into positive. The clowns get a relentless graphic experience that humour is a powerful social context – whether planned or spontaneous. I believe the humour given and received and the results seen have made these trips magical for most.

Designing for Fun

I would like to offer a few suggestions for individuals and groups who wish to put more humour into their lives and conflicts:

- Each person might embark on a journey of self-discovery. Find what is fun for you, and put these findings into practice. If indeed humour is important, it's essential for each person to develop and act on their own sense of humour, and expand its borders at all times.

- Make laughter, fun, and play a basic ethic of your community. This is not a frivolous decision. Time and money must be allotted for this humour in action. A party is not an indulgence, rather the liturgical celebration of community.

- Design into your environment places that are for play. There arc all the obvious, indoor and outdoor playgrounds, but also costume trunks, toy closets (child and adult), stage prop collections. Places like lakes, tree houses, fields and gazebos are fertile ground.

- Nurture and attract those members of the community who bring a natural sense of play. Make an effort to find and keep guests whose presence leaves the same impression. This new fun blood is very important over the long haul.

- Creativity attracts humour and play. Value all aspects of art and creativity as essential to community life, not as luxuries.

- Put great effort towards the deepest of friendships. Watch the role that humour has in making that possible. You may notice that, among friends, especially long-lasting ones, humour is a cement. So much humour is tied up in the memories of a community.

- Have a fantasy jar and encourage group mates to put into the jar descriptions of fun events they would like. Dip often into the jar and act accordingly.

- Take a huge number of risks toward being foolish.

- Once conflicts arise, do not belittle them by 'laughing them off'. Communicate them in several ways. Make sure everyone has his or her chance to speak. The point of humour is not to gloss over the intensity, rather to provide a ground where all can be communicated and resolved. Be receptive to lightening up on the subject no matter how involved. I've encouraged couples fighting to go ahead and say things, but try it all while naked, and jumping up and down.

- Be patient with people who are not funny. Everyone can be.

Patch Adams MD is the founder and director of the Gesundheit! Institute, a 25+-year-old project to address the problems of health care delivery in the USA. Fifteen thousand people passed through from 1972 to 1983 alone. He never charged any money and he never accepted health insurance or carried malpractice insurance. He integrated all the healing arts and to present a wellness context, he integrated medicine with performing arts, fine arts, crafts, agriculture, nature, education, recreation and social service.

Patch has been a public clown for over thirty years, using humour and joy as potent tools for conflict resolution. A film based on the life of Patch Adams, starring Robin Williams as Patch, has recently been released to critical acclaim and the proceeds from this have enabled Patch to realize his dream and begin building his ecologically designed community hospital. Gesundheit! Institute, 6855 Washington Boulevard Arlington, Virginia 22213 USA

5 Local, Bioregional & Global Outreach

Broadening the Ecovillage Movement

Robert Gilman
interviewed by Kosha Anja Joubert

In 1991, you set out a definition of an ecovillage that was to become a standard. You defined an ecovillage as a:
- *Human-scale*
- *Full-featured settlement*
- *In which human activities are harmlessly integrated into the natural world*
- *In a way that is supportive of healthy human development, and*
- *Can be successfully continued into the indefinite future.*

Fifteen years have passed since then. What was your vision then, and what is it today?

My vision then, which was fortunately shared by many people, including Ross and Hildur Jackson, was that a time would come when most of society would both want to and have to live in better harmony with each other and with the natural world; that we would both want and need more wholeness in the microcosm of the immediate human-scale community around us. In that definition I was envisioning a 'new mainstream' of both towns and city neighbourhoods that would take many decades to emerge. My vision is the same today. The only difference is that we have all learned more about such human-scale communities and we are closer to a time when these can grow into being the mainstream for human settlement.

What do you see as next steps for the ecovillage movement?

As I said in my presentation at the GEN+10 conference, I see most of the communities that are part of GEN, and that often call themselves 'ecovillages', as centers of research, demonstration, and teaching, but not 'villages'. This is meant as an observation, not a criticism. The first step needed to be such 'laboratory' communities. I am happy to see still more of these centers of research, demonstration, and teaching come into being, *and* they will find their fuller purpose as we also shift more attention to retrofitting existing towns and neighbourhoods. For me, the next step is to help such existing regular communities discover their ability to fulfill the various parts of 1991 definition though sustainable living in community.

How can we mainstream the ecovillage-experience, the idea of sustainable living in community?

The essential first step is to see ourselves in a complementary, rather than a superior, relationship with those who are leading 'mainstream' lives. Many of the people who are doing wonderful things in various GEN communities are personally willing to be quite bold in their lifestyle experimentation. Yet if you look carefully at this, it often becomes clear that their experimentation is possible because the larger society provides a more stable context – thanks to all of those mainstream lives.

The next step is to see our communities, not as complete unto themselves, but as centres of research, demonstration, and training that *need* their complementary relationship with mainstream communities to fulfill their mission.

Beyond, I recommend finding willing partners in existing mainstream communities and build from there. Go first where you are welcome and welcome those who are already interested.

How can we keep the essence of the movement true while reaching out into mainstream?

A lot depends on what you feel is the essence. If you feel the essence is 'alternative', if you associate the essence with a feeling of having 'found your tribe' or with that quality of being willing to boldly experiment with your life, then you will have a hard time keeping that essence and being effective in reaching out into the mainstream. You can serve better by staying in the laboratory.

But if you see the essence as the desire to live in harmony within yourself, in harmony with your neighbours, and in harmony with the natural world, then you have an essence that is more universal.

Today's ecovillage movement has both a personality and an essence. If the movement starts to include more mainstream communities its personality will change – perhaps to the disappointment of some of its current members. I believe, however, that we can both keep and grow deeper in our understanding of the essence. The appeal of sustainable living in human-scale communities is very broad.

If you see the essence as the desire to live in harmony within yourself, in harmony with your neighbours, and in harmony with the natural world, then you have an essence that is more universal.

I can see that what the world needs more than building new structures is retrofitting the old, physical as well as social. How can social structures, designed to fit a hierarchical, highly individualized and socially isolating society, be retrofitted? How can a weak civil society, with self-absorbed citizens be revitalized? In villages? Suburbs? Cities? In the US? And in other parts of the world?

So much depends on changing the patterns of communications, and often that means opening channels of communications that are now either non-existent or weak. Specifically how this is done and which channels need to be opened depends on the situation. For example, a village in the global South may have good internal communications (although important links may be missing if you look closely enough) but the village suffers from a lack of good communications with the wider world. In North American suburbs you have the opposite problem. 'Hierarchical, highly individualized, and socially isolating' is a description of communications patterns as well as the social structures that are built on these patterns. Introduce new communication patterns and the social structures will also change.

Which methods of communication have you found most helpful in your work within Langley?
- *In 1-1 communication*
- *In groups*
- *When communicating with the world 'outside' the community / ecovillage*

I would say that what has been most helpful has been to use many different methods of communication. In Langley we use:

- Intentional 1-1 face-to-face conversations
- Spontaneous 1-1 conversations on the street, in the post office, etc.
- Telephone conversations
- Scheduled small-group meetings (less than about a dozen people)
- Large-group 'town meetings' (from 40 to well over 100 people)
- Online web-based conferencing
- Email
- Video (on DVDs) of previous meetings and presentations.

These all play a role and their strength is in the way they mutually reinforce and complement each other. In each of these we do our best to set a tone of respect and inclusion. Everyone has an opportunity to communicate, and with so many channels, no one is able to dominate or control the communications.

In an article from 1985, called 'What's Needed: What we need to know and do to be effective cultural midwives', you wrote: 'The strategy is thus simply this: Be aware of our historical situation, become completely at home with the skills and spirit of win-win group process, and then apply these skills to building new model institutions, seeds for the future.' Are you applying this strategy in Langley?

Yes. In applying this strategy in Langley, we are also doing what we can to translate our ideas into terms that local people are comfortable with and move at a pace that the community can assimilate.

Can you define steps for successful local outreach for communities?

It begins internally with your own 'beingness'. What is the self-story that you tell yourselves within your community? Are you sufficiently at peace with your own life-path that you can celebrate the life-paths of others? Can you see your community and the surrounding society as

Town Meeting

complementary partners in an evolutionary process? How much of your motivation for outreach is based on fear and how much is based on love and a confident inner peace? I am not suggesting that you need to be 'perfect' before you can step out. Rather it helps to have some self-awareness of your own human limitations to bolster your compassion, humility, and patience.

The next step is to find partners in the local communities who already see the value of what you have to offer. Build out from there based mostly on practical, locally relevant activities. Focus more on the quality than on the size of your projects.

Listen a lot. See yourselves as co-creators with your partners, co-creators of something new that combines strengths from both partners. Don't expect mainstream communities to become carbon-copies of your community. Rather, experience the creative delight of unfolding the deeper essence of 'sustainable living in community' in new forms.

As you listen, you will likely discover opportunities to be helpful. Jeff Bercuvitz has wonderful advice in his article on Community Animation (http://www.context.org/ICLIB/IC33/Bercuvit.htm). His five-step app-roach is: think big – start small, take stock of your assets, have fun, just do it, and ripple out.

As you do this, keep looking for ways to open up fresh channels of communication. These may not be as 'dramatic' as new buildings or other big projects, but they may have more lasting effect on changing the system.

Patience is hugely important. Keep remembering that you are part of a long human adventure and that the current 'Great Turning' on the planet extends over decades, indeed centuries. This is not a short-term emergency that needs to be fixed so that you can get back to 'normal' life -- the planetary transformation *is* your life.

How can we lower the threshold for people to become involved?

Compared to the huge step of joining an intentional community, almost anything you can do to help retrofit an existing community will be easier for most people. It is great if you can offer a 'menu' that provides different levels of commitment and personal change. That way people can decide for themselves what is a doable, meaningful step for them. My sense is that it is better for many people to have success with small steps and then be eager for bigger ones than it is for them to feel challenged by big steps they may not choose to take.

How do you see the future of the broadening ecovillage movement evolving?

With a lot of love. If we can see our goal as fostering sustainable living in community and celebrate the many different forms that essence can take, we will be in good shape.

In organizational terms, I see a growing 'ecosystem' of groups playing different roles in the movement – everything from the 'on-the-ground' centers of research, demonstration, and training; to specialized consulting groups, to urban neighbourhoods, to towns and villages, and to various networks and associations weaving these together.

As the ecovillage movement broadens, it will encompass a wider diversity of political, philosophical, and lifestyle points of view. If our hearts are big enough to hold this diversity while we actively engage with all of the challenges within us and around us, then the ecovillage movement will be a great blessing – for all of us.

Dr Robert Gilman is one of the midwives of GEN. In 1991 he and his late wife Diane wrote the report for Gaia Trust, 'Eco-Villages and Sustainable Communities,' and then worked with Gaia Trust to lay the foundation for GEN. A former astrophysicist, in the mid-'70s he decided that 'the stars could wait but the planet couldn't' and shifted his attention to global sustainability, futures research, and strategies for positive cultural change. In 1979 he and Diane founded Context Institute (www.context.org) to focus on these issues. Today, he is translating ecovillage concepts to the mainstream as a City Councilman in the small town of Langley, Washington. He and his new wife Lianna are also among the co-founders of the Langley Community Forum, an innovative face-to-face and online 'open space' that is changing the character of governance in their town (www.langleycommunityforum.org).

Capra makes the case for a spiritual activism that involves engagement in local and bioregional politics. She describes politics as the art of balancing human and environmental needs and describes how global and national initiatives need to be applied at a local level.

Politics as Spirituality

Capra Carruba

To understand how communities can influence politics, on a local level and beyond, it is best to look at concrete examples. In this article I describe what has worked for us in Damanhur, in the hope that our experience may be helpful for others. We call the translation of our philosophy into politics 'bio-regionalism'.

Our concept of bioregionalism is based on the presumption that, within the environment, there is a harmonious balance between all forms of life, including human beings, as regards territory, resources, economy and society. Politics is the capacity to bring these different aspects together. All elements have to be reconciled with one another. Evolution means to constantly improve this balance. Politics means bringing order, and creating advantages for all involved, improving the life of all and avoiding stagnation. Life means movement, change and transformation. This is the basis of our concept of spirituality.

If you deal with spirituality, you also have to deal with politics; otherwise you lack what is needed to carry these aspects into society. Dealing with politics is a logical consequence for us. We are different from more radical groups who generally consider politics to be corrupt. It is true that politicians move in a different world with its own particular rules but we choose to put certain principles into practice, to act instead of waiting for others do it. In this sense, we begin with concrete action, initiatives that are integrated into already existing activities. The only possible road is one of moving forward together.

First Steps

We wanted to find people or political movements that were open to our vision of life. In the early years, we contacted people rather than political parties. The major interests and politics of Italian political parties are complex. It is best to find individuals who have proven political capacity. After speaking with all sides we found a few people who were more independent from the party they belonged to. We exchanged ideas about programmes, projects and visions.

During the last few years this experience has proved both difficult and interesting. At a certain point it was no longer sufficient to present ourselves as motivated and open-minded volunteers, as an interesting group ready for innovation and experimentation. It became important to found our own political movement. The focus for us was not the creation of a political party but a political movement, which we founded in 1995 as 'Con Te per Paese' (With You for the Country). This gave us a platform from which

Local demonstration by Con Te per il Paese on residency rights

to propose ideas and to cooperate with others – first of all with individual politicians rather than political parties. The majority of 'Con Te per il Paese' members are Damanhurians but the association is also open to others. We see ourselves as a political movement which is active all over Italy and we are open to working together with other political movements on a European level. Within 'Con Te per il Paese', we have applied the same principles that characterize the philosophy of Damanhur: an open mind, thinking big, far reaching projects that go beyond the present situation, long-term goals that bring about useful benefits at a local level. This typical Damanhurian vision has produced good results over the last ten years.

Our Process was Gradual & Systematic

We have always participated in politics at a local level. Since the mid-'80s we have had representatives on the local town council of Vidracco. In the beginning only one councillor represented Damanhurian citizens in this small town of 500 people. A leap took place in 1995 when four Damanhurians were elected on to the council and since 1999 Damanhurians have formed the ruling majority with a Damanhurian as Mayor. We also participated in the local elections of other towns and over ten years we have been elected in nine districts. We now have 22 elected council members.

Our goal is to revive the life of the valley. We proceeded systematically at first by analyzing the political, economic and geological resources of the area. This led, for example, to the installation of a double water circulation system in Vidracco, in order to reduce wastage of good drinking water and provide a separate system for gardens and car washing etc. Many measures were of a purely practical nature: improving street lighting especially for the

elderly population to whom more light means more security; or providing incentives for voluntary work, which has allowed us to organize care for the elderly and our own Red Cross Station, operating 24 hours a day.

Vidracco Council meeting.

Vidracco also has its own volunteer Civil Protection team that intervenes on behalf of the population in cases of bad weather, water shortages, snow and other emergencies. We are also involved in the management of town planning which has been remodelled according to ecological interests. It is now possible to use materials and architectural elements such as glass walls to collect solar energy as a prerequisite for energy saving houses. Such innovation was not foreseen by the old planning regulations.

How Local Politics can Influence National Politics

We are closely involved with local initiatives. Working at a local level helps us to understand what is applicable and what is not. The principle is always the same: We seek to apply national, and sometimes global models and initiatives at a local level. Even a small territory needs to move like an entire nation. For example, we are suggesting that major agreements, like the Kyoto Protocol, are now ratified in our valley instead of waiting for the official order from national government. This is also true for using renewable energies, reducing pollution and waste management, as has already been realized in many other European countries. Now we have door-to-door collection of separated recyclable waste in the town and have significantly reduced the quantity of dumped refuse.

A region can apply the same principles as a nation. Regional examples can become a model for the entire country, demonstrating that alternatives can work well. This way politics becomes more alive, dynamic and based on experience rather than rhetoric.

Bioregion in Balance

Small and traditional forms of local production are crucial in meeting local needs.

We need concrete solutions that meet the needs of the population. Let's take mobility: You cannot simply demand that people do without private cars – an alternative must be suggested which raises the quality of life. The goal is always to increase the quality of life for the entire area. What is at stake is not only the balance of the Earth, but also the wellbeing of the local population. Small and traditional forms of local production are crucial in meeting local needs. This guarantees the quality of services and the quality of food.

The Region has to develop autonomously not in an isolated sense but freely deciding how it wishes to exchange with the rest of the world. Bioregionalism is a concept of exchange and dialogue. We do not want to create happy islands detached from the world and its problems. What is needed is exchange, a politics that looks in all directions, that satisfies both the body and the mind and includes art and culture. This is only possible through good communication. This is the vision that we contribute to the Green Party as well as in local townships, councils and bigger entities like the Region of Piemonte.

Going Green

Over the last ten years we have also participated in the politics of the Province and the Region, participating in assemblies and collaborating on evaluations of political programmes. The only political party that comes close to our political vision is the Green Party. We do not agree on all points but we have many elements in common. This collaboration is still fairly young and has only become solid over the last two years. Today almost all Damanhurians are members of the Green Party and we have officially joined a political party – something we have never done before.

Why have we decided to do this? We are in a race against time. Even though we have always participated in politics, it was obvious that things accelerate once you are organized and with 'Con Te per il Paese' – we have had concrete successes. The greater our presence and direct participation, the more things have proceeded. After a Damanhurian was elected Mayor of Vidracco it became obvious that direct participation brings greater results and faster. We chose to join the Green Party so that we could introduce our ideas; to promote the fact that politics must always unite big ideals with practical solutions that can be applied at local as well as a regional and national level. We have introduced our ideas, ideals and proposals within the Green Party in order to see them realized more quickly.

But it has been far from easy. Interacting with the Greens is a complicated and difficult business because the party already has its own structure. There have been discussions, confrontations and let's say 'dynamic' situations which are not always easy because within the Green Party, as in all groups, there are different factions with different interests. We entered a rather lively situation contributing our experiences alongside everybody else's proposals. It has been a great challenge to transmit our holistic understanding of the environment, which does not see human beings and the economy as inevitably in conflict with the protection of nature.

Remedy & Strategy: a Joint Effort

We see politics not as an individual concern, but as one that needs to be organized by homogenous groups, which share similar ideas. You cannot improvize programmes and projects. What is needed is structured discussion, elaboration and exchange. Most of all politics needs individuals who are capable of developing concrete and realisable proposals.

We organized a weekly meeting to bring together elected councilors with people who are interested in politics but have no official role. Within a few months we created a workgroup of thirty to forty people. The minimum amount of time invested is two to three hours a week. This is enough to involve people and develop ideas. It is also useful because it allows those with an official role to have an outside perspective. This confrontation is fundamental because it generates ideas, proposals and offers of support. Within an organized group you can discuss and confront the most important issues and take a position. We also use voting by a show of hands in cases of opposing points of view. This way of working is simple but effective. Decisions are taken together and supported by all.

Within the Green Party we move in this spirit. An organized group (Con Te per il Paese) carries more weight than an individual's point of view. We have a Damanhurian elected on the National Council of the Green Party. This body consists of approximately sixty people and discusses major issues at a national and international level. Another Damanhurian sits on the leading council in Piemonte. We also participated in the regional elections in support of the Greens. Obviously within Green Party meetings we do what we have always done: contribute our point of view. We are not interested in a passive presence. We want to contribute our experience, ideas and proposals. Our proposals are based on pragmatism because they derive from our experience as local council members. We understand the problems of the local people and the economy of the area. Perspectives and suggestions always have to be practical and verifiable at a local level.

'Con Te per il Paese' Election Campaign Statement

We support technological research, when technology is at the service of evolution, and does not disturb the ecological balance. We do not agree with conservatism or a return to the past.

GM-free Vidracco

Attention to the environment is fundamental. We demand a stop to the use of genetically modified organisms. This is not in opposition to research, but all choices must be made with maximum security in mind. We demand that genetically modified organisms (GMO) are tested on a long-term basis before they are used on open land.

The quality of food is fundamental as far as the improvement of the quality of life for human beings and animals is concerned. Organic agriculture oriented towards quality creates new markets for producers of organic products.

We support fair trade, which in our terms includes: control of products, prioritising products on the basis of fair trade, supporting small, local producers who guarantee this ethic. In our area we have contributed on a small scale by declaring Vidracco a GMO Free territory, applying a logic that could be applied to a much larger area.

We want support for renewable energies at a national level and beyond that support of technological research to improve materials – in other words, to focus on ecological decisions, which also become economic decisions. We support small power plants producing renewable energy instead of large power plants that are hard to control (like nuclear power) and create serious pollution.

Our vision of society is multi-ethnic, uniting people ready to act. This means respect for all individuals independent of their origin, religion or colour …

Voluntary work is one of the instruments we propose at a local and regional level, because it orients society towards solidarity.

Our latest move: the recognition of associations and communities by national and regional governments as caretakers of specific areas including the delegation of the right to govern.

Summary

We support a bioregional perspective for areas such as this valley but also for the Province of Turin and the Piemonte Region. Bioregionalism blends with the Damanhurian vision of a society in transformation, where consumer habits, social structures and relationships to nature are profoundly changing.

The Mayor of Vidracco in Shenzen, China, receiving a United Nations CCC Award on behalf of Damanhur for its sustainability programmes and ability to integrate into the local area.

For many years we have promoted a vision of the environment where there is balance between human beings and the environment. If there is separation, a conflict is generated between the environment and human beings, which may lead to unbalanced choices, as the last fifty to sixty years demonstrate. A perspective of either/or, promotes the interest of one side to the detriment of the other. Joining both aspects together is a philosophical matter. It means considering the environment as a single organism, a holistic concept, and one we cannot go beyond.

This article is based on an interview with Roberto Sparagio, journalist and member of the town council of Vidracco. He is responsible for tourism and ecology. He has lived in Damanhur for over twenty years and is known as Coboldo Melo.

Christine Schneider was born in 1968 in Northern Germany and has lived, since 2001, in Damanhur, where she chose the name Capra Carruba. She has studied political science and has worked as a consultant in Organization Development and training. In Damanhur, Capra is the contact for international communities and is in charge of the ValdiChy project (www.valdichy.org), assisting friends of Damanhur from all over the world to settle in the valley. Capra teaches Esoteric Physics, plays the flute and accompanies guests through Damanhur. Her great research interest is what makes communities work, translating the experience of Damanhur to other/future communities.

capra@damanhur.it

Using the tool of 'Outcome Mapping' Agnieszka Komoch argues that paying more attention to the conscious design of our networks will enable us to more effectively realize our purpose. We will be better able to influence the mainstream from our niche; engage with the world around us, expand our boundaries and be conscious of our edge.

Alliances at the Edge
A Roadmap for Social Change

Agnieszka Komoch

Networks & Edges

Networks are often seen as means of exchanging information, stimulating learning and reaching out to gather support for a project. The emergence of networks in the last decades points to the fact that they fulfil a need. However, we often think of a network as a horizontal, homogeneous, ever-expanding web of contacts, where we encounter likeminded people with whom we feel safe and acknowledged. In this form a network might loose some fertility. Just as in permaculture, where the designer pays particular attention to the edge (or the boundary) between two elements because this particular area is key to diversity in any ecosystem, there is a richness of exchange and encounters happening 'on the edges' of any given project. Conscious design, when creating support networks, might help access this richness.

One question to ask when building relationships and strategic alliances relates to the purpose of any given relationship. What do we want to achieve? Get people to take actions against GMOs? Obtain funding for the project? Change the local development plan to be able to build an environmentally friendly low impact co-housing project? Influence the national policy regarding CO_2 emissions? Whatever the purpose is, we need to think about our influence and ways to increase it. Influence has a lot to do with resources, endurance and often with one's rank or status, but it can also be linked with our capacity to establish the right alliances and partnerships.

Web of Connections

The first step in the conscious design of networks is to assess all the connections we as participants in the project have, identifying likeminded people and organizations, as well as those who we need to influence in order to advance the cause. In general, relationships of influence occur where diverse worldviews meet. If among our web of contacts we can identify those whose actions and attitudes we need to address in order to make a change, we are already mapping out the edges of the project and its sphere of influence. This is the area of creative tension, where we deal with diversity and have the opportunity to make it work to our advantage. Diverse points of view, even adversaries, are needed to sharpen the edge, revise messages and strategies and expand our worldview.

Some criteria that can be useful in the process of mapping out our contacts and their potential contribution to the project are:

- Expertise
- Power of decision-making
- Access to funding
- Contacts with authorities or other groups
- Interest in the project
- Willingness to engage directly

Often, when setting up a community oriented project or advocating more sustainable lifestyles we face opposition or mistrust, e.g. from local government, the church or from neighbours. Our adversaries, just like our supporters, need to be included in the process of mapping out the web of connections.

In practical terms five questions are useful in such an analysis:

- Who are the project's natural allies, supporters and, equally, potential adversaries?
- What are their interests and goals? (Are there any mutual benefits; how far along the road can we meet the opponent; how would it be to be in their shoes?)
- With whom can we work directly? In other words: who is within our reach?
- Who are we hoping to influence through the project?
- How can we include them in the process?

Some relationships are naturally strong. Others will require considerable effort to bear fruit. Terri Willard and Heather Creech in their book *Strategic Intentions** talk about the following elements of **engagement strategies**:

- Providing information: at this initial stage information is disseminated to make decision-makers, the broad public and institutions aware of the project and its goals.
- Nurturing relationships: following up on enquiries, face-to-face meetings, formalising contacts, engaging in conversation, reflecting together and responding to requests.

* Terri Willard and Heather Creech, *Strategic Intentions – Managing knowledge networks for sustainable development*, International Institute for Sustainable Development, Canada 2001.

- Joint actions: e.g. finalising an agreement or jointly identifying ways of advancing the project.

These are time- and resource-consuming tasks and we cannot always be sure that the outcome will be what we really hoped for. However, the power of alliances also lies in the unexpected and in our ability as a group to deal with surprises and unplanned results.

Outcome Mapping

Outcome Mapping,* a method for planning, monitoring and evaluation which has been used worldwide by NGOs, community groups and institutions, has introduced the concept of 'boundary partners'. These are people, groups or organizations with whom we work directly and whose actions, attitudes and relationships we hope to influence and ultimately change. No doubt this can be seen as a controversial concept, but what is interesting is that this category makes us focus on relationships, points to power imbalances and issues of control, draws our attention to available resources and ultimately brings us back to the vision of the world we want to live in and makes us aware of the type of change that needs to happen in order to bring us closer to making that vision a reality.

Outcome Mapping can be useful in long-term projects because it outlines the paths leading to the realization of the vision, starting with building relationships. Once the web of contact has been analyzed, boundary relationships singled out, and needs and possible contributions identified, the project members can formulate the **desired outcomes** for each boundary partner. Depending on the context and nature of the relationship, this can happen together with the potential partners. Transparency, the ability to engage in dialogue, the capacity to communicate one's needs and expectations and conveying the role we foresee for others, increase trust and the likelihood of a buy-in. Ideally the partners should have a chance to bring in their own perception of their role, and the outcomes from the relationship that they feel are within their possibilities and resources. This is how we can bring participation and dialogue into the project and at the same time have the opportunity to size up its relevance.

How Does This Bring Us Closer to the Vision?

* Put together by Sarah Earl, Fred Carden and Terry Smutylo of International Development and Research Centre (IDRC) in Canada, Outcome Mapping served as an inspiration in writing this article.

Simply because we are interconnected, because our boundaries change constantly as we interact, and because a critical mass is needed to create a permanent change of state. It is important to remember that change, the big 'tipping point' we dream of, is made up of small steps. These can be assessed, monitored and hopefully traced back to the actions we have implemented.

Being aware of the process of change is just as important as the ultimate result. The path is the goal.

Deliberate change of course does not happen without a considerable effort on our side. Our contribution to the process of change we envisage can be more effective if strategies are focused on those within our sphere of influence and their behaviours. As the next step in the Outcome Mapping process, team members can brainstorm about what they can do to instigate the desired changes in attitude, relationships and actions of boundary partners. There is a clear 180 degree change of perspective here: from looking at what the project needs to make the vision happen and who we need to work with, we focus on the strategies we can implement in order to foment the change in others.

It is important to remember that change, the big 'tipping point' we dream of, is made up of small steps.

Alongside the strategies of engagement outlined above, Outcome Mapping suggests six types of strategies:

Strategies aimed at particular groups, individuals or organizations:

- What can be done to produce immediate output? e.g. providing information about the project, presenting research results, and good practices from other contexts. In other words: things you do to 'convince, tell and sell'.

- What will be done to build capacity? e.g. convening meetings and trainings, provoke new thinking.

- How will sustained support for the boundary partner be provided? e.g. mentoring, support network, providing regular guidance.

Strategies aimed at the groups, individuals or organizations environment:

- What will be done to change the physical environment or policy? e.g. access to higher powers, establishment of guidelines and incentives.

- How will you use the media or publications? e.g. creating pressure from outside by using the media.

- What networks/relationships will be established or used? e.g. alliances with networks and bodies able to influence.

The strategies used will, of course, be dependent on the type of relationship. They will vary if we engage with a local authority, start a support network or try to obtain support from experts. They do not have to be seen as prescriptive. They do, however, help us become aware of the resources and our potential, and make influence tangible.

There are a multitude of tools that are useful in project design, in branching out and engaging in developing new, often challenging relationships. Outcome Mapping is one such tool. However, what makes it different is that it deliberately calls attention to the fact that when we, as project members, embark on this path we interact, learn, gather experiences and evaluate them – we change as well, as we are also being influenced and change our activities, attitudes and relationships. The change we bring about flips back on ourselves. This is a two-way process in which mutual learning can, all of a sudden, become a reality.

Case Study: the Ecovillage of Lebensgarten

The ecovillage of Lebensgarten in Northern Germany has recently faced challenges related to plans of opening a motorcross park just 2 km from the settlement. The park would be designed for city dwellers wanting to enjoy motorized sport during the weekends. This project was perceived as controversial if not directly threatening to the continuing existence of the community, not only because it would mean increased traffic, noise, pollution and risk of vandalism, but it also questioned the values of the community and the standard of life created there over the 20 years of its existence. As a pioneer in solar energy, having put the first solar car in the whole region on the road, Lebensgarten is a promoter and an example of a lifestyle that preserves existing resources, rather than exhausts them for the sake of a quick ride. The area designated for the development has mainly been untouched by humans since the 1960s and with its 13 km² become a biotope where many endangered species found their niche. Used as an ammunition factory during the Second World War, the place witnesses death and suffering of thousands of workers from Eastern Europe and the spirits of the nazi past weight heavily over the whole area. All that taken into a consideration, we thought that the place deserved something better than being run down by adventure hungry bikers.

… we thought that the place deserved something better than being run down by adventure hungry bikers.

We decided to take action, when we one day saw the project being announced on the municipality's website and articles in the local press talked about it as if it was already happening. Rather quickly we identified our allies and potential supporters from the village of Steyerberg. Each one of the community members analyzed their personal contacts and we realized we had connections to Friends of the Earth, regional politicians and economists. We knew that we could count on particular persons in the village (the ones that always supported Lebensgarten) but that it would take an effort to get the support of the broad public, who most likely passively would welcome the project. It was also clear to us that little help was there to get from the local politicians (who were already making the project their flagship even before it was officially approved by the town council) and the town mayor. With years of training and practicing non-violent communication and mediation, it wasn't difficult for the community members to adopt an attitude of openness and dialogue towards the promoters of the project. We knew that it was unwise to create 'us' versus 'them' dynamics or focus on differences. We focused on finding common grounds and a true win-win solution for all involved. That piece of land is after all an enormous resource, which could enhance the region even more, if its use was designed with the needs of its nearby inhabitants in mind. We saw it as our civil duty to start a debate about sustainable development in the region, inform the inhabitants, involve them in the discussion and put pros and cons of the motorcross park on the table. We have analyzed what the different stakeholders in the project (the municipality, the inhabitants of the village, the shopkeepers and the hotels) would gain from it and although the project would not reward local businesses considerably, we realized that we needed to create (and publicize) a vision for the land that would be far more attractive to everybody and economically viable as well.

After a couple of meetings we designed a plan of action, primarily targeted at the investor and the villagers. At the same time a competition for an alternative development plan for the land started.

Through our analysis of allies and supporters we were able to count on assistance form the local chapter of Friends of the Earth (FoE) and a specialist in tourism development. They brought in the dimension of legislation regarding endangered species as well as the latest information about current trends in leisure activities in Germany.

Our strategies aimed at the villagers and the investor

- Producing immediate output
  - (a) Villagers and the investor: we presented the facts about the project, p the reports form Friends of the Earth and research about trends in tourism in Germany which did not promise any economic gains from motorcross parks to neither investors nor local businesses.

- Building capacity: through the dissemination of reports and information about alternatives we did present a more nuanced picture and new awareness emerged among our boundary partners
  - (a) Villagers: we called for public meetings and facilitated the discussion.
  - (b) The investor: following the advice from FoE a group of senior community members invited the investor (and the town mayor) for a walk through the woods bordering with the area, presented our point of view and tried to persuade him to abandon the project.

- Sustaining support for the boundary partner
  - (a) Villagers: we started to create a civil society which would be based in the village and welcome the villagers wanting to inform themselves or voice their concerns (whether pro or contra the project); we offered our facilities for meetings and designated contact persons.
  - (b) The investor: we kept the communication line open.

Strategies aimed at the environment of the villagers and the investor

- Strategies to change the physical environment or policy:

    We were not in position to change or establish policies, which could influence the villagers nor the investor.

- Use of the media:

    The press was fed with all the information; community members wrote open letters, which were published in the local press.

- Networks/relationships established or used:

    We established closer relationship with the archive documenting local history from the war times; invited experts, created stronger links with FoE, contacted befriended regional politicians, hoping to provide more qualified information for the investor and the villagers.

We will never know what kind of effect these strategies had. A couple of months later the investor, for unknown reasons, decided to withdraw from the project. Needless to say: we were relieved. However we did take notice of one unexpected outcome: when plans for windmills and a biogas utility for the same piece of land emerged some months later, Lebensgarten was consulted first.

Agnieszka Komoch has worked as independent consultant with organizations and institutions, which propose concrete solutions to our present environmental and social crisis. Themes of her work include ecovillages and complementary currencies among others. She was actively involved in Global Ecovillage Network, helping establish its European branch during five years.

Agnieszka has an MA in Latin-American Studies and Semiotics from universities in Denmark, Spain and Argentina.

info@ultimoround.com · www.ultimoround.com

5 Local, Bioregional & Global Outreach

Bioregional Outreach
Educational Outreach
Global Outreach

235

Daniel Greenberg, the founder of Living Routes, shows what academia and ecovillages can gain from one another. Together, we can transform higher education into a rich soil that grows knowledge and projects that support the regeneration of our planet.

Ecovillages – Academia

Daniel Greenberg

We are living in a unique time, not just in human history, but in *planetary* history. From the war in Iraq to the war on rainforests; from global markets to global warming – it is clear we *must* learn to live in ways that honor all life. Yet, as a species, humans seem almost evolutionarily unprepared to address the global issues facing us. For the most part, business is going on as usual; governments– at best –are thinking ahead only to the next election; and, as Oberlin Professor, David Orr has said, 'We are still educating the young as if there were no planetary emergency.'

We now need to move beyond the industrial era and begin to train leaders for the 21st century – leaders who know how to *heal* the Earth and build durable economies and sustainable communities. But how? Einstein once said, 'We can't solve problems by using the same kind of thinking we used when we created them.' So perhaps we also need to move beyond the ivory towers of traditional academia and create campuses and pedagogies that are better able to educate for a sustainable future.

Worldwide, ecovillages are striving to create high quality, healthy life-styles *and* low ecological impacts. These ecovillages are developing and refining ecological and social tools such as community-scale renewable energy systems, ecological design, organic farming, holistic health and nutrition, consensus decision making, and mindfulness practices such as yoga and meditation.

Ecovillages are increasingly being used as 'campuses' where students learn about sustainability while actually living it. Ecovillages such as Crystal Waters (Australia), Findhorn (Scotland), and Auroville (India), and in North America such as Sirius, EcoVillage at Ithaca, The Farm, and Earthhaven, have already had considerable successes as educational centers and in creating ongoing partnerships with government agencies, research centers, and schools of higher learning. And organizations such as Living Routes are helping to build bridges between ecovillages and academia by creating college-level semester programs based in ecovillages around the world.

Why Academia needs Ecovillages

To understand why ecovillages offer ideal campuses for sustainability education, we need to compare them with traditional universities. Regardless of what classes students take, the following list illustrates the hidden curriculum, or 'metanarrative' as Chet Bowers would call it, that students learn simply through their day-to-day participation and involvement:

Living Routes students engage in a sharing circle at Sirius while preparing to travel to Auroville, India

Conservative vs. Experimental

Universities tend to be burdened by cumbersome bureaucracies and are slow to change. In fact, the basic structure of universities has not significantly changed since the Middle Ages.

Ecovillages are physical and social 'laboratories', experimenting with new technologies, social structures, and worldviews. They tend to have a trial and error mentality and are quick to adjust to changing conditions, challenges, and opportunities.

Hierarchical vs. Heterarchical

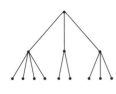

The power structure of universities is very top-down, with power emanating from the president down to the provosts, deans, faculty, and – at the bottom rung – students. The hidden agenda is one of 'power over' and submission to authority, which is consistent with the conventional attitude that humans are meant to dominate and subdue nature.

In ecovillages, there is a wide diversity of relationships and members tend to interact on more or less an equal footing. Individuals might cook a meal together one day, sit in a budget meeting another day, and perhaps help harvest vegetables on yet another. These interdependent sets of relationships help members get to know each other on many levels and better understand the complexity of living systems.

Competitive vs. Cooperative

Universities are competitive on all levels – among students for the best grades; among faculty for grants, tenure and recognition; and among schools for prestige and endowments.

The sense of belonging that students experience within ecovillages both awakens and fulfils a need that many did not even know they had.

While competition exists within ecovillages, the norm tends toward co-operation with members assuming as much responsibility as they are willing to handle. The success of individuals is typically viewed as inherently tied to the success of the community as a whole.

Fragmented knowledge vs. Transdisciplinary

Universities have responded to the exponentially increasing rate of knowledge generation with ever more sub-specializations within disciplines. Pat Murphy, director of Community Service in Yellow Springs, Ohio, refers to the 'silo' mentality of higher education where institutions 'stockpile' knowledge within discreet containers that are functionally isolated from each other.

Ecovillages recognize that real-life issues rarely exist within the boundaries of disciplines. For example, the decision to put up a windmill requires knowledge within the fields of appropriate technology, engineering, regional and community planning, governance, and even sociology and anthropology. The decision to create an organic farm crosses disciplines of agriculture, nutrition, philosophy and ethics, business, education, and communications among others. While able to train specialists, ecovillages are uniquely positioned and equipped to train much-needed *generalists* who posses 'lateral' rigor across disciplines to complement 'vertical' rigor within disciplines.

Academic Community vs. Living Community

Many students claim that 'gaining a sense of community' is a primary motivation to attend college. While this is certainly available, it is also true that most relationships in academia are mediated by specific, rather narrow roles – student/teacher, fellow researcher, classmate, etc.

If a sense of community is the goal, wouldn't it be more fulfilling to immerse oneself in a 'living' community where members have a wide range of relationships, hold a common vision, and are committed to each others' long-term growth and development? Small class-size, the use of authentic assessment methods, and the creation of 'learning communities' in which students have opportunities to deeply reflect on and share about their experiences further support their learning and growth.

I believe humans are 'hard-wired' for community and tend to resonate with human-scale institutions in which they can both know and be known by others. Margaret Meade, the noted anthropologist, observed that for 99.9 per cent of our evolution, we lived in tribes. Many people in modern, 'developed' countries have lost a sense of community so thoroughly that their closest acquaintances are characters on TV shows. The sense of belonging that students experience within ecovillages both awakens and fulfils a need that many did not even know they had. And once nourished, this sense of belonging tends to expand to include ever broader communities – both human and non-human.

Theoretical vs. Applied

Academic types tend to stay in their heads – and their armchairs – and maintain a detached, theoretical perspective of the world. Researchers use the myth of 'objectivity' as a rationale to stay removed from their subject matter and, consequently, often create knowledge, but rarely wisdom.

Ecovillages, in order to survive and prosper, must focus on practical knowledge and wisdom that can be applied in real-world settings. Theory is in the service of 'what works' rather than the other way around. Ecovillages are inherently 'experiential' – a word that many universities are loath to even use. Students often claim they learn more through internships and service learning opportunities than in even the best seminars.

Secular vs. Spiritual

Not only are most universities very hands-off, they also tend to separate our heads from our hearts – and typically only care about our heads. Consequently they tend to support a Cartesian view of the universe as a soulless machine to be manipulated and controlled by humans.

While some are explicitly religious, most ecovillages embrace a larger, more eclectic spiritual container in which members are supported to be 'in process' and engaged with large questions of life and meaning. Yoga, meditation and silence are common features of many ecovillages and students on Living Routes programs have pursued vision quests as a way to deeply reflect on their relationship with themselves, each other, and the world.

Students at Findhorn meet with long-term member, Craig Gibson in an underground Kiva

Large Footprint vs. Small Footprint

Universities are beginning to incorporate more ecological design and building, but for the most part they are still incredibly resource intensive institutions and not very attuned to their impact on their region or the world. Recycling and compact fluorescents are recent phenomena on many campuses and very few campuses even attempt to buy food locally, not to mention organically.

Ecovillages strive to live well, yet lightly. While many assume ecovillages aspire to self-sufficiency, this is rarely accurate. Most look to their bioregion or watershed as the unit of land and culture that should become more self-reliant. Ecovillages often serve as regional catalysts for reducing ecological impacts by supporting local initiatives such as organic agriculture and local distribution networks so resources do not have to be shipped great distances.

Cross-Cultural vs. Cultural Immersion

Most campuses enroll students from a variety of cultural backgrounds. Yet typically these lifestyles and traditions are subsumed under the melting pot of the academic culture with few opportunities for cultural expression or exchange.

In ecovillages, perhaps because they are 'living' rather than 'academic' communities, there tends to be fuller expressions of members' cultural backgrounds through festivals, rituals, language, and food. Even further, in traditional, indigenous ecovillages, students have the opportunity to truly

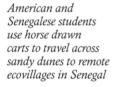

American and Senegalese students use horse drawn carts to travel across sandy dunes to remote ecovillages in Senegal

immerse themselves in vivid and full-featured cultures that both honor the past and are consciously reaching towards the future. For example, on Living Routes' programs in Senegal, US and Senegalese students join together to explore sustainable community development within indigenous ecovillages, which provide rich contexts for cross-cultural exchange and understanding. These programs are frequently life-changing experiences in which students experiment with and adopt wholly new ways of being and thinking.

Problem Oriented vs. Solution Oriented

Last, but perhaps most important, universities tend to be primarily focused on dissecting and understanding 'problems'. It is obviously critical that we continue to study and better understand the serious local and global issues facing us. But there comes a point when students 'get it' and need to either *do* something about it or risk becoming overwhelmed with negativity and despair. Worse, some students even become emotionally numb in an unconscious effort to defend their hearts against the seemingly insurmountable social and environmental problems facing humanity and the Earth.

Some students even become emotionally numb in an unconscious effort to defend their hearts against the seemingly insurmountable social and environmental problems facing humanity and the Earth.

Ecovillages give students important opportunities to be a part of the solution and learn how they can make a positive difference in the world. They are not utopias, but after spending time living and learning in an ecovillage, students can never again say, 'It can't be done', because they see people wholly devoted to right livelihood and creating a sustainable future. It then comes back to students to ask themselves, 'What am *I* going to do? How can *I* make a difference in my own life and in my own community?'

Why Ecovillages need Academia

The above comparisons may seem like an argument to run, not walk, away from traditional academia, but there are also important reasons to build bridges and work together.

First, academia is changing. With an increasing internationalization of the curriculum, interest in community partnerships, and recognition of the need for ecological design and interdisciplinary research, universities are beginning to see ecovillages as natural collaborators. Also, technological changes such as the internet and distance learning are making the large infrastructures of campus-based universities increasingly irrelevant and out-dated.

Second, universities are not going away anytime soon. In the US, higher education is approximately a $350 billion/year business. That's the GDP of Belgium! And this is not counting the *trillions* of dollars invested in facilities and resources. And universities are where the students are! Two out of every three high school graduates in the US go directly to college and nationwide more than 16 million students are currently enrolled. Worldwide, there are approximately 88 million college students (more than the population of Germany!) and this number is expected to increase to 100 million by 2010 and possibly 150 million by 2025.

Third, ecovillages need help in order to reach their highest potential. As advanced as ecovillages are in terms of providing campuses for sustainability education, I believe they are still in *kindergarten* in terms of what is truly needed to educate professionals capable of building the institutions and systems required for a sustainable world to be possible. While programs offered through Living Routes and individual ecovillages are a good start, we need to further collaborate with academia to create 'communiversities' where students can spend *years* in ecovillages and other related organizations and gain the background and skills needed to enter the workplace as professionals in fields as diverse as appropriate technologies, habitat restoration, sustainable agriculture, group facilitation, holistic health, ecological design and green building.

The fourth, and most important, reason for ecovillages to reach out to academia is that college-age students represent a powerful leverage point in the world's 'Great Turning toward a more Ecological Age', as Joanna Macy refers to it. Many talk about members of the college population as 'emerging adults' in that they are mature enough to ask the big questions yet also open to radical alternatives and new life directions. Emerging adults are key to the dissemination of emerging paradigms and the world desperately needs leaders who are able to think – and act – outside of the box. The novelist Frederick Buechner once wrote that, 'Vocation is the place where one's deep gladness and the world's deep hunger meet.' Never before has this been more true – or necessary. Building bridges between ecovillages and academia is literally building bridges to a more sustainable future. What an amazing time to be alive! What an honor to be a part of this Great Turning!

 Daniel Greenberg has studied and directed community-based educational programs for over 15 years. He visited and corresponded with over 200 US intentional communities for his PhD dissertation on children and education in community, and later spent a year at the Findhorn Foundation in Scotland working with children and families there. He is the founder and Executive Director of Living Routes, which develops accredited ecovillage-based education programs that promote sustainable community development. He lives at the Sirius Community in Shutesbury, Massachusetts USA with his wife, Monique and their two daughters, Simone and Pema.

Marian, who has been living and working in Senegal for many years, shares her experience of living at the interface of North and South. How can ecovillages from the North and the South learn from and support one another in meaningful ways?

South/North Interface in Senegal

Marian Zeitlin, Ismael Diallo, Oumar Diene & Henri Lo

The Healing Interface

Built on common foundations, the ecovillage movements in the South and the North are at opposite ends of a process that is coming full circle. As illustrated below, the cycle shown in Figure 1 rises from pre-industrial lifestyles on the left to the excesses of the global consumer economies at the top. It then tends back down, with the earth-restoring ecovillage movement, toward sustainable post-industrial lifestyles on the right. The challenge for peoples living at the Alpha and Omega of this journey is to exchange knowledge in the cultural, spiritual, environmental, economic, and technological realms in order to open the gates of a human-scale underpass across the divide at the bottom. In this way, the majority of the earth's population, living on the left, might not have to go through the disastrous industrialization and globalization process that currently threatens human survival.

Indigenous Third World communities need to access and appropriate post-industrial technologies that permit them to live in dignity and comfort in the modern world without being exploited by global industrial and market forces. Post-industrial peoples need to relearn indigenous knowledge and wisdom destroyed during colonization, industrialization, and global commercialization. The best of the high road and the best of the low road need to join forces. The goal for both South and North is to discover solutions together, as symbolized by the key and to create a harmonious and sustainable world.

In this work, the ecovillagers of the world's poorest regions, who continue to attempt to survive while practicing traditional economic and cultural lifestyles adapted to their ecosystems, provide an interface for the North to rediscover priceless information. Their data banks of 'old growth' knowledge are as valuable as the 'old growth' rainforests and other ecosystems in which they live.

Fig 1   Joining Forces to Find our Way Home

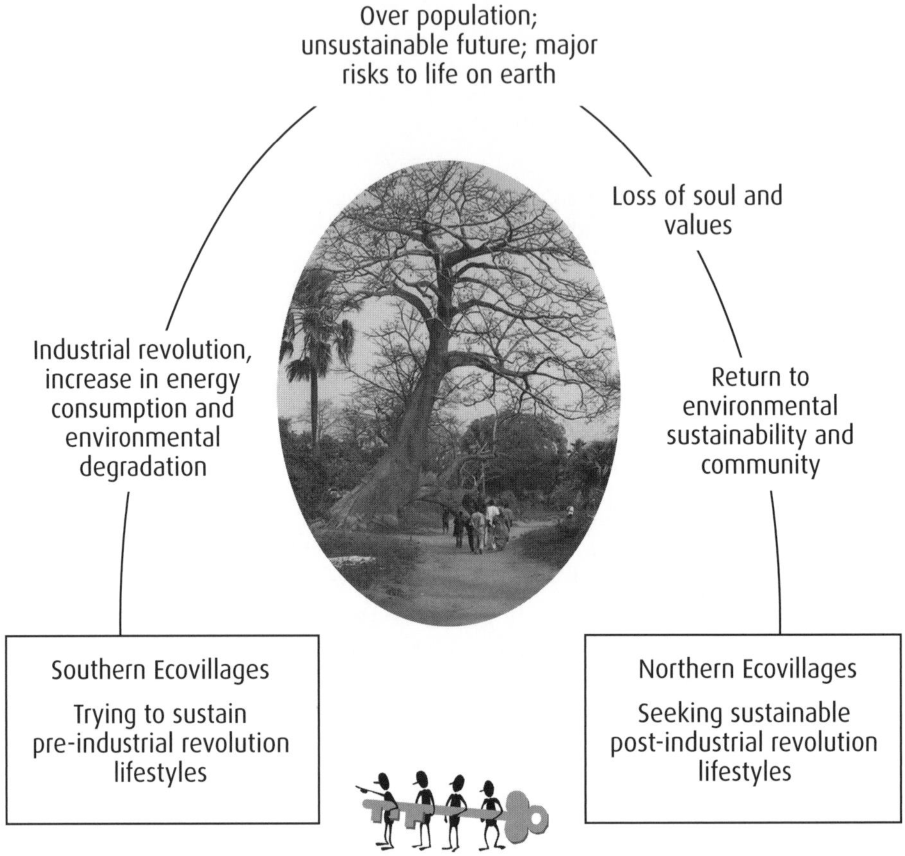

Over population;
unsustainable future; major
risks to life on earth

Loss of soul and
values

Industrial revolution,
increase in energy
consumption and
environmental
degradation

Return to
environmental
sustainability and
community

Southern Ecovillages

Trying to sustain
pre-industrial revolution
lifestyles

Northern Ecovillages

Seeking sustainable
post-industrial revolution
lifestyles

Common foundations in the South & the North

Pre-and post-industrialized peoples share an urgent desire to repair the earth, and very similar feelings concerning the relationship between individuals and communities and the planet on which we dwell.

Desire to repair the planet

The wealthiest and the poorest communities both keenly feel the need to reverse the withering of supportive values, beliefs and social structures and the upsurge of destructive economic and environmental practices and changes on our planet.

Ecovillages in the North and in the South, attempt to the best of their understanding and capacity to protect, preserve and create habitats that foster environmental, economic, social, cultural and spiritual health, diversity and self-expression, supported by low-impact ways of life and appropriate technologies.

Similar perceptions of the earth

Love for and feelings of loyalty towards the earth are shared by the Northern and Southern culture ecovillage movements. In talking about these feelings and perceptions, people tend to bring arguments into play that more or less explicitly echo and support the Gaia hypothesis. Gaia is the name of the ancient Greek goddess of the Earth. The Gaia hypothesis, shared by members of the Northern ecovillage movement, holds that the planet and its biosphere form a self-regulating or homeostatic system, in which life forms, atmosphere, physical features and climate co-determine each other in a manner that preserves the integrity of the system as a whole. The Gaia concept bridges spiritual views in both the South and North of the earth as a loving mother on the one hand and scientific concerns for the self-regulating interrelationships between species diversity, soil quality, climate and other features of the biosphere, on the other. Those less educated intuit what scientists conclude.

The Gaia hypothesis holds that the planet and its biosphere form a self-regulating or homeostatic system, in which life forms, atmosphere, physical features and climate co-determine each other in a manner that preserves the integrity of the system as a whole.

Acting locally

Ecovillages draw their significance from the fact that self-regulating systems cooperate hierarchically. As in the human body, self-regulating cells underlie self-regulating organs, such as the liver, and other body structures. These homeostatic and self-regenerating structures form the physical bodies of higher life forms that are self-regulating at the individual level. Human beings consciously and unconsciously regulate their own well-being and form self-regulating social groups. Following this chain upward implies that self-sustaining grass-roots communities, formed by humans and the other life forms and the physical features of their environments, are fundamental building blocks or micro-ecosystems that make up the world as we know it. It implies that behavior that protects the needs of these local human and ecosystem settlements also protects the global needs of humans, other life forms and the planet.

Herein lies the science behind the motto of the environmental movement: 'Think globally, act locally.' Ecovillages 'act locally' in a holistic way that creates and maintains self-regulating sustainability at the community level. Ecovillagers, South and North, tend to live on earth as if they were living parts of the living bioregions of a living planet.

Shared analysis of the problems

Ecovillages in both Northern and Southern environments typically identify the same categories of issues affecting the health and sustainability of their communities, namely ecology, ecomomy, worldview and the social. A preoccupation with the need for improvement across these same domains unites ecovillages and sustainability programs worldwide across cultural and economic boundaries.

The deep longings of Southerners and Northerners converge. In visioning exercises, the dreams of the least modernized, deeply rural villagers strongly resemble those of the most modern and urban.

Readiness for ecovillage solutions

Many Northerners and Southerners are ready for the ecovillage movement, but in somewhat different ways. Northerners tend to have greater material resources, more technical education and more individualistic cultural traditions that encourage greater divergence from mainstream thought and action than Southerner cultures. On the other hand, Northern readers of this chapter should realize that the devastation that drives change runs deeper in the South, where many villagers and city dwellers feel wrenched by poverty from their indigenous livelihoods, values, ecological and community practices and diverse cultures.

Many feel they are losing the struggle to survive in increasingly degraded and overpopulated environments with economies weakened by global market forces. Loss of hope of surviving on their ancestral lands leads elders to encourage their youth to dream of immigrating to the North and to abandon efforts to improve local living conditions that they view as hopeless or temporary. Therefore the concepts of the ecovillage movement may come to many Southerners as an answer to prayer, and a call to return to reconstruct the golden age of their ancestors. For these reasons, Senegal, like other countries of the South, is fertile ground for creating new dynamic ecovillage-networks.

Village meeting in Senegal

Roles of Northern & Southern Ecovillages in the Protection of the Planet

It is important to note that boundaries between the 'North' and 'South' are not entirely clear, since the world as a whole is increasingly divided between the global consumer class and the global poor. Rich countries have large pockets of poverty, while the wealthy, who rule poor countries, often live exaggerated consumer lifestyles. Therefore the generalizations below are not foolproof. Typically, global consumers in poor countries live in the cities, and it is the rural areas of the global North and South that differ systematically. In a number of cases, elite intellectuals in poor countries have created or are creating 'Northern' style ecovillages. At least two ecovillages, Louly Ngokom in Senegal and ODI in Nigeria, are integrating Northern and Southern approaches in the communities.

However, Southern ecovillages, using Senegal as an example, do differ in a number of respects from ecovillages in the industrialized countries. These differences call forth different approaches to Ecovillage design and to Gaia Education.

The construction of the interface requires levels of commitment that run far deeper than the profit motive.

Preserving the Earth's surface

As mentioned above, one way to think of ecovillages or eco-communities, rural and urban, is as fundamental building blocks or paving stones of sustainability. We also can use images of ground cover, skin or connective tissue, protecting the surface of the planet and its biosphere, together with wilderness lands in which Gaia's cycles are relatively uninterrupted. We may view the ecovillage movement as the great work re-growing the protective cover of the planet. Thinking in these images, indigenous peoples or eco-systems peoples still live in relative harmony with their land and engage in livelihoods that more or less protect the integrity of its surface membranes.

Vast areas of the South still are relatively protected in that their human inhabitants are traditional organic farmers, village dwellers, homesteaders or nomads. Although the global market, which transforms nature, land and humans into commodities, advances rapidly into these areas, vast protected territories remain to be salvaged in the South. By contrast, in the North, ecovillage acreage exists in the form of bandages that cover small patches of lands that otherwise are heavily damaged by chemical pollution, erosion, roadways imprisoning wildlife, destructive water management, etc. In the North damage to the Earth's surface already is fairly complete.

Changing the paradigm

To place a greater focus on North or on the South alone, however, would be a mistake. The famous quote from anthropologist Margaret Mead, 'Never doubt the ability of a few dedicated individuals to change the world,' refers

State of the art technologies in the North can join forces with the collective consciousness and egalitarian flow of human beingness preserved in the South to transform the planet …

to ways in which transformational ideas and trends can gain force, and create global changes in worldviews and lifestyles. With current information technologies, the ecovillage movement is hardly limited to any particular part of the planet. State of the art technologies in the North can join forces with the collective consciousness and egalitarian flow of human beingness preserved in the South to transform the planet, not only at the ecovillage level, but at top policy levels. When social paradigms change, physical and social conditions can swiftly follow.

Major Differences between the Two Sides of the Interface

Communities of choice in the North vs. communities of necessity in the South

'Northern' ecovillages typically are intentional communities of 10 to less than 500 members. Through participatory planning, they first purchase land and then design and create their homes, workplaces, organic farms or gardens and common areas in harmony with the natural environment. Socially, culturally and spiritually, they strive to create vibrant communities grounded in sustainable local economy and in essential social services, including education and health care. People with financial resources and strong educational backgrounds create this type of ecovillage. As they commit to a sustainable ecovillage lifestyle, however, they struggle to survive the challenges and financial hardships that come with life choices that are uncommon in their societies. The northern ecovillages are communities of choice, whose members choose freely to join and leave the group.

In Senegal, ecovillages are villages that have requested membership in GEN Senegal (GENSEN) and have participated in an accreditation exercise in the form of an educational and participatory appraisal of how far they have already advanced in the protection of four dimensions of the village's ancestral heritage: Society and Culture, Natural Resources, Economics, and Habitat. The first six ecovillages, who met together monthly during the year 2001 to create GEN Senegal, produced the forms that serve both to create ecovillage awareness and to accredit the villages.

They usually are low-income rural traditional villages of 100 to 5,000 members, who belong to the village by necessity, since each member depends on the other members for survival in relative harmony with a fragile environment. Their inter-related families have lived together on the land for generations. In Senegal a local village association serves as the administrative and educational presence of the ecovillage, responsible for leadership and for teaching ecovillage values and practices to the rest of the village.

Living on the Margins in the North vs. the Mainstream of Society in the South

In relationship to government, availability of public and development assistance funds, and network dynamics, the national Senegalese network of ecovillages, GENSEN differs from its mother network, GEN Europe.

Whereas ecovillages are as yet somewhat marginal in the EU planning and funding process, the ecovillage concept is accepted as part of the mainstream in Senegal.

In many African countries, a combination of the lack of government resources, and the active, self-reliant dynamics of traditional villagers led years ago to policies of delegating the protection of natural resources to rural villagers and in particular to their women's groups. The Global Environmental Fund (GEF) for example, targets its Small Grants Program to rural villages working together with non-governmental organizations (NGOs) that provide the villagers with training and other forms of technical assistance. A major goal is to teach and engage villagers in protecting and rationally harvesting endangered natural resources on protected national park lands. Ecotourism is one of the government's main strategies for assisting villagers to generate revenue to make it unnecessary for them to harvest endangered species.

Active collaboration and mutual aid across network projects in the South

The fact that NGOs act as technical intermediaries between funders and villages in Africa has led GENSEN to include the NGO's as members of the network. The founders of these NGOs tend to be idealistic entrepreneurs eager to help villagers to improve their environmental and social conditions, and hence share their services across the network. In Europe, technical expertise resides within the Ecovillages themselves.

GENSEN headquarters, and the EcoYoff Living and Learning Centre offer regular training programs that bring representatives of the ecovillages together in different villages. During these trainings, the visiting ecovillage reps work together with the local villagers to put in place the ecological technologies that are the subject of the training. This creates a communal assistance dynamic and inter-village sharing across the villages. The annual reforestation work camps and ecovillage fairs held during the rainy season are regional events planned and executed by the ecovillages of different regions working together. GEN Europe members collaborate virtually over the Internet in writing funding proposals magazine articles. They congregate physically to carry out publicity events.

Challenges of Education and Outreach at the Great Divide

The best teaching materials on how to create ecovillages have been written and published by Gaia Education. However, these draft materials are primarily intended for modern educated persons seeking to create ecovillages on the Northern model. Senegal's EcoYoff and Living Routes programs encounter the following problems in teaching and being taught by semi-literate and illiterate indigenous peoples:

- We experience role confusion and a double agenda. As teachers, we also are learners voyaging into the unknown. We may feel that we are making a pilgrimage to revisit ourselves tens, hundreds and sometimes thousands of years back in time, hoping to retrieve and protect lost knowledge.

- Discovering our lost relatives in an unknown hidden valley, suddenly exposed to threats to their environment, we cannot simply explain to these villagers what to do. We must accompany them on their journey.

- We, and this includes African intellectuals and university students who didn't grow up on the land, cannot fully feel as they feel, think as they think, or act as they act, either individually or in terms of group dynamics.

- We have difficulties creating appropriate teaching aids and explaining abstract concepts.

- Many of the decision-makers and authorities in traditional culture and technologies guard their secrets to be taught only through initiation or to trusted and designated insiders.

- They (and we) are unable to fully understand:
    ◊ How modernization threatens their livelihoods and invades their lifestyles.
    ◊ What livelihoods truly will be capable of supporting them under modernizing conditions.
    ◊ The value to them, us and the world of the old ways that many are abandoning.
    ◊ How to move beyond cultural inertia to incorporate appropriate technologies, such as hygiene practices that lower illness and death rates and solar cooking that protects their ground cover.
    ◊ How we from the North can incorporate into our lives the richness that they possess and that we have lost.

And satisfactions of living in the crucible

The interface where North meets South, in poor indigenous regions, is the crucible which new and old ways fuse to restore the earth. Being part of this process can be intensely inspiring. Ways to go there include courses, internships, volunteer visits, research, participatory action research, and development projects involving experts, students and villagers. And also, the continuous work of creating a knowledge highway at this interface requires months and years of unpaid good citizenship devoted to crafting our post-industrial ecovillage world. Internet, Skype, webcams and other communication technologies help to make the choice of Northerners to live and work in the South more and more similar to living anywhere on the planet. Fortunately, the magic of the old ways and the power of transformation in the crucible attract Northern and Southern settlers to spend increasingly longer periods of their lives here.

Marian Zeitlin, PhD directs the EcoYoff Living and Learning Center established by GEN in 2001, in Yoff, Dakar, Senegal. EcoYoff is the training center for the 33-member ecovillage network of Senegal (GEN Senegal) and offers internships and university courses in écovillages with the Living Routes program. Ismael Diallo is the President; and Oumar Diene, PhD, the Secretary of GEN Senegal and assistant EcoYoff program director. Henri Lo, PhD teaches sustainable development at the University of Dakar and is academic director of EcoYoff's Living Routes semester programs.

Specifically written for young people, this article describes the living legend of La Caravana and its roots in the idealism of the '60s. Travelling across South America La Caravana has been both a mobile experiment in community living and an artistic and inspirational form of outreach – now poised for one of their greatest adventures.

Caravana Arcoiris por la Paz
Bioregional and Planetary Outreach in South America

Alberto Ruz

Back in the 1960s

Back in the 1960s, when I was in my twenties, part of a generation of rebels and dreamers, John Lennon described many of the most profound visions of the world we wanted to live in. He invited us to IMAGINE a world without wars, jails, mental hospitals, borders, hunger, fear, unjust governments, corrupted political parties and fundamentalist churches. And he said that, yes, we may all be some dreamers, but that we were not the only ones. And he foresaw that if more visionaries, poets, activists and social workers arose everywhere on the planet, the world could change. John Lennon also declared one day that 'The dream was over', and he was shot in the street, for no apparent reason, just because there is always someone out there who thinks that the world is OK as it is, and that nothing can be changed anyway, whatever we try to do.

We grew up with these two options, and as the years went by, most of my friends decided that it was pointless to try to create a better world, that the Matrix had taken over, and that it was better to adjust to things as they are, and to take advantage of the system as much as possible, and for as long as it lasted. A few of us opted instead to continue trying to do things that might improve not only our personal situation, but the situation of the rest of the world too. Maybe little things, maybe very small projects, but at least we decided not to give up, and we continue even today, in our sixties, creating a world as we imagined it when we were young.

In this piece, I will share with you some stories about my own life, because they also illustrate the lives of many others like me – people doing little things to preserve hope in the hearts of young people – the heirs of this planet.

After four years of academic life in various faculties of my university in Mexico City, I found that none of the careers they offered me could fill my need to know all the things that I hungered to learn. I wanted to learn about other cultures, help the dispossessed, try new experiences, learn how to use my hands and not only my head, speak other languages, meet people from all walks of life, create plays, write stories, make films, play music, live with my best friends … and build our own community.

The more I read about what was going on in the rest of the world, the more I thought and believed that something radical needed to be changed in the whole system, and that if we did not start to make those changes, we could not expect others to do them for us. We did not have a clear idea of what we wanted, or of how we could build it, but as Jim Morrison said in one of his songs … 'We wanted the world, and we wanted it … NOW!!!!'

Protest and resistance were our main tactics, first in our homes, then in the class rooms, the campus, the streets, and finally in all the main cities of the four continents. In 1968, when I was 23, it was as if we, the radical young people from North America, Mexico, Europe, Australia and Japan, had become a planetary urban countercultural guerrilla force supporting the anti-colonial and anti-imperialist struggles in Latin America, Vietnam and many African nations. At the same time, another part of us, was becoming a peaceful army of colourful hippies, raising the banners of Peace and Love and asking for the manifestation of PARADISE NOW!!!

… if we did not start to make those changes, we could not expect others to do them for us.

Get Back to the Real World?

Following the big cultural and revolutionary parties, festivals, concerts, sit-ins, be-ins, marches and barricades that we raised to confront the mighty powers, the feeling was that 'the dream was over' and it was time to 'get back the real world'. A lot of young people got scared or tired from the beatings, the jails, the persecution, the trials, marginalization, scarcity, and from all the problems raised from trying 'new ways' without having a clue how to make them sustainable. Frustrated by attempts to create new 'open' couples,

Live your dreams!

families, communes, farms and urban co-ops, we ended up with many of the same problems of 'out there': power struggles, gender wars, dependent economies, fanaticism, drug abuse, freedom without responsibility, disorientated children, and a lack of recognition from the rest of the world.

I personally experienced many of those failures but, with a few others, began learning from our mistakes, got onto our feet and continued walking. As Lao Tse says, the path to freedom is a long one, and it always starts with a single step. By the mid-seventies, having been part of the counter cultural revolts in Mexico, the United States, France, Spain, Holland, Italy, England, Germany and Scandinavia we formed, with an international group of people, a solid collective nomadic tribe that we baptized in India – the Hathi Babas Transit Ashram Commune. And we took theatre as our path, both to preserve our unity, and to have something to offer to the communities we visited on our journeys.

As a travelling company, after 13 years on the road, we found that we could continue to live as an extended family, at one point consisting of seven buses, 20 adults and 12 children born in the four corners of the world. We also discovered that we were not alone in our search. In 1976, we encountered the Rainbow Nation at an inter-tribal gathering in California, and for the next decade we helped strengthen the loose network of heirs of the '60s, that now adopted the name of Rainbow Warriors.

Huehuecoyotl

In the early '80s, we decided it was time to abandon, or at least rest, our old buses for a while, and start building a more solid community. A few years later, we founded Huehuecoyotl, an unusual ecovillage up in the Tepozteco mountains of Central Mexico. For the next 14 years of my life, Huehuecoyotl became the centre of all my activities. I gave it all my passion, time, and resources until it became an open and recognized centre for the arts, ecology and all non-sectarian forms of spirituality. Over the next 24 years, thousands of people visited this experimental laboratory of ecotopia, and took part in one or many of our multicultural and educational events.

Huehuecoyotl has also become a cauldron where many local, national and international actions have been cooked up.

Since 1984, Huehuecoyotl has also become a cauldron where many local, national and international actions have been cooked up. Activists and representatives from the Rainbow Nation, from the international Bioregional Movement, from the 13 Moons World Peace movement, from the Global and American Network of Ecovillages, and many other networks; indigenous leaders and spiritual guides from different paths; and artists from all over the world, have met and performed, given lectures and workshops, held meetings and congresses, celebrated ceremonies and enjoyed festivals respecting all paths and practices. Today, students from universities in Mexico, the United States and Europe, converge every year, to follow courses on an extraordinarily wide range of topics ranging from traditional healing and the wisdom of the elders, through consensus facilitation and ecovillage living, to African drumming, capoeira and the making of audiovisuals. And, perhaps

Play time

primarily, to experience what we have saved from our original dream of an alternative community, based on a set of values other than the Matrix.

In 1990, Huehuecoyotl was also the birthplace of a movement bringing together groups from all over Mexico – the Consejo de Visiones para la Accion Bioregional, a southern adaptation of the best principles of northern Bioregionalism. This event spawned annual gatherings, each one in a different bioregion, hosted by a local group or loose network of movements. A highlight was in 1996, when we organized the First Bioregional Council of the Americas, bringing together more than 1,200 activists from over 30 nations to a Peace Village we set in a place called Meztitla.

La Caravana

Meanwhile, also in 1996, with a group of young adventurers and a couple of veterans from the '60s, I decided to start a new project that we named La Caravana Arcoiris por la Paz (Rainbow Peace Caravan). Its main goal, besides traveling in the South, was to share our experiences, both with the people participating in the journey, and with the communities and individuals we would meet on the way.

Since we set off almost 10 years ago, the Caravana Arcoiris has become, for some, a 'living legend'. It will never be an ideal project, because ideal projects only exist in our imagination. They are the product of our expectations, illusions, dreams or nightmares. Reality is always much more fluid and complex than that. The Zapatista Mayan indigenous people say: 'It is not enough to dream now, we need to wake up ...' And once awake, I would add, to start creating the vision you had in your dream. A cultural hero from the past, said once that it is always better to 'die in the attempt' than to 'die on your knees' thinking that whatever you do, things will allways be the same. And that is why the Caravana, regardless of anything else, is a great project for all those who come in contact with it.

The Caravana has, in its more than nine years of travelling, spent time in most of Central America, Chiapas (southern Mexico), Guatemala, San Salvador, Honduras, Nicaragua, Costa Rica, Panama and the Kuna Islands. Then, after many adventures, we managed to get our bus across the Darien pass by boat and into Colombia. Once on firm land, we spent over a year in each one of the following countries: Venezuela, Colombia, Ecuador, Peru and Chile, as well as several months in Amazonia, Argentina, Uruguay and, now in Brazil, from where I am writing this story.

On our journey we have visited many indigenous communities. This year we will visit the Tucano, the Xavante and the Xingu here in Brazil. Each one of these people holds a piece of the unique puzzle that defines the rich diversity of this continent. Having the opportunity to spend time with the people of these nations has made me richer than any job could had made me in the meantime. We also shared the best of ourselves, and I hope we gave as much as we took.

We have visited dozens of small rural villages, and spent, sometimes, long seasons in the heart of some of the biggest, most crowded capitals of South America. In each one we have left traces of our walk. In each one we at least presented a play, did a workshop, or shared an audiovisual story. In many we did ceremonies, big or small circles, organized events, concerts, Peace Villages, bioregional and healing gatherings, and even international Vision Councils – in Peru in 2003 and in Brazil in 2005. In each one of these countries we now have friends and family that continue sharing with us, send us news of how things we planted have grown, how seeds we have left in their hearts have turned into new projects, and how the hope that we have offered has been transformed into a flowering garden of beauty.

... we now have friends and family that continue sharing with us, send us news of how things we planted have grown, how seeds we have left in their hearts have turned into new projects ...

Nobody who comes to the Caravan, for a short or a long time, leaves unaffected. Not all leave happy. Many have strong criticisms about things we have not resolved, things we have disregarded, and we always hear them. We can't always change the things we would like to change, but life itself forces us, sooner or later, to do the things that we neglect. We are not all the ecologists we would like to be. We are not always as impeccable as we would like to be, but that is a lifelong task. The path is full of changes and, sooner or later, we will be faced with the things we need to face to become better human beings.

The Present

Right now, the Caravan is preparing to take a gigantic leap. We have committed to do a one-year 'Tour of Brazil' with the support of the Secretary of Culture, visiting 'living points of culture' – a project started a couple of years ago to support local communities in sharing their cultural heritage with the

Travelling in buses

rest of the nation. We will act as both an incentive to those communities, and as a witness to the rich biodiversity of Brazil. We will share what we learn, through images and stories, with the rest of the world. After ten years of trying, we are about to start a project that represents some of our wildest dreams. We are sure we will do a good job. In our next story we will be able to tell you more about our adventures, our successes and our challenges.

In the meantime, I leave you with this short, but very spicy testimony and chronicle, hoping it will be inspiring to some of you, and that some new ideas, visions and projects may also result from this exchange. My best to you all, and, as an old Gypsy saying reminds us: 'May we always roam with hunger'.

Have a good and safe journey, now y siempre....

Alberto Ruz Buenfil, Born in Mexico City, 1945. Forty years dedicated to studying and serving as an international networker make Alberto Ruz a first line pioneer, veteran and historian from the ecovillage and bioregionalist movements. Co-founder of Huehuecóyotl ecovillage in Mexico (1982), founder of the 'Caravana Arcoris por la Paz' (1996) and itinerant focalizer for ENA (Ecovillage Network of the Americas) in South America since 2000. Ashoka fellow (2002), and adviser to GEN (2003). Partner to the Brasilian Ministery of Culture's program 'Cultura Viva' (2006-2007).

www.lacaravana.org · subcoyotealberto@yahoo.com.

involved closer connection between Ladakhis and Westerners. We set up the 'Farm Project' where Westerners have a chance to spend a month living and working with a Ladakhi farming family. The project helps both sides to gain a more accurate impression of each other's lives and cultures. The interest and involvement of these Westerners in farming is helping to restore Ladakhi self-respect.

We also began a program called **Reality Tours**, which enables Ladakhi leaders to travel to the West to see it for themselves. Exposing people to both the negative and the positive aspects of the West helps dispel many of the misconceptions about 'modern' life, and leaves participants with a better sense of the benefits of their own culture. The tours also expose them to the growing concern for the environment around the world, thus providing support and inspiration for ecologically sustainable development within Ladakh itself.

The director and secretary of the Women's Alliance of Ladakh recently travelled to the UK on a reality tour, which became the subject of a German/French documentary. During their tour, the women saw various aspects of 'western reality', both positive and negative. They visited an old peoples' home, a homeless shelter, a landfill and explored the underside of London life.

The women visited a natural health clinic, a co-housing group, a healthfood store and another shop selling organic clothing. They also toured a city farm in the heart of London, a large organic farm in Berkshire and a farmers market. Both women are farmers in the Himalayas and were particularly interested to see the resurgence in organic and sustainable farming methods in the UK. Seeing trends like these in the West helps Ladakhis to see that there is a growing concern among Westerners for the environment, human health and society. This in turn helps Ladakhis to understand the value of the traditional way of life in Ladakh, much of which is still intact.

Reality Tours are one way of helping people in the East understand the reality of the West. We all have much to learn about each other so that we can protect the wide diversity of cultures on the planet. This is essential to a harmonious, sustainable future.

For the author's biography, see page 82.

5 Local, Bioregional & Global Outreach

Bioregional Outreach

Educational Outreach

Global Outreach

Showing the West to the East

Helena Norberg-Hodge

The Cult of the West in Media

In the west, we have become thoroughly accustomed to the distorted reality portrayed in media and advertising. Most of the time we are barely conscious of the effects. My experiences in Ladakh, Bhutan and elsewhere in the 'developing' world have shown me, however, that the impact is widespread and extremely damaging.

Today, the cult of Western consumer conformity is descending on the less industrialized parts of the world like an avalanche. 'Development' brings tourism, Western films and products and, more recently, satellite television to the remotest corners of the Earth. All provide overwhelming impressions of luxury and power. Advertising and action films give the impression that everyone in the west is rich, beautiful and brave and leads a life filled with excitement and glamour. In the remotest corners of the planet Barbie, Madonna and the Marlboro Man are familiar icons.

For millions of young people in rural areas of the world, modern Western culture appears vastly superior to their own. Every day, they see incoming tourists spending as much as $1,000 – the equivalent of a visitor to the US spending about $50,000 a day. Besides giving the illusion that all Westerners are multi-millionaires, tourism and Western media images also help perpetuate another myth about modern life – that we never work. It looks as though our technologies do the work for us. In industrial society today, we actually spend *more* hours working than people in rural, agrarian economies. But that is not how it looks on television.

In the commercial mass culture which fuels this illusion, advertisers make it clear that Westernized fashion accessories equal sophistication and being cool. People are even encouraged to reject their own ethnic and racial characteristics – to feel shame at being who they are. Around the world, blonde-haired blue-eyed Barbie dolls and thin-as-a-rake cover girls set the standard for women. It is not unusual now to find East Asian women

with eyes surgically altered to look more European, dark-haired Southern European women dying their hair blonde, and Africans with blue- or green-coloured contact lenses aimed at 'correcting' dark eyes.

The one-dimensional, fantasy view of modern life promoted by the Western media, television and business becomes a slap in the face for young people in the 'Third World'. The people they learn to admire and respect on television are all 'sophisticated' city dwellers with fast cars, designer clothes, spotlessly clean hands and shiny white teeth. Yet they find their parents asking them to choose a way of life that involves working in the fields and getting their hands dirty for little or no money, and certainly no glamour. It is hardly surprising, then, that many choose to abandon the old ways of their parents for the siren song of a Western material paradise.

People are not aware of the negative social or psychological aspects of Western life so familiar to us: the stress, the loneliness and isolation, the fear of growing old alone, the rise of clinical depression and other 'industrial diseases' like cancer, stroke, diabetes and heart problems. Nor do they see the environmental decay, rising crime, poverty, homelessness and unemployment. While they know their own culture inside out, including all of its limitations and imperfections, they only ever see a glossy, exaggerated side of life in the West.

Lifting Illusion – Looking at Reality

For the last three decades, I have been working with Ladakhis and Westerners to counteract the damage inflicted by the glamorized image of the West that one sees everywhere now in Ladakh. Paradoxically, these efforts have

Communities
New Opportunities for 'International Solidarity'

Leila Dregger

I am writing this text in the wake of a peace pilgrimage through Israel and Palestine, in the early months of 2006. The pilgrimage was organized by the Peace Research Centre of Tamera, Portugal and was led by its co-founder, Sabine Lichtenfels. Over 40 people from Israel, Palestine and many other countries walked for 25 days through the divided Holy Land. We listened to stories on all sides, witnessed conflict in many ways, meditated at the Wall and shared our thoughts and feelings. Our vision was to bring healing through thinking and acting in community instead of separation. Doors opened which for a long time had been closed.

The pilgrimage was an example for political action carried by the spirit of community. It opened up a new perspective on international solidarity.

International Solidarity

Solidarity means to perceive one self and others as being part of a larger whole. Solidarity means mutual help and active support for each other. It is the source of enormous power. Solidarity is the realization that there is no fundamental difference between my neighbour and myself. What happens to any human being on earth might happen to me, too, and in a way is happening to me. We are all – man, animal, plant, victim or aggressor, enemy or friend – part of the same larger whole. The tears of a Palestinian woman could equally be mine. The child in need in South America could be my child. The tortured man in Syria could be my son or my lover. This is the track of a political heart.

When taken one step further this entails that I could be the aggressor, the so-called enemy, too. 'As long as we do not recognize that the guard of the concentration camp could be us, too, it will happen again,' says Claude AnShin Thomas, Zen Monk and Vietnam Veteran.

A scene from a theatre piece performed by Tamera members at many places in Israel and the Westbank during the pilgrimage

The term 'international solidarity' is approximately one hundred years old. Early, during the first wave of industrialization, the socialists made a discovery: a worker in Germany had more in common with a worker in America or Russia than he had with a bourgeois of his own country. Class and profession weigh more than nationality. The socialists formulated the common experiences of the worldwide working class. Along those lines they unmasked the strategies of capitalism. Factory workers, going on strike for better working conditions, knew that a worldwide movement stood behind them. Together they managed to experience their power to change their situation.

The consciousness of international solidarity spread into other areas. More and more science awoke to the fact that we are *one* humanity, living on *one* planet, that we are all sitting in the same boat. The ecological movement recognized the global threat to our home planet by environmental pollution. Environmental groups worldwide extended the new term of international solidarity to animals, plants, all creatures and future generations.

Meanwhile, in the age of global networking, this kind of thinking has become a matter of course. The more strongly Human Rights Organizations, Women Organizations, Refugee Organizations, Animal Protection Societies and Development Organizations act in the sense of international solidarity, the higher their effectiveness becomes.

International Solidarity and Community – History of my Journey

Long live international solidarity!

I called out this slogan countless times. It was written on the banners we carried in demonstrations. Solidarity with El Salvador, with Nicaragua, with Palestine, with countries and people I did not even know. But I knew that, at least partly, they suffered as a result of the life style we maintained in the Western world. I fought this political fight with fervour – against exploitation, against war, against US imperialism, against the way of life of my parents. I have never wanted to be part of a world in which one side sits cosily in the living room while the other side dies of war and hunger.

Nevertheless, the people we fought for remained curiously abstract. I knew what I was fighting against. But I did not know what I was fighting for. My motivation was pure anger. But in the long run this was not enough. I began looking for other perspectives allowing me to build a vision of a new world together with others, full-heartedly and with much ardour to live it.

Why is it that to maintain our social live style we have to exploit people, landscapes and animals in far corners of the world? What hunger is hidden behind the need to consume? What would an alternative life look like? Why do we go home alone after a demonstration? Could solidarity become the basis of our entire lives? Twenty years ago the first Forums (see pages 128-33) were held in German cities to discuss these questions publicly. I remember when hundreds of young people after demonstrations in Berlin and Cologne sat together in old factories or cinemas trying to find out how to change their lives. Communities sprang up by the hundreds. Soon the experience was made that it was much easier to feel a sense of community in the face of a political enemy than to actually live it. The communication process around the organization of every day life, around love relationships, religion, power and money was a greater challenge than the organization of a mass demonstration had been.

It was much easier to feel a sense of community in the face of a political enemy than to actually live it.

After an initial phase of blooming the communities basically produced the same world that they had initially intended to change. Hidden behind our revolutionary masks we proved to be anguished, jealous and power hungry petty bourgeois! We had to change ourselves if we wanted to help change the world. Ghandi said, 'We have to be the change we want to see in the world'.

At this point many communities give up. Others begin to concentrate on inner processes, ideas, and difficulties in such a way that they forget their original purpose in the world. 'To hell with Vietnam, I have a problem with orgasms,' the German student revolutionary, Rainer Langhans, is supposed to have said. International solidarity demands from us to look at our dark sides in order to change them, and in the process not to stop working for solidarity and peace in the world. This work is a source of power.

Many communities have failed in this process. Those who succeeded have gained a large wealth of experience and knowledge. For the political movement this knowledge could prove to be very precious:

- Know-how of how food and energy supplies can function independently of industry and state
- Know-how around healing independent of pharmaceutical industries
- Know-how around truthful communication
- Know-how around conflict resolution
- Know-how around conquering separation and loneliness, the main suffering of the human being

All these are areas of knowledge are now being brought into the global peace movement, into the movement of international solidarity.

The expression of international solidarity in the form of demonstrations, appeals and proclamations found its highlight in March 2003. Many millions of people all over the world marched in the streets in international solidarity with the people of Iraq. The largest peace demonstrations ever flooded the towns of Berlin, Athens, New York, Barcelona, Rome, Sidney and many more. All the same, the war took place with all its terrible consequences. Although 80 per cent of the population of Europe was against the war, we could not prevent it from happening. Probably even ten times as many demonstrations would not have sufficed to stop the superpower of worldwide capital and the armament industry.

To demonstrate against war and then carry on living as usual is obviously not enough We need to remember that this war was made by people. Behind all injustice and terror there are always people – and people are, finally, reachable. There must be a possibility for global effectiveness that is based on a connection to people.

Obviously there is a link missing in our tactics. Maybe the time has now come for the experience of community to contribute to a leap in quality needed in international solidarity.

Community as an Antidote to Separation and War – Impressions

The Peace Pilgrimage

The Peace Pilgrimage through Israel/Palestine was a good example of such a leap in quality. This Pilgrimage became possible only because of the background of long-term community experience of our leading team, mainly of Sabine Lichtenfels. She was able to create an atmosphere of trust even in the most difficult situations.

Wherever they go they carry with them white banners and wear white scarves with the word 'Grace' written on them.

In November of 2005, 40 people walked through Israel and the Westbank. Amongst them there are Israelis and Palestinians, Germans, Swiss, Americans and other nationals. The youngest is 16, the oldest 71. International solidarity has brought these people together. They are on a pilgrimage that leads them through Arabic and Jewish places. They meet peace workers from both sides, they speak with young Hamas fans in Palestine and with surviving victims of suicide attacks in Israel. They witness street fights and visit military camps in which teenagers are trained to go to war. They visit refugee camps where people live in indescribably cramped conditions, some since up to 60 years, dreaming of their villages and homes. They visit the ruins of Arabic villages, empty, with only the wind sweeping through. Wherever they go they carry with them white banners and wear white scarves with the word 'Grace' written on them.

They sleep in tents and in olive groves, in communal buildings of the PLO, in Israeli Kibbuzim, in refugee camps, in Bedouin tents and in the homes of Palestinian clans. They meditate by the wall that seals off the occupied territories, they help with the olive harvest, visit the Holocaust Museum.

Meditation in front of the Israeli Separation Wall in the Westbank

They witness conflict on every imaginable level.

They do not find an enemy.

They only find people.

People whose pain, anger and fear they share. They also find courage and the longing for peace in unexpected places.

Israelis travelling through Palestine

Most of the participating Israelis travel through occupied territory for the first time. Fear and absurd regulations have kept them from doing so up to this moment. For the first time they witness the 'other side' and expose themselves to the emotions that come up when facing the effects of the politics of their own government. Feelings of guilt, helplessness, despair and anger mix with an almost panic-like fear. Under the protection of the international group they discover the human face of the enemy. Many moving scenes are happening.

"Welcome, welcome," says Yousran, our host in a Palestinian village. "Our house is your house."

"Thank you," I say. "This is Michal. She comes from Israel."

"Israel?"

There is a moment of paralysis. Yousran has never met an Israeli who is not wearing a uniform before. Then her face twitches. "Welcome, welcome, this house is your house." A conversation begins which neither of them has ever had before. Today Michal keeps in touch with Yousran and supports her financially so that her daughters can finish their studies.

Counteracting the virus of separation

A wall, 600 km long cuts through the so-called Holy Land. Israel-Palestine is a land where the principal of separation is stretched to its limits.

Crossing a checkpoint – entering the Westbank

Cultures, religions and nationalities are divided. The walls of fear, ignorance and anger seem impenetrable.

During our pilgrimage we are searching for an antidote to the virus of separation. In our daily sharing circle we witness moving realizations and decisions, often pertaining to the smallest and most ordinary daily occurrences.

"You never look at me," says Mustafa to Daniel in the sharing circle. "You talk with everyone else except with me. Why is this so?" Daniel, an Israeli peace worker realizes that he has grown up in a society that has taught him not to see Arabs as human beings. From then on the two of them have a lot to say to each other.

"I have never met people like you," says one of our Palestinian guides. "You all look as if you were married to each other." In his culture community exists only in terms of an extended family.

Meeting soldiers

Soldiers stop us in an olive grove in the Westbank. They are Bedouins (Arab Israelis) who are part of the occupying troops. Their task is to suppress their brothers with whom they share the same faith. Sabine asks them to let us carry on with our sharing circle. What a surprise! They ask to be permitted to join us. The apple goes around, passes from one to the other. The one who holds it speaks. The soldiers in uniform, with helmets and machine guns listen. They are not much older than our youngest participants and are visibly drawn between duty and interest. When the apple reaches them they put their guns down.

"You are doing the right thing," one of them says. "I would love to go along with you."

Another: "I do not believe in peace. Why not? If the children here are hungry I give them to eat. They take it, but when I turn around they throw stones at me. No, I do not believe in peace, because THEY do not want peace."

We have heard these words often: we want peace but the others don't.

Fayez is a Palestinian farmer whose land was destroyed by Israelis. For years he has been in jail. He guides us through the Westbank. When the apple reaches him he gives an unforgettable speech:

"I see everything that has destroyed my life reflected in your uniforms. Not in you, but in the uniforms you are wearing. You are young. I can see in your eyes that

Sabine Lichtenfels convinced Israeli soldiers to join the sharing circle

you are not married yet. I feel what your parents feel when you leave the house in the morning." At this moment he starts to cry vehemently. "Your parents are afraid, they are afraid that you might die. They feel just as I do when I see my children. My children are 15 and 17 and since our land has been destroyed the walls of their rooms are full of posters depicting suicide bombers. I am afraid that my children will one day take revenge on your children. We need to stop this. Now. You say that you protect your brothers. I honour you for that. But I am your brother, too. You ought to protect me as well."

The soldiers are stunned. Never before have they heard the enemy talk like this. One of them gets up and brings him water. Fayez has never had the opportunity before to talk to soldiers in such a way.

Jewish settlements

We also visit Jewish settlements. Our Palestinian friends warn us that the settlers are 'bad people'. These settlements, their access roads and dozens of checkpoints cutting through the entire Westbank, make it impossible for Palestinians to travel freely. And again we meet humans, not enemies. Strangely enough, it feels like looking into a mirror. We can't ignore the similarity between these settlements and any European residential area. Finding fault with the state of affairs here, means finding fault with our European way of living: ignorantly shut oneself off from ones surroundings, not wanting to see the neediness of the neighbours, to take from them land, rights and mobility … The only difference is that in Europe those who are exploited and shut out are farther away!

The settlers share with us stories of an almost child-like faith which tells them that God wants to have them in this country. We see their need for justification and their being strangers *vis-à-vis* the world, also their fear and confusion. But, as they notice that we have not come to judge them but want to understand them they also share with us their questions and their wish for peace. Certainly these people are no enemies. The enemies are the ignorance and the indifference.

The virus of separation is rampant not only amongst Israelis and Palestinians. Everyone meets this virus a thousand times through the daily challenges of being together on this pilgrimage. 'I have fought so much in my life. It is incredible how much war there is inside of me, although I have the word *peace* written on my banner.'

We refuse to be enemies. What does this sentence mean when applied to our own life and love for each other? An older female participant, a real veteran of the peace movement says: 'It is for the first time that I am together with a group for this length of time without internal fighting breaking out.' The way of community proves to be a real antidote against the virus of separation.

We have planted another seed of peace.

Finding fault with the state of affairs here, means finding fault with our European way of living: ignorantly shut oneself off from ones surroundings, not wanting to see the neediness of the neighbours …

Peace Performance in a schoolyard in the Palestinian town Anata, which is walled in by the separation wall

For sure the children will throw stones again when we leave, the soldiers will put more children in jail, settlers will attack farmers or vice versa. Many doors that opened may close again. But a vision has been created and a core group has committed itself to the building of a permanent Peace Research Village in the Middle East.

Conclusion

After 20 years, the term *international solidarity* has been put in another context through my experiences. There are now names, faces, life stories, fates, mutually shed tears and shared experiences connected to it. Solidarity connotes sympathy and understanding.

In community I have learned to see the walls I draw between others and myself. These same walls, in a larger context, lead to conflict and war. In community I have learned to open doors. Community has allowed me to grow, offering new opportunities every day to break down the walls around my heart. It is a life-long path and I am grateful for it. May these experiences repeat themselves within a global context.

Political work in terms of *International Solidarity* and *Building Community* are two sides of the same coin. When they come together we enter into an exciting human adventure. I perceive this combination to be a great resource for the resolution of conflict on our planet and for the creation of another world.

More information about the planned Peace Research Village in the Middle East: www.prvme.org.

Solidarity connotes sympathy and understanding.

Leila Dregger, 46, is a journalist and agriculturist from Germany. She has been committed to political activism since she was 17. She was the publisher of the women's magazine *The Female Voice – Politics of the Heart*. She has been living in communities for many years and has visited communities in many parts of the world. From 2006 onwards, she participates in the peace experiment Monte Cerro which is taking place in the community of Tamera in Portugal. Her vision is to build up a school for peace journalism.

Wolfram Nolte sets out his vision for how living in communities and ecovillages contributes to the planetary consciousness that is needed to avoid ecological disaster.

From Local Communities to the World Community
More than a Dream?

Wolfram Nolte

Is it just a dream that ecovillages or other community-based ways of living can change the world? Are they more than the last islands of a romantic nostalgia? A good intention, but not fitting for a new shaping of the world?

We have to take such questions seriously. If we focus on the unbalanced state of our planet there seems to be little or no hope. If, however, we look deeper at the underlying evolutionary and spiritual forces that carry us, we can discern a promising picture in which community thinking, feeling and acting play their part.

I want to describe how the beauty of our blue-white pearl in space can touch us and encourage people to a more global and planetary way of thinking. As I am alarmed by the actual state of the world in which this beauty is endangered, I will follow the vision of Pierre Teilhard de Chardin who believed that a united humanity can evolve. I ask what sort of inner and social conditions we have to develop and I try to show some perspectives for a planetary peace policy in which ecovillages play a critical role.

The Blue-White Pearl in the Universe

In 1948, Sir Fred Hoyle, a cosmologist and science fiction writer, said,

> The moment a photo of this planet is taken from space, there will be a significant transformation of thought processes in humanity's history.

Thirteen years later the Russian Jurij Gagarin circumnavigated the Earth and became the first man ever to contemplate our planet from space. Following this, over 200 astronauts and cosmonauts came back to Earth transformed. Cosmonaut Oleg Makarow said,

People who have been out in space have recognized that, in spite of their differences, they agreed on one thing: They strongly felt they were citizens of the world, with a strong feeling of responsibility to preserve this unique planet we all share. They had understood that with this simple aim in view, all difficulties, differences of opinions and obstacles have to and can be overcome.

The picture of the Earth in space has become the symbol of this simple aim, namely that life on Earth has to be protected and preserved.

'Fear has to disappear from this planet.'

Could it be that those views of our planet have already contributed to what one of the world's leaders said in the 1980s, 'Fear has to disappear from this planet.' Gorbachev's words and his policy of bringing the cold war to an end, momentarily opened us up to new possibilities of living peacefully together on this planet. Human consciousness was not yet ready to react to this situation by truly opening up their thinking to the future. Fear and mistrust took the upper hand and old ways of thinking – profit seeking, a win-lose mentality, and domination – still prevail. So far the new millennium is more than ever characterized by fear and fatalism.

But there remains that look from outside at the blue-white pearl in the blackness of space and our experience that walls can crumble, iron curtains can open up and stuck situations can become more fluid. These experiences are also the legacy of the last century. In 2000 the General Assembly of the United Nations declared this year as the year which would introduce, world-wide, a culture of peace and called on all people, governments and nations to work towards this goal. Today the stakes are high: we have to develop a new world-embracing culture of peace, solidarity and sustainability by promoting a lifestyle in which all living beings have room. Aware of the destructive consequences of globalization, this task has to be visualized as world-wide. The time for individual solutions is over. Regional and national levels are too restrictive and can no longer exist separated from global development. All projects concerning our future need to be compatible world-wide. But where will the power, optimism and know-how come from?

The Dream of a Planetary Community

Fortunately a different, more hopeful way of looking at the development of mankind is possible. It has its origin in a deeper understanding of evolutionary processes and takes into consideration far bigger periods of time. Evolutionary seeker Pierre Teilhard de Chardin named this process 'planetarization'. Teilhard de Chardin sees the evolution of mankind as a process of increasing community development. He was interested in the development of cohesion between people, rather than in the outer forms of living together that are the focus of most historians and sociologists. This leads him to a different way of seeing the world.

Teilhard de Chardin uses a vivid picture to describe the different phases of mankind's evolution on Earth. He sees them as waves moving on the surface of an imaginary globe from its south pole to its north pole. The south pole represents the starting point of human evolution and the north pole its final destination. The first phase he calls the building of communities in expansion. He describes this as a diverging movement, humanity expanding over the globe and thus taking possession of the Earth. Through an ongoing process of increasing differentiation different cultures came into existence and within these cultures different individuals started elaborating their individuality. Once the equator has been crossed humanity can no longer expand. The building of community henceforth continues as a growing together. Growth no longer takes place on the surface level of the world but in the depths. From now on humanity has the chance and, indeed, the duty to develop a deeper consciousness of its inner bonds, thus growing more and more into its true role as the eye and steering organ of creation. As Peter Russell, a researcher into human consciousness, puts it: comparable to the nerve cells of the brain, which long to link up to the phenomenon of human consciousness, humans can build up the global brain of Gaia, the collective body of wise intelligence of our planet.

And where are we standing today? To stay with Teilhard de Chardin's picture, for the last hundred years we have been in the process of crossing the equator. The change of hemisphere is a critical turning point, as the direction of movement changes from divergent to convergent. The same should be true for our way of thinking: away from its outward direction towards inner space, away from confrontation towards cooperation. With this two million year old attitude of wanting to expand we venture into this new phase which demands an attitude of joining up, of linking up with the underlying wholeness.

There is no guarantee we will succeed. With its free will humanity can impede this development and eliminate itself. Teilhard de Chardin describes the struggle as follows:

> The individual is overtaken by a deadly fear to loose its own small 'I'. This happens when we are dominated by the imagination that we can be swallowed up by a seemingly blind totality. Planetarization is then experienced as a totalitarian process. The individual rebels against being part of a bigger entity, for it wants to use human society as a stepping stone to find its own independent, individualistic solution for life's problems.

This is an accurate and foreboding description of the current process of globalization. On the surface the linking up of humanity takes place with incredible speed – by telecommunication, the flow of capital and goods, tourism, catastrophies and wars. We feel pressure because we lack that inner connection – the communication 'from heart to heart', as Teilhard de Chardin calls it – which alone makes it possible to connect with others.

The Significance of Community Life

For years peace movements and ecological movements have tried to increase humanity's readiness for peace and ecological responsibility by using protest and information, sometimes with considerable success. Through intensely growing global competition, however, old aggressive patterns are reactivated. How can you motivate people to go for peaceful and sustainable development in such a climate?

During the recession of the 1920s and '30s a similar situation occurred. We have interesting correspondence from these years between Einstein and Freud, both pioneers of 20th-century thought. Whereas the latter went exploring the mystery of the universe, the former set out to explore the human soul. The scientist asked the psychologist whether he could see a solution to the problems of rearmament, aggression and war. Freud's answer was that men are torn between their instincts of aggression and love, and that peace is only possible if strong emotional bonds develop between people.

Robert Muller, former undersecretary at the UN, concludes from this correspondence, 'Patriotism has united mankind on a national level. It is our big historical challenge to develop love between all the inhabitants of the planet and to motivate them to love the Earth itself.'

Doubts show up immediately: how is it possible to love all the inhabitants of the planet and on top of this the planet itself? Whose heart is that big? Esteem, respect, caring – yes. But love? To love truly even one person is difficult. Even to love ourselves is not always possible and often we manage it only in a narcissistic, conceited, egotistical way.

The universal love which embraces the Earth and all beings living on it cannot be taken for granted. It shows up more like a shooting star in our lives! Everyone knows these peak experiences – moments when we feel connected with everything – and the question why do we live has become redundant.

... it is possible to develop a lifestyle that protects natural resources, frees us from pointless consumption and leaves us time to develop and satisfy our non-material needs ...

I am convinced that universal love can be encouraged to grow so that gradually it becomes our normal feeling state. It grows when, in our daily life, we act lovingly towards the Earth and our fellow beings. This is where the importance of a communal lifestyle comes in. In a co-operative living context we can integrate ourselves and our family into a wider context. We adjust our own needs to those of others, and we learn to trust. Here it is possible to develop a lifestyle that protects natural resources, frees us from pointless consumption and leaves us time to develop and satisfy our non-material needs, such as the need for human connection and love, for beauty in nature and arts, for truth and for unfolding one's own creativity. To be successful, communities experiment with new forms of communication, decision making and conflict resolution.

Dieter Duhm, community explorer and co-founder of the community Tamera in Portugal, sees community as a universal form of living that is necessary for a healthy development of life:

Community was and remains the natural humus for trust and solidarity. If this humus is lacking, uprooted men become violent and ill ... Community is an intermediate level in the evolution of life that cannot be circumvented. It links the individual with a higher order and sharpens the senses for the whole ...

People who live in such an organism don't live according to the principles of comparison and competition but fulfil life's need for diversity and completion.

What is so special about ecovillages and communities is that not only are theoretical concepts of ecological social and human lifestyles being developed but their viability is being tested and developed in real life. They become the most important fields of research, schools of life which society badly needs if it wants to survive. They practise looking for, and finding, answers to the most serious challenge of our time, namely, how to develop an attitude of all embracing love of the Earth and all her creatures and to express this in the world.

I do not pretend that ecovillages and communities are the only possibilities able to meet this challenge. Informal networks such as neighbourhoods, groups of friends and spiritual and cultural circles, are also developing community spirit. As the systemic researcher, Fritjof Capra, says: 'The biggest challenge of our time is to initiate viable future oriented communities and help them grow.'

The Big Turning

The development of sustainable communities and their worldwide networks are the bases for a new type of politics born from a spirit of cooperation. However, communities by themselves are not the solution. They are only the paradigmatic part of the solution. That is to say, out of their lived experience they are able to provide an acute perception of the problems, appropriate methods and a matrix of solutions. This process has to be accompanied by spreading a communal and ecological way of thinking into towns and districts. Here communities can serve as catalysts and initiators. There is nothing like a living example to change people's minds. Graham Bell, a specialist in permaculture, argues, 'In my opinion it is the dialogue you lead with your neighbour that changes the world.'

When they start out, however, ecovillages and communities are generally considered to be foreign bodies in their environment. They are busy with their own problems and have little energy left to build up good relations and develop common projects with their neighbours. But as time goes by they develop to become attractive centres in their region offering the population new economic, social and cultural possibilities. The Federation of Damanhur in northern Italy for example, the Findhorn Foundation in Scotland and the Zegg in Germany demonstrate community living in their regions. Helena Norberg-Hodge, a critic of globalization, sees 'the development of independent bioregions based on ecovillages as maybe the most radical way to combat dependency on the world economy.'

For these efforts to be successful in the long term, politics must change at both national and international levels. We have to be ready to converse with other groups and individuals with their own concerns (poverty, unemployment, violence, fear of future, etc.), and not just trumpet our own ideals.

We have to be ready to converse with other groups and individuals with their own concerns ... and not just trumpet our own ideals.

Communities need to make this step into the surrounding society to avoid stagnation and isolation, to avoid becoming swallowed up by social and political developments which threaten not only their existence but all life on this planet.

Similarly, society needs the experience of communities, and above all of co-operative thinking, if it wants to find new solutions. After the breakdown of state socialism there is a vacuum in our political discourse. There is no longer any serious discussion about radical social alternatives as a convincing vision offering a viable future for all inhabitants of the planet.

More than other alternative groups and NGOs, communities have to offer society the living experience that a co-operative and ecological way of life is possible. We have expertise to share in a wide range of subjects. How is it possible to bring together a supportive, communal lifestyle, economic solidarity, ecological awareness, and self-determined work? How can we raise our children? How can our culture and arts be produced by the people themselves? How can we promote the creative potential of all women and men? How can love and friendship grow between men and women? How is sympathetic communication possible? How can we end conflict and achieve peace in a non-violent way? Our movement has answers and solutions to share to questions such as these.

Joanna Macy, a specialist in deep ecology, said that this big transformation is also a challenge. It happens simultaneously on three levels: Firstly, it is expressed through criticism of the prevailing circumstances which are being countered by actions of resistance directed at slowing down the process of destruction. Secondly, and simultaneously, proposals of fundamental alternatives and of building up alternative structures and new experiments have to increase. Thirdly, we need a change in consciousness, widening our capacity for the empathy that makes us aware of our interdependence and our intimate connection with the Earth's body.

Awakening to the World Community

The planet needs a meaningful vision of how nearly seven billion inhabitants can live in peace, evolving into a responsible organ instead of mutating into a cancerous growth. The new direction of politics has to be planetary, but based on strong self-reliant regions. Already some tasks can only be solved at a planetary level, such as the restoration of destroyed natural spaces, responses to catastrophies, working for disarmament and peace, fair regulation of the world economy, and the realization of political and social human rights.

The basic question 'What are the primary goals of the evolution of humans and humanity' has to be complemented by questions such as 'What, how and how much shall we produce? (after all, preserving the planet is at stake)', or 'How will we distribute wealth? (the happiness of humanity is at issue)'. The answers to such questions can no longer be left with economic experts. It is in the interest of the Earth and all its living beings that they be answered by the entire human community.

The 'United Nations' needs a living worldwide network of 'United People', a network of men and women from all countries, professions, confessions, ways of life and organizations, people who are able to organize resistance against globalization and whose visionary thinking develops beyond the narrowness of possessions and power, and who start to build up sustainable, sociable forms of living all around the world

It is my dream that all these people communicate and cooperate with each other to form eventually a movement that ultimately will enable all people to lead a good life. This movement is locally anchored and brings people together so that a new world of self realization and solidarity can be developed. It builds up ecological forms of living combined with the best in regional self-sustainability and self-determination. What underpins this movement is a common caring for life in general. This form of love provides security in a world that is about to move away from provincial structures towards hitherto unknown new forms of cohesion.

What is needed more than any new organization is a new kind of connection at the spiritual and heart levels. This new linking-up serves as a source of orientation and strength for all those who feel inspired to work for the necessary change: towards a way of thinking and feeling that takes into consideration all of humanity. Through this new solidarity, our collective force expands until trust grows and fear is banned from the Earth.

Many of you know what the American Indian, Vine Deloria, said:

> Only tribes will survive.

In this deep truth I hear the message:

> Humanity will only survive if it unites to form one tribe, one world community.
> This is both a dream and a necessity.

Wolfram Nolte, sociologist and independent journalist, has lived for 20 years in different communities in Great Britain, Italy and Germany. For the last six years he has lived and worked in the ecovillage of Sieben Linden, Germany. He is editor of the Eurotopia pages on cooperative living in the magazine *Kurskontakte*.
He organizes and guides trips to ecovillages and communities in Europe (eurotopia-tours) and offers seminars on deep ecology and community building.

In this interview, Vandana Shiva shows how colonialism has returned as globalization, and deepened as a colonization of life itself. She inspires us to return to the feminine principle and include spirituality in our search for local solutions to the global questions we are facing.

Local Solutions to a Global Problem

Vandana Shiva

Based on interviews done by Geseko von Lübke, compiled by Kosha Anja Joubert.

Vandana Shiva, you come from a third world country, from India. What critique do your offer on the western industrial growth system?

I think the significance of the third world critique of western industrial growth is that unlike the West the South cannot fool itself about where the growth came from. For the West it is very possible to say that the industrial growth of England was related to its magical technologies and its brainpower. For us in the third world it is so clear that it is related to colonialism, to control over our economies, to slavery, to capturing an entire continent's population and making them work on the cotton fields of America. So the costs were always very clear to us: the monetary costs and the people cost, the social cost and the cost of destroying other economies.

Is colonialism a chapter in the history of humanity that has been closed?

Colonialism hasn't gone away. In fact, it has returned as re-colonization. Colonialism has returned as globalization. Globalization, in fact, is worse because while maintaining all the old forms of domination of western powers over non-western cultures, what you have is an addition: the colonization of life itself. Something that the old colonialism could not do! What is being colonized now is the inner space of living beings, human beings, animals and plants. In addition to all the old style colonialism, this colonialism is a colonization of the future itself. It is denying us a future.

How do you suggest we change our attitude towards the economics of life?

The most important restriction in the concept of western economics and of western science and technology is the fragmentation of looking at a small bit of the whole picture only. What we in India and the whole movement that criticizes globalization reject, is a growth that is based on destruction. We want a growth that is honest to itself about what it destroys. If it is real growth, it will destroy as little as possible, because it will build on what exists rather then on the ruins of what went before.

Does this mean that our western concept of growth is based on an error in our way of thinking?

There are two levels to the present definition of growth in patriarchal systems. The first level has destroyed our societies by assuming that if you produce for yourself you are not producing. It has declared that very productive women are not productive. It has declared that subsistence peasants who meet all their needs and who do not depend on governments for welfare or on corporations for a job are unproductive. With the progress of globalization this definition has been expanded even further. We are made to believe that societies whose economies produce mainly for the needs of their own nations are not productive enough. Following this second level in the definition, growth takes place when we sell everything we produce on the international market and import everything we need from other nations. This rewards the rule of capital over the rule of life.

What intention do you see standing behind this worldview of fragmentation and this economic system of globalization?

The will to control! The will to control everything is what is most destructive. But it is even more absurd because it is totally impossible to really control. You cannot control through manipulation. I think ecology has taught us that the only real control comes through self-control. This means that societies need to be given the capacity to make their own decisions about their ways of life. One good example is birth control. Self-control and self-decision in reproduction is the only solution. But they cannot take place unless people have control over their land and over their livelihoods, because what is reproduced is not just the biological species. In human societies what is reproduced is a social formation, a whole society. When a large part of a society lives under conditions of insecurity, all kinds of demographic problems start. In the North there are not enough children to reproduce society, and in the South there are too many.

I do not believe that anything can be achieved through the kind of population control that is being practised at present. All the millions of dollars and all the millions of contraceptives sent to the South do not have

Self-control and self-decision in reproduction is the only solution.

the effect in terms of regulating numbers because they do not address the basic issue. The basic issue is: freedom for organisms, social formations, and societies to organize themselves.

On which levels should change take place?

We need to respect nature and treat nature as our family, the way we are taught in societies like India. We need to realize that we live in the earth family. Humans are not a privileged species. We are just one more species on the planet. If we end the colonization of nature, we end the ecological crisis.

The same is true for the colonization of women. If men from industrial societies set the standards and define woman as the inactive, unproductive gender, then women are called unproductive even though they might be working 20 hours a day in rural societies. Creative women start being defined as secondary sex.

We need to end the colonization of whole cultures, through the taking over of land and natural resources, including biological resources, and the genes in their plants.

Does this mean that the effort for change needs to take place on both the personal and the political plain?

We can only build what we already are. What builds the process is strength and energy, and a sense of power. What we can recognize in the movement for change is a new notion of power. I call the old notion of power patriarchal power. It is not a masculine form of power in the sense that every man biologically carries it – that is not the issue. But western society has constructed itself following a world view based on the idea that certain men are more superior than other humans, including other men unable to dominate, bully, destroy and be aggressive. So, we need to change the cultural concept of power. Real power comes from within. Real power turns firmly to oppose any form of oppression. Real power empowers the other and empowers oneself, instead of building on the extinction of the other as the basis of the power of the self. In the Indian tradition we have the concept of Shakti, a metaphor for the cooperative force that is the all-pervading energy in this universe. It is this Shakti that we must bear to bring to the fore in this transformation.

Real power empowers the other and empowers oneself, instead of building on the extinction of the other as the basis of the power of the self.

What does Shakti mean?

In our cosmology Shakti is the creative principle. In this cosmology nature is recognized as creative force. Trees grow from their seeds and they renew themselves. Every year the grass renews itself. Streams renew themselves, the water cycle goes on without any human help. This tremendous activity is the creative force of nature. It has been identified as the feminine principle. But this principle is not just out there in nature, because nature is not out there. We are an integral part of nature. The creative principle is a part of men as much as of women. Many modern cultures deny the existence of this original creative force. However, the recognition of Shakti is tantamount to the honouring of the miracle of life itself. Recognizing this power makes us humble, it makes us recognize that we are not the masters over life and death.

What is the connection between this concept of Shakti and globalization?

The feminine principle has disappeared in western cultures. At the root of every culture lies its myth of creation. Since the industrial revolution, since the emergence of capitalism, what we basically have is a new creation myth. This myth denies that creation takes place in nature and that women are generators of life. Instead, it would like to define destructive acts which men have engaged in as creative acts: acts of throwing bombs on other societies, acts of finding new pesticides, acts of finding new genetically modified organisms that pose a threat to biodiversity on our farms. These acts of destruction are seen as acts of creation.

Acts of destruction are seen as acts of creation.

In this myth, it is assumed that capital itself creates. It is assumed that if you invest in seed industry, you are creating new seeds and therefore you can own these seeds as property. You can then force peasants to pay you royalties for seeds and treat them as thieves if they save seeds on their farms, even though you yourself have taken those seeds from nature. This myth turns the natural relationships between humans and between humans and nature on its head. It rewards the pirates and thieves and punishes the conservers and caretakers of nature.

What would the vision of a society look like that turns away from patriarchy to embrace the feminine principle?

Recovering the feminine principle would set genuine growth back on the agenda. It would allow our forests to grow back. It would allow biodiversity to return to our farms. It would allow people to first meet their own needs and then put surplus into the market. It would allow for self-sufficiency, self-reliance and self-determination. That would be real growth. Together with nature, people and whole societies would flower. Growth would no longer be a fictitious figure in the profit reports of multinational corporations, who are today able to move three trillion dollars of total fiction around the world.

On what ethics would such an economic and cultural system be based?

First, any new ethics must be healthily related to traditional ethics. The ancient systems of human organization can show us what makes long-term human survival possible. So we do not have to create the first wheel in ethics. All we need is to recognize that humanity has had many faces and many histories.

Humanity has brought forth beauty, responsibility, and sustainability. It has also brought forth destruction and violence. It is our responsibility to choose the parts of that legacy of the human spirit which we wish to inherit.

The second basis for a new ethics is the fact that theory and practice have to evolve hand in hand. For me hope comes from the continuity of life, life with all its complexity and in its constant dynamic change through evolution. Hope does not arise from a theory. This continuity of life, these life processes, create the obligation for us to defend them. I do not believe that hope grows from thinking of a future out there and then trying to pull ourselves towards it. Thinking of the present we feel the need to defend its richness. This is how we will increase positive values: values of sharing, of giving, of nurturing.

These values have been made to look like deficiencies in humanity. Here is the flip in our minds that we have to achieve. This is what I mean with recovering the feminine principle. Everything that has been treated as third rate: caring, assessing slowly, introducing change in a responsible way, connecting responsibility to rights and so forth are characteristics of good societies. The key hope that young people can have today is to say: We have a right to the future! Tell the multinationals that they have no business in colonizing our future. We will defend it, we will join in creative constructive campaigns that widen our space and give continuity to life.

How can we change something as big as globalization?

I think the globalization process offers us tremendous opportunities for change precisely because it is so destabilizing. The outrage about the fact that every bit of production anywhere in the world needs to fit into a global economic system to be given viability is growing. This system is making so many people redundant, not only in the south but also in the north, that we will be forced to find an alternative in which local control over our economy and our decision making become possible again. Local control over decision making – about jobs, livelihoods, natural resources – is becoming a survival imperative. It used to be a survival imperative only for the South, which is why in our environmental movements people are prepared to offer their lives. When we fight against the building of a dam we basically say that we'd rather die than let them build this dam. When the Chipko movement wanted to stop logging in the Himalayas, they embraced the tree, and said 'you can kill me, before you cut this'. In the South, it has been an issue of survival for a long time. But now for the first time because of globalization and the deregulation of commerce it is becoming a global problem.

Can local solutions solve global problems?

The only way to solve the global problem is by local solutions worldwide. I do not believe that there is anything that is purely global. Everything that is global has local roots. Global pollution has its roots in local pollution.

The group that created the institutions of World Bank and GATT has all the characteristics of a small, local culture. It is an elite of powerful men of European descent. If you map it out in terms of contemporary tribes, it is a very small tribe which behaves as if it is a global tribe and treats every other tribe as a local tribe. It is time that people realize that these powerful managers also form only a local tribe, with the addition that they are functioning on a very wide scale. They carry a very bureaucratic mentality and narrow interest and simply do not hold a large enough vision to enable a future for our planet and its people. The solutions must therefore necessarily be local. This does not mean local in one place. Local means that people regain the control over their daily lives, and this needs to happen everywhere. The moment it happens everywhere you have a global solution.

Is this process of 'regionalization' primarily important in the South or is it a global imperative for survival?

I think under economic globalization, the colonized part of the world is most strongly threatened through the process of recolonization. But even the Western privileged part is threatening its own future and its future generations with joblessness, hopelessness, and little perspective for a life beyond money and profits. People are dispensable, and most people do not find a possibility to live meaningful lives. Societies are supposed to support their members in finding the meaning to their lives. We need a shift in consciousness now – and in this, the North can learn from the South! We don't have to wait for the corporations to give us jobs. We need to recreate our own livelihoods, our own communities and our own networks of mutual help and self-help. We have to resist all the laws that corporations are creating to make it illegal for us to look after ourselves and each other.

The Western privileged part of the world is threatening its own future and its future generations with joblessness, hopelessness, and little perspective for a life beyond money and profits.

What are the main steps that we need to take?

I think a lot of change can be achieved through changing our way of looking at the concept of growth. If we start recognizing that growth takes place when people work with nature to create real things, real food, good fabrics, good housing, in all diversity, then we will recognize that those people who have been imagined to be poor, are in reality not poor. Then we could stop destroying their way of living and their culture in the name of bringing them progress. We would then realize that three quarters of the world is actually economically growing, while one quarter is destroying itself and the rest. This could encourage and empower us. Three quarters of humanity are able to look after themselves and the real challenge is for the destructive one quarter to change their ways. This shift in consciousness is needed in the West. It is the mind in the West, which has been most deeply colonized. 500 years of colonization are distilled into our history textbooks and our whole educational system. The young people of the West are made to live the myths of capitalist patriarchy and continue them.

Can change take place in an evolutionary fashion, or is a revolution needed?

Is it going to be evolutionary or revolutionary? I think that split is a very western split, revolution meaning drastic, dramatic, very often violent change, and evolution meaning slow change, in small steps. But that would take too long. We need a radical transformation – in that sense the change must be revolutionary. If we are too slow, the destruction itself will be revolutionary. The destruction can be so radical and so rapid, that any containment of the destruction has to be equally rapid, otherwise it will not work. But as far as the question of gentleness and nonviolence is concerned, change needs to be dramatic, but also very peaceful, with no direct violence to other human beings.

If you talk about new ethics, new values, new worldviews, then this also touches upon the deepest layers of human culture. Does the cultural change entail a new form of spirituality?

I think if we recover the sense that within nature and within us there is an internal self-organization that guides us, we start to have the capacity to question the propaganda of the economic growth system. We learn to laugh at or ignore the advertisement campaigns that accompany global capitalism, rather then allowing our minds to be colonized. This is indeed also a spiritual revolution. What is spirituality? Spirituality basically means having the ability to tap into our inner sources. In this way, we strengthen ourselves internally against the onslaughts of all external violence that otherwise manage to bond us in fear. To be free of fear means you must be resilient inside. Through spirituality societies have supported their members to develop this inner resilience.

Dr Vandana Shiva is trained as a Physicist. In 1991, she founded Navdanya, a national movement to protect the diversity and integrity of living resources, especially native seed, the promotion of organic farming and fair trade. Navdanya's efforts have resulted in conservation of more than 2000 rice varieties from all over India and have established 34 seed banks in 13 states across the country. In 2001 she started Bija Vidyapeeth, an international college for sustainable living in Doon Valley in collaboration with Schumacher College, UK. Through her books *Biopiracy, Stolen Harvest, Water Wars*, Dr Shiva has made visible the social, economic and ecological costs of corporate led globalization. Biotechnology and Genetic Engineering are another dimension of Dr Shiva's campaigning internationally. Dr Shiva's contributions to gender issues are nationally and internationally recognized. Her book, Staying Alive dramatically shifted the perception of Third World women. Among her many awards are the Alternative Nobel Prize (Right Livelihood Award, 1993), Order of the Golden Ark, Global 500 Award of UN and Earth Day International Award.
www.navdanya.org

Further Reading

Aberley, Doug (ed.), *Boundaries of Home: Mapping for Local Empowerment,* 1993, New Society Publishers

Abraham, Ralph, *Chaos, Gaia, Eros: The Three Great Streams of History*, 1994, Harper San Francisco

Abram, David, *The Spell of the Sensuous*, 1996, Vintage Books

Adams, Patch, *Gesundheit: Bringing Good Health to You, the Medical System, and Society through Physician Service, Complementary Therapies, Humor, and Joy*, 1998, Healing Arts Press

Andruss, Van *et al*, *Home! A Bioregional Reader*, 1990, New Society Publishers

Anzaldua, Gloria and Moraga, Cheri (eds), *This Bridge Called My Back: Writings by Radical Women of Color*, Kitchen Table: Women of Color Press.

Aung Sun Suu Kyi, *Freedom from Fear and Other Writings*, 1995, Penguin

Auvine, Brian, *et al*, *A Manual for Group Facilitators*, 1977, Center for Conflict Resolution

Avery, Michel *et al*, *Building United Judgment: A Handbook for Consensus Decision-Making*, 1981, Center for Conflict Resolution

Bang, Jan Martin, *Ecovillages: A Practical Guide to Sustainable Communities*, 2005, New Society Publishers

Beck, Don Edward and Cowan, Christopher, *Spiral Dynamics: Mastering Values, Leadership and Change*, 1996, Blackwell Business

Berg, Peter, *Discovering your Life-Place: A First Bioregional Workbook*, 1995, Planet Drum Foundation

Berry, Thomas and Swimme, Brian, *The Universe Story*, 1992, Harper San Francisco

Bohm, David, *On Dialogue*, 1996, Routledge

Bohm, David, *Wholeness and the Implicate Order*, 1980, Routledge

Bond, George, *Buddhism at Work: Community Development, Social Empowerment, and the Sarvodaya Movement*, 2004, Kumarian Press

Bornstein, David, *How to Change the World: Social Entrepreneurs and the Power of New Ideas*, 2004, Oxford University Press

Bray, Margery, *Sexual Abuse – The Child's Voice – Poppies on the Rubbish Heap*, 1997, Jessica Kingsley Publishers

Briggs, Beatrice, *Facilitation and Consensus Manual*, www.iifac.org

Brown, Juanita and Isaacs, David, *The World Café. Shaping our Futures through Conversations That Matter*, 2005, Berret-Koehler

Butler, Lawrence and Rothstein, Amy, *On Conflict and Consensus: A Handbook on Formal Consensus Decision-Making*, 1998, Foods Not Bombs Publishing

Buzan, Tony, *How to Mind Map*, 2002, HarperCollins

Capra, Fritjof, *The Web of Life: A New Understanding of Living Systems*, 1996, Anchor

Chambers, Robert, Participatory Workshops. A Sourcebook of 21 Sets of Ideas and Activities, 2002, Earthscan

Chambers, Simone, *Alternative Conceptions of Civil Society*, 2001, Princeton University Press

Chappell, David W (ed.), *Socially Engaged Spirituality: Essays in Honor of Sulak Sivaraksa*, 2003, Kumarian Press

Chopra, Deepak, *Perfect Health: The Complete Mind/Body Guide*, 1991, Harmony Books

Communities Directory, Fellowship of Intentional Community, updated regularly

Christian, Diana Leafe, Creating a Life Together: Practical Tools to Grow Ecovillages and Intentional Communities, 2003, New Society Publishers

Christian, Diana Leafe, *Finding Community: How to Join an Ecovillage or Intentional Community*, 2007, New Society Publishers

Dawkins, Peter, *The Science of Life: Discovering the Sacred Spaces of your Life*, 1998, Weiser Books

Dawson, Jonathan, *Ecovillages: New Frontiers for Sustainability*, 2006, Green Books

De Bono, Edward, *Six Thinking Hats*, 1999, Back Bay Books

Diamond, John, *Holism and Beyond: The Essence of Holistic Medicine*, 2001, Enhancement Books

Doyle, Michael and Straus, David, *How to Make Meetings Work: The New Interaction Method*, 1993, Jove Books

Duhm, Dieter, *Die Heilige Matrix*, 2001, Synergie

Duhm, Dieter, *Towards a New Culture*, 1993, Verlag Meiga

Durrett, Charles, *Senior Cohousing: A Community Approach to Independent Living*, 2005, Ten Speed Press

Earl, Sarah, Carden, Fred and Smutylo, Terry, *Outcome Mapping: Building Learning and Reflection into Development Programs*, 2002, IDRC (International Development and Research Center), Canada

Eisler, Riane, *Tomorrow's Children: A Blueprint for Partnership Education in the 21st Century*, 2000, Center for Partnership Studies

Elgin, Duane, *Promise Ahead: A Vision of Hope and Action for Humanity is Future*, 2000, Quill

Elworthy, Scilla, *Power and Sex. A book about Women*, 1997

Eppsteiner, Fred (ed.), *The Path of Compassion: Writings on Socially Engaged Buddhism*, 1988, Parallax Press

Featherstone, Cornelia and Forsythe, Lori, *Medical Marriage: Partnerships between Orthodox and Complementary Medicine*, 1997, Findhorn Press

Feldenkrais, Moshe, *Body Awareness as Healing Therapy*, 1994, North Atlantic Books

Fisher, Roger, Patton, Bruce and Ury, William, *Getting to Yes – Negotiating Agreements without Giving In*, 1983, Penguin Books

Foster, Steven and Little, Meredith, *Vision Quest – Personal Transformation in the Wilderness*, 1988, Prentice

Gaskin, Ina May, *Spiritual Midwifery*, 2002, The Book Publishing Company

Gleick, James, *Chaos: Making a New Science*, 1988, Penguin

Gordon, James, *Manifesto for a New Medicine: Your Guide to Healing Partnerships and the Use of Alternative Therapies*, 1997, Addison-Wesley

Heider, John, *The Tao of Leadership*, 1985, Humanics New Age

Helmick, Raymond and Petersen, S J and R (eds), *Forgiveness and Reconciliation*, 2002, Templeton Foundation Press

Hildur Jackson (ed.), *Creating Harmony: Conflict Resolution in Community*, 2000, Gaia Trust/Permanent Publications

Holloway, John, *Change the World without Taking Power: The Meaning of Revolution Today*, 2002, Pluto Press

Jackson, Hildur and Svensson, Karen (eds.), *Ecovillage Living: Restoring the Earth and Her People*, 2002, Green Books

Jaworski, Joseph, *Synchronicity. The Inner Path of Leadership*, 1996, Berret-Koehler

Jensen, Derrick, *A Language Older Than Words*, 2004, Chelsea Green

Johnson, Don Hanlon, *Body, Spirit and Democracy*, 1994, North Atlantic Books

Johnson, Don Hanlon, *Body: Recovering Our Sensual Wisdom*, 1992, North Atlantic Books

Kaner, Sam *et al*, *Facilitator's Guide to Participatory Decision-Making*, 1996, New Society Publishers

Kanner, Allen D, Roszak, Theodore and Gomes, Mary E, *Ecopsychology: Restoring the Earth, Healing the Mind*, Sierra Club Books

Kaufmann, Stuart, *At Home in the Universe: The Search for the Laws of Self-organization and Complexity*, 1995, Oxford University Press

Kelsey, Dee, *Great Meetings! Great Results*, 2004, Hanson Park Press

Klein, Allen, *The Healing Power of Humor*, 1989, Tarcher

Kligler, Benjamin, *Integrative Medicine*, 2004, McGraw-Hill Professional

König, Karl, *Man as a Social Being*, 1990, Camphill Press

König, Karl, *The Camphill Movement*, 1993, Camphill Press

Lazslo, Erwin, *Evolution: The Grand Synthesis*, 1987, New Science Library

Leafe Christian, Diana. *Creating a Life Together*, 2003, New Society Publishers

Lewin, Robert, *Complexity: Life at the Edge of Chaos*, 2000, University of Chicago

Lovelock, J E, *Gaia: A New Look at Life on Earth*, 1979, Oxford University Press

Macy, Joanna R and Brown, Molly Young, *Coming Back to Life: Practices to Reconnect Our Lives, Our World*, 1998, New Society Publishers

Macy, Joanna, *Despair and Personal Power in the Nuclear Age*, 1983, New Society

Manitonquat, *Return to Creation*, no longer available

Manitonquat, *Ending Violent Crime: A Report of a Prison Program that works and a Vision of a Society Free of Violence* (www.futureworld.dk/society/books/nonviolence.htm)

Mathews, Dylan, *War Prevention Works, 50 Stories of People Resolving Conflict*, 2001, Oxford Research Group

McCamant, Kathryn and Durett, Charles, *Cohousing: A Contemporary Approach to Housing Ourselves*, 1994, Ten Speed Press

McLaughlin, Corinne and Davidson, Gordon, *Builders of the Dawn*, 1986, Sirius Publishing

Meltzer, Graham, *Sustainable Community: Learning from the Cohousing Model*, 2005, Trafford

Merrifield, Jeff, *Damanhur: The Real Dream – The Story of the Extraordinary Italian Artistic and Spiritual Community*, 1998, HarperCollins

Metcalf, Bill, *From Utopian Dreaming to Communal Reality: Co-operative Lifestyles in Australia*, 1995, UNSW Press

Mindell, A, *River's Way: The Process Science of the Dreambody*, 1986, Viking-Penguin-Arkana.

Mindell, A, *The Leader as Martial Artist: An Introduction to Deep Democracy; Techniques and Strategies for Resolving Conflict and Creating Community*, 1992, HarperCollins.

Mindell, Arnold, *Sitting in the Fire: Large Group Transformation Using Conflict and Diversity*, 1995, Lao Tse Press

Mindell, Arnold, *The Deep Democracy of Open Forums*, 2002, Hampton Roads

Morgan, Gareth, *Images of Organization*, 1986, SAGE Publications

Pearse, Innes and Crooker, Lucy, *The Peckham Experiment – a study of the living structure of society*, 1985, Scottish Academic Press

Pearse, Innes, *The Quality of Life – the Peckham Approach to Human Ethology*, 1979, Scottish Academic Press

Peat, David, *Synchronicity: The Bridge between Matter and Mind*, 1987, Bantam

Peck, Scott, *A Different Drum*, 1988, Touchstone

Perlas, Nicanor, *Shaping Globalization: Civil Society, Cultural Power and Three-folding*, 2003, New Society Publishers

Perry, Danaan, *Warriors of the Heart*, 1995, Findhorn Press

Plotkin, Bill, *Soulcraft*, 2005, Arun

Rosenberg, Marshall, *Nonviolent Communication: A Language of Compassion*, 1999, PuddleDancer Press

Rosenberg, Marshall, *Speak Peace in a World of Conflict. What You Say Next Will Change Your World*, 2005, PuddleDancer Press

Sahtouris, Elisabet, *Gaia: The Human Journey from Chaos to Cosmos*, 1989, Pocket

Satprem, *The Mind of the Cells*, 1982, Institute for Evolutionary Research

Satyana Institute, *Principles of Socially Engaged Spirituality*, www.satyana.org

Schmookler, Andrew B, *The Parable of the Tribes: The Problem of Power in Social Evolution*, 1984, University of California

Schultz, Beatrice G, *Communicating in the Small Group: Theory and Practice*, 1989, Harper & Row

Schuman, Sandy (ed.), *Handbook of Group Facilitation*, 2005, International Association of Facilitators

Schwarz, Roger, *The Skilled Facilitator: Practical Wisdom for Developing Effective Groups*, 2002, Jossey-Bass

Seamon, David and Zajonc, Arthur (eds), *Goethe's Way of Science*, 1998, State University of New York Press

Senge, Peter, *The Fifth Discipline*, 1994, Currency

Shaffer, Carolyn R and Anundsen, Kristin, *Creating Community Anywhere*, 1993, Jeremy P Tarcher

Sheldrake, Rupert, *A New Science of Life*, 1995, Park Street Press

Shields, Katrina, *In the Tiger's Mouth: An Empowerment Guide for Social Action*, 1994, New Society Publishers

Shiva, Vandana, *Staying Alive: Women, Ecology, and Development*, 1994, Zed Books

Somé, Malidoma Patrice, *Ritual: Power, Healing and Community*, 1995, Gill & MacMillan

Somé, Sobonfu, *The Spirit of Intimacy. Ancient African Teachings in the Ways of Relationships*, 1997, Quill, HarperCollins

Somé, Sobonfu, *Welcoming Spirit Home: Ancient African Teachings to Celebrate Children and Community*, 1999, New World Library

Spangler, David, *Revelation: The Birth of a New Age*, 1976, The Rainbow Bridge

Starhawk, *The Fifth Sacred Thing*, 1993, Bantam

Starhawk, *Truth or Dare, Encounters with Power, Authority and Mystery*, 1988, Harper & Row

Starhawk, *Webs of Power: Notes from the Global Uprising*, 2002, New Society Publishers

Stengl, Martin *et al* (eds), *Eurotopia: Directory of Intentional Communities and Ecovillages in Europe*, 2005, Eurotopia Verlag

Sulak Sivaraksa, *Culture, Conflict, Change: Engaged Buddhism in a Globalizing World*, 2005, Wisdom Publications

Sulak Sivaraksa, *Global Healing: Essays and Interviews on Structural Violence, Social Development and Spiritual Healing*, 1999, Thai Inter-Religious Commission for Development

Thich Naht Hanh, *Peace Begins Here: Palestinians and Israelis Listening To Each Other*, 2005, Parallax Press

Thich Nhat Hanh, *Creating True Peace: Ending Violence in Yourself, Your Family, Your Community, and the World*, 2003, Free Press

Thich Nhat Hanh, *The Art of Mindful Living: How to Bring Love, Compassion and Inner Peace into Your Daily Life*, 2000, Sounds True

Travis, John and Ryan, Regina Sara, *Wellness Workbook*, 1988, Ten Speed Press

Tutu, Desmond, *No Future without Forgiveness*, 2000, Image

Van der Ryn, Sym and Calthorpe, Peter, *Sustainable Communities: A New Design Synthesis for Cities, Suburbs and Towns*, 1986, Sierra Club Books

Vasant Lad, *Textbook of Ayurveda*, 2001, Ayurvedic Press

Von Lüpke, Geseko and Koch-Weser, Sylvia, *Vision Quest. Visionssuche: Allein in der Wildnis auf dem Weg zu sich selbst*, 2005, Knaur

Von Lüpke, Geseko, *Politik des Herzens, Gespräche mit den Weisen unserer Zeit*, 2006, Arun Verlag

Walker, Liz, *Ecovillage at Ithaca: Pioneering a Sustainable Culture*, 2005, New Society

Wheatley, Margaret, *Leadership and the New Science. Discovering Order in a Chaotic World*, 1999, Berrett-Koehler Publishers

Wilber, Ken, *A Brief History of Everything*, 1996, Shambhala

Wilber, Ken, *A Theory of Everything: An Integral Vision for Business, Politics, Science and Spirituality*, 2001, Shambhala

Wilber, Ken, *Sex, Ecology and Spirituality: The Spirit of Evolution*, 2001, Shambhala

Willard, Terri and Creech, Heather, *Strategic Intentions. Managing knowledge networks for sustainable development*, 2001, International Institute for Sustainable Development, Canada

Wong Kiew Kit, *The Complete Book of Chinese Medicine: A Holistic Approach to Physical, Emotional and Mental Health*, 2002, Cosmos Publishers

Zinn, Howard, *The Power of Nonviolence: Writings by Advocates of Peace*, 2002, Beacon Press

Internet

Center for Nonviolent Communication – www.cnvc.org – Books, tapes, courses, etc.

Community at Work – www.communityatwork.com – Workshops on facilitation skills, organizational development, and more

Institute for Cultural Affairs – www.icaworld.org – Facilitation and group process trainings around the world

International Association of Facilitators – www.iaf-world.org – Sponsors an annual conference, group facilitation listserv, publications

International Association for Public Participation – www.iap2.org – Trainings and publications related to effective citizen involvement

International Institute for Facilitation and Consensus – www.iifac.org – Beatrice Briggs, director. Website, electronic monthly publication, courses

Process Work Center – www.processwork.org – Trainings based on the work of Arnold Mindell

The Natural Death Handbook published by the Natural Death Centre – www.ac026.dial.pipex.com/naturaldeath

More books from Permanent Publications

   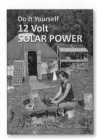 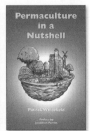

   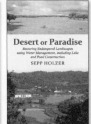 

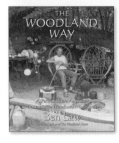   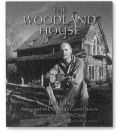